The Black Woman's
ATTITUDE
And The Men Who Want To Love Us

Identifying the Root Cause Behind the ATTITUDE

Jerri Lynn

To Velencia
Thank you for
your support

Jerri Lynn

Copyright information

Printed in the United States of America
ISBN 978-0-9881872-0-7

Most of the Bible scriptures in this book have been quoted from the New International Version (NIV); these are other versions that were used.

King James Version (KJV)
New Century Version (NCV)
New Living Translation (NLT)
American Standard Version (ASV)
Amplified Bible (AB)

Like Minds Publishing
www.likemindspublishing.com
info@likemindspublishing.com
ronyea@likemindspublishing.com
817-754-0503

A Message from the AUTHOR

These stories in their entirety, do not belong to one
woman or man.

This is a **GREAT BOOK that I believe will definitely impact your life,**
*and it's an **EXCELLENT read.***

*I WOULD LIKE TO SAY, BECAUSE Of THE SERIOUS AND
PAINFUL SUBJECTS IN THIS BOOK, IF YOU ARE IN A
DISCUSSION GROUP, I ASK THAT YOU ONLY ANSWER
THESE QUESTIONS ALOUD IF, YOU FEEL CONFIDENT
THAT THE PEOPLE IN THE GROUP HAVE YOUR BEST
INTEREST IN MIND AND THAT THEY WILL NOT USE YOUR
INFORMATION AGAINST YOU, NOR FOR GOSSIP.*

Dedication

First and foremost, I dedicate this book to my Heavenly Father, and my Lord and Savior Jesus Christ, who planted this seed in me and entrusted me to give birth.

I also dedicate this book to the woman who has the courage to seek the root cause behind her *Attitude.*

*And, to the man who is willing to try and understand her, because he **loves** her.*

About The Author

Jerri Lynn, Empowerment Guide, Motivational Speaker, Playwright, and Author, has written a book and created a stage play tailored for both men and women in the compelling story, *"The Black Woman's Attitude And The Men Who Want To Love Us."* For more than six years, Jerri has spoken at various events and churches in different states, sharing the message, "When women are healed, and equipped for success, the entire family benefits." Jerri empowers women through an open, bold, and direct forum, WOMAN TALK, and is now presenting her self-help messages through other formats such as books, DVD's, and CD's, and soon, theatrics and film.

Jerri's inspiration for her messages comes from God. Although she has encountered major setbacks and challenges in life, many while writing this book, including over coming three brain surgeries, and no computer or typing skills.

Her faith alone with her passion for helping women to heal and be set free, as well as bring unity to familiars, has made her more determined than ever. This book is the first of Jerri's series of self-help messages; with one finger she has pecked over 300,000 words, a testimony that with God all things are possible.

Acknowledgments

Words cannot express how proud and thankful I am to my children for supporting me during my difficult times. Although we didn't always agree, Thank You for lovingly supporting me.

To my first born, son and daughter-in-law, Ray and Nichelle, who are my biggest financial supporters, and my Voice of Reason. Thank You for protecting me personally; and, Thank You for serving and fighting for our country in the U.S. Military. You make me proud, and I salute you.

To my oldest daughter, Tori Lynn, who has not only been a financial supporter, you have sacrificed much of yourself to get me through. You are my shoulder and my rock; and you always have my back. Thank you so much for all you do.

To my youngest daughter and son-in-law, Ronyea and Robert, my balancers. Whenever I sway to the left, you give me a reality check that keeps me grounded. You are always right there, ready to jump in and help when I need you. Although I don't say it enough, I really Appreciate and Thank You.

And last but not least, to my youngest son, Michael, who has sacrificed the most. As a teen, you gave up many school activities without complaining, to literally help took care of me when I was seriously ill. You have grown up to be a fine young man who I am very proud of. Your self-less generosity is to be commended. Thank you, and Thank You for serving our country; I also salute you.

I would also like to give a big Thank You to my cousin-in-law, Stacy Norton, for sharing with me from a male's point of view, some of your experiences as a manager, and for being the inspiration that lead me to write about, *The Black Woman's Attitude*.

To all the models, Thank You for helping me bring the stories to life.

And to the brave woman who allowed me to share their stories in order to help other women heal, THANK YOU.

Contents

Introduction

I would like to start this book by first saying, I am not speaking for every black woman. So if you are a black woman who read this entire book and couldn't identify with any of the different attitudes, then you are one of the black women I am not speaking for. But, for the black women in the world that will read this book, get real, and admit they can identify with any of these *ATTITUDES,* and are ready to be healed, then I challenge you to read this book with an open mind and allow Jesus to minister to you.

This journey of self-discovery has helped me have a healthier and happier life. It's also allowed me to touch the lives of women across the country.

I will share with you my tips and strategies, as well as the brave women who have allowed me to share their stories in this book, to encourage you to look in the mirror and identify the root cause for your attitude.

This inspirational book will give insight on some of why there's such a breakdown in communication between the black man and the black woman.

Finding the root cause can help enhance your relationships and help you have a healthier and more fulfilling life. You see, it may seem that black women are full of attitudes, antagonisms, and anger, but that's not the truth. We're about so much more than that. This book will help you pull back the layers of your own experiences and begin to heal.

So come on sistas, let's talk!

When We Have A Good Man, What Do We Do?

"If only I had a good man!" How many of us have said this? We SAY we want a good man. We even PRAY and ask God for a good man, a good Godly man in fact. Then when we get him, what do we do? We punish him for everything every other man has done to us. We make him pay an even higher price for the hurt, pain, and shame that we feel from past relationships.

After we have beaten the brother's spirits down and the relationship has been sabotaged, we then come to our senses and realize what we had. Now it's too late! He has moved on to someone else. We wish we would have been honest and said to him before it was too late, "I'm sorry for the way I've treated you. It's not your fault, you are a good man. I want to love you and allow you to love me; however, I can't because, subconsciously, I'm blaming you for what those other men did to me. I know it's not right but until I'm healed from my issues, I can't help it. Because I don't understand what's going on *within* me, my frustration comes across as an *attitude*."

It's sad how we push good men away. This is the reality of too many black women. Then we wonder why we can't get or keep a good man. Well maybe

> Sistas, we can't keep pushing good men away.

we should look within and find the root causes of our *attitudes*. This discovery changed my *life* and my *attitude*.

•

Discussion Question:

Men: Have you found yourself in situations where you felt you were being punished for the abuse of other men? Did you wonder if there were some deeper issues she could be dealing with or did you just label her as a black woman with a bad attitude?

Women: Do you find yourself making one man pay for what other men has done to you? Why do you think you punish the good man? Is it possible you need to be healed?

I Want To Make You Happy, But I Don't Know How

One night as we lay in bed, Jeff, my husband of nearly three years, said to me, "I want to make you happy, but I don't know how." Where did that come from? I thought. After all, we had just finished making passionate love. We had a really good marriage, or so it seemed, so what did he mean when he said, "I want to make you happy, but I don't know how?"

While lying there with his arms wrapped around me like a blanket, we began to talk. I tried as hard as I could to convince him that, in my eyes, he was doing everything right to make me happy. As we continued to talk, suddenly, he did something that many women say their men usually don't do; he opened his heart and allowed me in. He told me he felt something was missing in our marriage. "I'm not quite sure what it is but I know something is missing. Although we go through the motions of love, I can see it in your eyes and feel it in our most intimate moments that something is missing. Whatever it is, I know it has nothing to do with the beautiful home we live in or the nice cars we drive. I've even noticed you around the children. Don't get me wrong, you are a good mother and you do an excellent job providing for them, but truth be told, I can see something is missing," Jeff said. I looked away. He gently touched my chin and turned my face back toward his. Jeff then asked with a serious stare, "I need you to be honest and open with me, what is this emptiness I see in your eyes and feel when I hold you?"

I took a deep breath as thoughts raced through my mind. I was trying to decide if I should open the can of worms from my past or should I just continue to pretend that I was okay. He was right, something *was* missing. There was a problem but even I wasn't sure what that problem was. I just knew deep within I wasn't happy because there was a void. How could I tell him that he will never be able to make me happy as long as there was a void in my heart?

> Real happiness comes from within.

The *something* missing in our marriage had nothing to do with my husband. I WAS A BROKEN WOMAN! Getting married and having children did not mend my broken pieces, nor did it fill that void that was in my heart. If only he knew how badly I wanted to love him *and* the children.

I desperately wanted to be whole, but what I needed *they* could not give me. I was in a battle and the battle was within me. Jeff was right and I knew it. There was something missing indeed and for many years I didn't know what it was because I didn't know who I was.

Not knowing who I was put a strain on our marriage. It kept me from giving my all to my family. Jeff, not understanding, perceived it as rejection as we grew more distant. Neither of us really knew the root cause of our declining marriage or how to turn it around. Our immaturity did not allow either of us to stop and say, 'Yes there is a problem in our marriage, but, there is hope, it can be fixed. Our marriage is worth fighting for!' So, rather than seek help, professionally, through ministry, or wise couples with wisdom, a year later, we did what so many couples do when the marriage become uncomfortable; we chose to divorce.

Isn't it interesting how quickly we throw in the towel when faced with situations that we don't understand, make us grow, or challenge us to *walk out our vows*.

What I have found, well for me anyway, by not dealing with my brokenness or the void in my heart, I ended up having that same experiences over and over again, *only* with different men.

•

Discussion Question:

Men: Despite your effort to make your wife happy, do you ever feel something is missing? Are you willing to open your heart and allow your wife in? Do you understand there's a difference between her not *doing* anything about her problem, and not *knowing* what to do about her problem? If you recognize there is a problem, are you willing to hang in there and find the root cause? Or, do you feel it would be easier to just throw in the towel? Are you frustrated because you don't know what to do?

Women: Do you feel something is missing from your life? Do you find the love from your husband and children is just simply not enough? Have you found it difficult to experience inner joy and happiness in your life? Do you feel the relationship between you and your husband is changing for the worst? Are you frustrated because you don't know what to do?

We Can't Give
What We Don't Have

It was years after that bedtime conversation with Jeff that I discovered what was missing. The missing piece was self-love. Because I didn't love myself I could not give love nor receive love.

For many women, lack of self-love is the root cause behind the attitudes. Some of us are so broken and beaten down by life that we lose touch with love. Many women reject the very notion of love before it ever starts. Over time this can cause us to see ourselves in a negative light.

For some women it started earlier in their childhood when adults around them, who were there to nurture and protect them, violate them instead, it creates issues they don't see themselves as deserving love, not even self-love.

When we don't have love in our hearts, we simply have no way of giving love properly. As a result, we build walls and project negative attitudes. We dress up our pain by applying makeup, keeping our hair done, and wearing bright smiles. We even get married and have children pretending to ourselves that *all is well*, but somewhere along the way we realize there is a problem.

The discovery of a problem can happen at any time. It can be in the still of the night after passionate lovemaking or in the midst of a heated argument. It can be in any number of situations when the realization sets in. When it does, we're faced with choices; do we continue as before or do we try to find the solution?

If you can relate then be encouraged. You don't have to continue to suffer under negative emotions because there is a solution. I finally realized there is only *one* who could fill my void, His name is JESUS.

It was after I invited Jesus into my life and accepted Him as my Lord and Savior that my journey of healing began. Sometimes we come to Jesus freely and willingly, but most often we don't turn to Him until we've exhausted all other options or we're desperate for a solution. What I have found is that, by accepting Jesus Christ in my life, He was able to mend my broken pieces and make me whole. He can do the same for you.

> Jesus can fill that inner void.

The world offers many solutions for dealing with poor self-worth and internal hurt. I believe any solution that does not include a spiritual component, Jesus Christ specifically, will not provide a lifelong solution to your problems.

Jesus loves us unconditionally. When we truly accept His love and the fact that He died for us, even with our faults, we can then begin to see ourselves through the love that He sees in us. From that point, we can allow the healing process to take place.

Let's explore why we hurt in the first place. In my case, I wanted to know when and how I became broken. I felt if I could understand where my pain started, I could begin to heal.

Through my journey with Jesus, I began to understand that Satan's sole purpose is to destroy us, even before we are born. One of the biggest tools he uses is deception by blinding us from God's love which leads us to self-destruction and lack of self-love.

In the past, church sermons didn't seem relevant to my particular situation until I made the link between my hurt and Jesus' healing. When I realized that inviting Jesus into my life, and aligning my desires with His Will was the key to feeling whole, I saw my spiritual life through new eyes. From that point on I could not keep quiet. God has given me an assignment!

As a result, I committed my life to help other women be set free by exposing taboo issues of life. Through my personal discovery and journey, WOMAN TALK, an open platform for women, was birthed.

WOMAN TALK is a forum for women to come together, take off their mask, and get real. The purpose is to empower women as they build character, self-esteem, self-awareness, and self-love through an intimate relationship with God. As the women learn their value, their self-worth grows.

I recommend that those who host WOMAN TALK be willing to commit to a four, six, or eight week group session. The women in the groups are from all walks of life; family, friends, or strangers. I have found that a mixture works best. Most women are reluctant to be open about their deep dark secrets in front of people that are closest to them, fearing that they may judge or view them differently. Sometimes it's through strangers being open about their lives that other women begin to talk.

•

Discussion Questions:

Men: Are you beginning to understand that the attitude may have nothing to do with you? Some women are broken and just can't give what you need until they're healed.

Women: Like the author, have you wanted to give or receive love from your family, but couldn't? Could it be that YOU are a broken woman?

WOMAN TALK

After launching, WOMAN TALK I received calls from all over the United States from women requesting to host sessions. One particular request I received was quite different. The caller was Tracy Jones, a hairstylist and my employer.

She asked if she could host an exclusive, WOMAN TALK session at her beauty shop. *Get Real Beauty-N-Cutz* was the shop Tracy co-owned with Mike Bentley. She emphasized "exclusive" because typically the women attending the sessions would invite other women once they saw the benefit in attending. However, Tracy made it clear that for this eight-week session, she was requesting that only she and her clients attend.

For the most part the women all knew one another. Seven of the women were her standard Saturday appointments and the other three came on different days throughout the week. This made eleven women, including Tracy.

Tracy expressed that after years of listening to her clients, who had also become her friends, talk about their lives, she was concerned that some of their issues were becoming very unhealthy. As a woman of God, Tracy tried to encourage them the as she could in a business setting, but felt they needed more. She knew the women needed help but she also knew the chances of them individually seeking guidance were slim to none.

Tracy cared about each of them and thought maybe they would be willing or at least open to the idea of receiving guidance as a group; that way they could support and encourage one another. She expressed it was also important to her that the women received guidance from a Woman Of God who would give bible-based knowledge and advice, so she contacted me. I will admit I was a little apprehensive at first. As I mentioned before, it has been my experience that people are more reluctant to really open up and get real in front of people they know.

I have spoken words of wisdom many times in each of these women's lives; in fact, that's how I got the shop name, "Ms. Speaks." However, being Tracy's assistant, and working in a business setting, I was not able to spend the individual quality time that the women needed. I was also concerned if the clients would be able to separate *Ms. Speaks*, the shop's assistant, from Ms. Jerri, the Empowerment Guide and Founder of WOMAN TALK. Therefore, I wasn't confident that much would be accomplished; nevertheless, I agreed.

Next, we needed to agree on a certain day and time of the week. Most of the women get their hair done on Saturday (believe me black women are not going to miss their hair appointment). Plus, several of the women made it clear that on Saturday nights, if they weren't at choir rehearsal, they would most definitely be at the club. Since the shop is closed on Mondays, we set the sessions for Monday evenings from six to eight.

I asked each of the women to send me a few of their main concerns before the sessions began so I could select an appropriate topic. What I observed from their synopsis was that most of the women's issues seemed to center around relationships with men and jobs. Their main concerns were:
Why is it hard to find a good man?
Why can't I keep a man?
Ain't no good men out there.
Why can't I get or keep a job?

Although they named these specific issues, it was obvious to me from talking to the women in the shop that they were carrying much deeper issues. Issues such as unidentified hurts and pains that even they didn't realize they had.

In order to find the root cause behind the attitude I first had to help them leave their pride at the door, take off the mask, and get real. I knew this would be a challenge because while the women knew each other, they didn't necessarily like one another.

"Hmmm…O-kay…Sooo!" I needed to make sure the women established an atmosphere of respect. I also needed a topic for the next eight-weeks that would address the women, their men, and their underlying issues. Then it came to me, the one topic that we as black women really don't want to address, but need to, is: "The Black Woman's ATTITUDE *and* The Men Who Want To Love Us: Identifying the Root Cause Behind the *Attitude.* "

•

Discussion Questions:

Men: Do you feel *Identifying the Root Cause Behind the Attitude* is important for both the woman and the man who wants to love her? Why?

Women: Where do you believe most women's issues stem from? How do you feel it should be addressed? Do you feel a group setting will be beneficial? Would you willing to open up in front of people you know?

First Session

DIFFERENT ATTITUDES OF BLACK WOMEN

A Look In The Mirror

Meet The Attitudes

"**S**o would anyone like to start?" I asked the women at our first WOMAN TALK session. I scanned the room but no one volunteered. I tried again, "Does *anyone* have anything to say?" Again, silence.

Just as I thought, the women sat there in dead silence with what appeared to be an attitude. Some stared at the ceiling, some looked out the windows, and others sat with their arms folded and legs crossed. It was clear; these women were reluctant to talk.

LaRita, known as **Ms. Drama Queen,** always had drama and on top of that, she was very angry. She was rude, talked loud, cussed like a sailor, and was ready to fight in a heartbeat. Her attitude clearly said, *"Y'all don't know me because baby, I will set it OFF up in here!"*

Shaquanda, LaRita's sidekick, known as **Ms. Ghetto Fabulous,** was very particular how she dressed. For instance, on that day her clothes and hot pink updo hair style matched her pink glitter eye shadow, two inch long eyelashes, and light pink shimmering lipgloss; all carefully chosen to show off who she was. She had four earrings in each ear and about eight bracelets on her arm. Her fingernails were so long they had begun to curve and she wore two rings on each finger. Her manicured toes hung over her shoes. You could smell her perfume a mile away. Her attitude said, *"People always stare at me. I know it's cause I look good!"* Both LaRita and Shaquanda sat there rolling their eyes and popping their gum.

Sitting with her chair slightly turned away from the two of them and her nose in the air was no-nonsense Elaine: **Independent, Educated,**

Successful, and Workaholic. Wearing a business suit and carrying a laptop, she was focused and very intelligent. She had very high standards and a list of qualifications a man must meet before she would even consider allowing him to get to know her. She makes it very clear, *"I'm independent, have my own home, car, career, and money, so unless he has what I have and more, I DON'T NEED A MAN!"* Her arrogant attitude can be a threat to an insecure man. She has very little tolerance for people she considers beneath her. Although she's not being downright disrespectful towards me it is obvious, by some of her comments that she feels I fit in that category. The attitude of, *"Why am I here wasting my time with these people?"* was written all over her face. As she sighed several times, she sat with a snooty and uppity look of disgust on her face.

Then there was bubbly Niecey, known as the **Selfish, Greedy, Religious, Shopaholic.** Niecey was only concerned about Niecey. She felt everything had to center around her. Her attitude said, *"Whatever Niecey wants, Niecey gets!"* Bubbly Niecey was out of touch with reality. It was hard to hold a down-to-earth conversation with her because she was constantly saying, "Praise the Lord"; even at inappropriate times. For instance, a person could be pouring their heart out to her, and while that person is literally crying, Niecey might be looking in the mirror fixing her hair, and all of a sudden with a big grin on her face she'd say, "Praise the Lord!" She acts as though she's never had a bad day. Her attitude comes across as, *Holier-Than-Thou*.

Ms. Veronica, **The Cougar and Diva,** nearly fifty years old, still acting and talking like she's in her twenty's (the age of the men she usually dates). She is very polished and sharp at all times and goes to great lengths to stay that way. She's together and she knows it. In her words, "A

DIVA doesn't TRY to be, she just IS!" Her attitude is, *I know I'm all that and a bag of chips!*

Ebony, the **Lazy, Trifling, and Naive Woman,** deals with baby daddy drama. Even on the day of our session, she rushed into the salon explaining how she thought she was going to be late, *"One of my* babies' daddy's *stopped by, and well, before he would give me some money for his child, I had to give him some sex first."* Her attitude just appears *trifling.*

The last woman to arrive was Tammy**, the Abused Woman.** Walking in slightly late, she gave a slight wave and immediately took a seat in the corner. Her posture was one of brokenness and low self-esteem. Appearing withdrawn and depressed she tried to display a smile but it was obvious she was wearing a mask. Her attitude sadly revealed *hopelessness.*

Tracy, the common bond to all the women, was known as, **Professional, Kind, and Caring**. However, like many beauty shops, her place was where you could get all the gossip and drama. Tracy's clients often shared their issues with her; what they didn't realize was that Tracy had issues too. But, how would they know since none of them ever asked her how she was doing? Her attitude was, *"Positive and encouraging."*

Three more of Tracy's weekday clients Lyric, Vanessa, and Evelyn, would be attending as well but they were not available for the first two sessions.

•

Discussion Question:

Men: Do you recognize any of these attitudes? What was your experience?

Woman: Can you honestly examine yourself, and *if* you can identify with any of these attitudes, will you admit it?

Attitudes And Hurts

As I glanced around the room at each of the women, I thought how fitting the topic, "The Black Woman's ATTITUDE *and* The Men Who Want To Love Us," seemed to be. From their body language I could sense attitude and hurt. I knew then that my work was cut out for me.

"Ms. Jerri, I mean, this ain't got nothing to do with this meeting or nothing, but I just wanna ask Ebony something before I forget," Shaquanda said in her usual loud and harsh tone, "Ebony, are you going to the club Saturday night?"

"Girl, I don't know. I have to wait and see if one of my babies daddy's is gonna stop by and give his child some money." Ebony responded naively.

"Ebony, why don't you just get a job so you won't have to depend on your children's fathers?" Ms. Veronica asked.

"I've tried to get a job Ms. Veronica, but shoot, it seems like every dollar I make working, the state deducts it from my welfare check. I think the system is designed to keep us down. That's why now, I'm trying to find some work where they won't take out taxes. I ain't gonna report it if they don't know it, shoot!" Ebony said as she rolled her eyes and pursed her lips.

"Being dishonest Ebony, is not the way to do it. Pray for direction, trust God, and then come up with a plan that will help you to not rely on welfare. Now, it may involve learning a skill, taking up a trade, or even getting a degree, but it will be worth it to not have to depend on your children's fathers," Tracy said sincerely.

> Faith without works is dead.

16

"In the meantime what Ebony needs to do is just go down and file child support on all her 'babies' daddy's.' Praise The Lord," Niecey chimed in.

"Shoot Niecey, if I did that, most of them would probably get put in jail because they ain't got no jobs," Ebony said rolling her neck like a snake charmer with her hand on her hip. "And if that happen then they won't be able to hustle and give me the little money they give me now!"

Trifling Ebony

Ebony was twenty-three years old. She had four children that have different fathers and she was pregnant with her fifth child; making a fifth father. But that didn't stop her from getting dressed every Friday and Saturday night and going out to the clubs looking for a husband. Usually, she didn't return home until the next  afternoon. Ebony blamed her children for her not being able to keep a man. As she puts it, "They are always fighting each other, crying, and needing things. I think that's what be running the men away." Ebony *says* she doesn't have any extra money to spend on her children but she makes sure she has money for a new outfit for the club; which is where most of her money goes when she's playing Bingo or the casino. Usually the same outfit she wears to clubs, she also wears to church. She feels as long as she has food stamps, she's providing for her children.

Ebony was afraid to invite men to her house because she never knew when one of her babies' daddy's was going to pop up. In order for Ebony to get them to do anything for their children, she had to have sex with them first; she didn't think anything was wrong with that.

She would stop in the middle of whatever she was doing when one of her babies' daddy's came by. Right in front of her children she would lead him into her bedroom to have sex. "Don't bother me until I come out of this room," she would tell them as she'd close the door. Once in the middle of cooking dinner, one of her babies' daddy's dropped by and insisted that she give him sex before he would give his child support. They didn't have time to go to the bedroom because she didn't want her food to burn. So, while actually standing at the stove, she pushed out her behind, and allowed him to raise her dress, pull her panties to one side, and have sex with her right in the open kitchen as she continued to cook. It didn't seem to matter to either of them that her children were watching TV in the connecting living room. *Hmmm, don't underestimate children, they are very smart, and they see a lot more than we think.*

Ebony doesn't seem to understand that those men are not doing her a favor when she has to give them sex before they give her money to help support their own child.

> We must hold men accountable to their responsibilities and not feel privileged when they help support the needs of their children.

Ebony's oldest child was eight; and just like Ebony, when she was about that age, her daughter has to be the caretaker of her younger siblings. When we think of the innocence stolen, we typically think of sexual abuse; but, did you know that robbing a child of their childhood is also "innocence" stolen?

> Sistas, we are not to HUNT, our position is to be prepared for the CATCH.

Ebony was the kind of woman that would step out looking like a million bucks but at home her place would be a mess. The laundry was piled high, dirty clothes and underwear was everywhere, trash was all over the floor. Her children were always hungry because she hardly every cooked, and they always looked mucky. When she's at home she spends most of her time sitting on the couch watching TV and talking on the phone. She doesn't shower, brush her teeth, or comb her hair all day unless she's going somewhere. She says she wants a husband but what type of man would put up with that? Most men would consider her life style, *NASTY*. The bible says, "HE WHO FINDS A WIFE, finds a good thing and obtains favor from the LORD." Ebony is not preparing herself to be a wife. The Bible doesn't saying anything about *she who finds a husband* either. Ebony should stop trying to find a husband and start working on becoming a WIFE and the right man will FIND her.

Ebony thought she was doing a good job raising her children but with her poor parenting skills she just appeared trifling. I wanted Ebony to realize the impact we as parents have on our children. So I asked.

"What Examples Are We Setting For Our Children?"

Mothers, our children are constantly watching us. We teach them, by our examples; especially our daughters. Most little girls dream of growing up and being like their mothers. Believe it or not, a lot of who we are is what they are learning to become, including our attitude.

Awww look, picture perfect!

19

However,

If we think for one second that our children are not watching us, we are fooling ourselves.

At an early age our children are mimicking us.

Parenting is not an easy job and I believe most parents are doing a great job with what we know to teach our children: cooking, cleaning, work ethics, and the value of education. When Ebony takes men to her bedroom and tells her children not to bother her until they come out; or, openly have sex in the kitchen while her children are in the living room watching TV, that's what she's teaching them.

Ebony also smokes weed everyday. As she puts it, "My mama smoked weed and drank everyday when she was pregnant with me and I turned out fine." Ebony saw nothing wrong with her lifestyle. Then again, why would she? It's the same way she was raised. She saw her mother's whole life center around men and drugs. I said a prayer for Ebony that she will begin to see herself through the eyes of God and realize that *she* and *her children* deserve better.

●

Discussion Question:

Men: What is your view of Ebony? What type of man do you feel would put up with Ebony? Do you feel a woman should hunt for a man or be the catch? If a woman has hunted you before, how did it make you feel?

Women: What is your view of Ebony? Do you know women like Ebony, not willing to file child support to help their children, in order to protect their men? Do you think it's possible that if Ebony were taught better, she would do better? Are you willing to sincerely help an, "Ebony" you know is trying her best, but needs a little help and guidance?

A Wise Woman Of God

She speaks wise words and teaches others to be kind.
Proverbs 31:26 (NCV)

Although the women meant well, I didn't want Ebony to feel she was being targeted so I felt it would be best to move to another subject. I noticed Niecey seemed annoyed, so I asked, "Niecey is something bothering you?"

Niecey reiterates, "Well, I just think filing child support would help Ebony. Praise the Lord! Plus, she wouldn't have to allow those men to keep using her, is all I'm saying. Praise the Lord!"

Knowing more about Ebony's personal business, Tracy added, "Ms. Veronica's idea about getting a job is something you could seriously consider as well."

Ignoring Niecey, "Tracy, I appreciate your concern and all, but you just don't know how hard it is or what I have to go through having four kids and dealing with different daddies, or what it was like being a teenage mother!" Ebony responded as she tugged at her too short skirt. It seemed that the tighter and shorter her clothes were the better she liked them. Even being pregnant didn't change that.

The conversation was on Ebony once again but enough was enough. I was just about to change the subject when I realized I didn't have to. It was obvious Elaine had set her mind on a different target; me.

Elaine abruptly and sarcastically said, "Ebony, Tracy may not know what you have to go through," then turning her attention to me, "But Ms. Jerri, you know, don't you? Didn't I overhear you in the shop mention that

22

you were a teen mom and that your four children have different fathers? Oh yes, and that you have been married several times?"

"Elaine, why are you bringing that up now? That's not new news. Ms. Jerri has openly shared her life experiences with us," Ms. Veronica said in my defense.

Elaine remarked back defensively, "I have personally never spoken with Ms. Jerri about her personal life, Ms. Veronica!"

"Yes, Elaine, you are right," I said. "My four children do have different fathers and yes I have been married several times. Three times to be exact."

"THREE TIMES!" all the women said in unison. They knew I had been married more than once, but no one had asked the exact number of times.

"I don't mean any harm Ms. Jerri," chimed in Niecey. "But what was wrong with you that you couldn't keep any of your husband's? I'm sure glad I don't have that problem. My husband and I would never think about getting a divorce. Praise the Lord!" She proudly boasted.

"To be honest, although I've been married three times, God revealed to me that I was never a wife. Remember the bible says, 'He who finds a WIFE…' That means she has to be prepared and have a wife's mentality BEFORE the marriage." I continued, "I never really had a clue what marriage was all about. I didn't know about the commitment, the seriousness, the sacrifices, the struggles, or the maturity that marriage requires. No one ever broke it down to me the way we do in our sessions. That's why I thank God for empowerment forums like WOMAN TALK that prepare women to have a successful marriage. You see, I learned life's lessons the hard way.

I gave birth to my first child at age thirteen and I dropped out of school in seventh grade. I went through most of my life ashamed because I couldn't read or spell very well. But, after I accepted Jesus in my life He took away that shame."

Elaine was the first to respond to this, "Ms. Jerri, I don't want you to think I'm trying to patronize you, but being Tracy and Mike's assistant; shampooing their client's hair, taking care of both conjoining suites, sweeping, mopping, folding towels, and whatever else is needed for the shop to run smoothly doesn't necessarily require the highest level of education. However, becoming a founder and CEO with little education is what I don't understand. Where do your credentials come from?" Elaine asked.

Tracy cut in, "Ms. Jerri, if I may interject, I would like to address Elaine because I think I know where she's trying to go with this." Turning to Elaine Tracy said, "Elaine, I know you already know that Mike, myself, and our clients gave her the shop name, "Ms. Speaks" because she speaks from a voice of wisdom. Ms. Jerri is not only an employee she is also my prayer partner, spiritual adviser, and dear friend. Her wisdom not only comes from a biblical standpoint, it also comes from her life experiences." Tracy continued, "Knowing the hardships, shame, guilt, embarrassment, and struggles she has gone through and overcome, including surviving three brain surgeries, I personally feel is encouraging."

Ms. Jerri Opens Up About Her Own Struggles

After Tracy finished speaking there was a pause. Although I was the guide, the attention was now on me. It was time I became transparent. So I said, "You can't imagine how I felt not being able to help my children with their school work as they were growing up because I dropped out of school so early. Although I have now found a measure of self-made success, I openly admit that my choice to quit school was a big mistake. It caused me added heartaches and I didn't want my children to ever experience what I had gone through. Yes, I was uneducated, but I trusted God and believed that all things were possible. If He could make a covenant with Abraham to bless his seeds, through faith, I believed if I lined up my will with His Will, God would make a covenant to bless me, my children, and my generations to come. I also believe James 2:26 says, 'Faith without works is dead,' so I instilled in my children the importance of education. 'God is faithful!' I often told my children, 'If you do your part, He will do His.'"

"I was not trying to belittle you Ms. Jerri, it's just that I have worked hard getting the best education in order to work my way to the top of the career ladder. Since you didn't finish school I assumed you were, well, illiterate," Elaine said, clearly believing her theory.

"Elaine, you of all people, being *highly educated,* as you say, should know not to assume. Praise the Lord!" Niecey said.

"I'm not illiterate Elaine, I taught myself to read by reading the Bible," I stated.

"Wait ya'll!" Ebony interjected, "I think I just had a light bulb moment! Ms. Jerri, even though you wanted to be a better reader, NOW I GET IT; just wanting it was not enough, you had to literally pick up a book and try to read. Is that what the Bible means by 'Faith without works is dead?'" Ebony asked.

"Exactly! It was my responsibility, and I'm proud to say that at the age of forty-nine, I passed the required tests and received my high school

> Never allow anyone to tell you it's too late. **It is NEVER too late!**

diploma. Besides Elaine, not finishing high school does not mean a person is illiterate," I answered.

"What about your children? How did they turn out considering you were unable to help them with their school work?" Ebony asked seeking encouragement.

I paused for a minute, "I was getting ready to say I'm not trying to brag. But yes, I am going to brag because I am very proud of my children. Three of my adult children have graduated from college and my fourth, the youngest, is currently attending college. My son-in-law and daughter-in-law are both college graduates. I have six grandchildren, the oldest has graduated from college, two will graduate from college in 2013, and the youngest three are toddlers."

I proudly continued, "My oldest son is a Major, and my daughter-in-law is a retired Command Sergeant Major in the U.S. Military. My oldest daughter graduated from college in three years on the Dean's List and President's Honor Roll, and is self-employed and an author. My youngest daughter graduated with honors, in the top ten percent of her class, featured in *Who's Who among Students in American Universities & Colleges*, owns her own publishing company, and is an author and playwright. My son-in-law is an Air Traffic Controller. My youngest son has been accepted into the Military Intelligence Field. My oldest granddaughter is a Registered Nurse, married to the man of her dreams, and expecting their first child. I'm going to be a great-grandmother!"

Proudly, I added, "I know that graduating from college is not the only means to success; success can mean different things to different people, but I do believe it is a key that can unlock many hard-to-get-through doors. I also realize that being a teen mom, uneducated, and having multiple marriages, according to society, makes me a statistic that should not have produced successful children or the generational lineage. However, God is faithful and He has given me the desires of my heart. Yes, my children are well educated and more importantly, they know the Lord and are beginning to walk in their purpose," I concluded.

Intrigued, Ebony asked, "Ms. Jerri, did you raise your children as a single mom?"

"Obviously not, Ebony! Did you not hear her say that all of her children were college graduates or is attending college?" Elaine said, not letting up off her theory. "Surely a single mom with a seventh grade education could not have produced *that*."

"Ebony, although I had my first child at age thirteen, I received tremendous help from my mother, (I don't know what I would have done without her) and from my step-father, a wonderful man; they continued to raise my son after I moved out. I chose to move nearby so that I could keep a relationship with my son as well as actively be involved in his school activities. Remember, I've also been married and divorced several times; but for the most part, I raised my children as a single mom," I responded, clearly understanding Elaine's confusion. You see, she didn't understand the concept that *WITH GOD ALL THINGS ARE POSSIBLE.*

Tracy added, "Ms. Jerri feels her assignment is exposing hidden bondage that keeps people from living their full potential. Her passion for helping people has also been evident; for she has loved and cared for more than fifty foster children through the years."

"FIFTY FOSTER CHILDREN!" again, the women all said in unison.

"Yes, children she felt were full of potential and had greatness inside; they just needed someone to believe in them. Her attitude is, *Empowerment.* So, as the host of these sessions, if any of you feel Ms. Jerri has nothing to share with you, you are welcome to leave," Tracy concluded.

•

Discussion Question:

Men: As the head of your household have you made a covenant with God? Do you have a spiritual father to whom you can be held accountable?

Women: Have you ever made a covenant with God? Do you believe it can happen? Are you willing to line your will with His Will? Do you overlook advice coming from someone you feel is beneath you or not as well educated? Do you know a Proverbs 31 woman to whom you can be held accountable?

Attitudes, Integrity, And Morals

"**C**an we PLEASE get back to my question?" Shaquanda asked, clearly wanting to bring the conversation back to the nightclub. "I mean don't get me wrong, all y'alls advice to Ebony is right and everything, but anyway." Shaquanda shouted, "Ebony! If one of your babies daddy's don't stop by to give 'his child' some money and you don't get to go to the club, can my cousin Nae Nae borrow yo driver's license so she can get in the club? The last time she went with us they wouldn't let her in. They come talkin' about she too young and she under age just because she seventeen."

"Oh, my, goodness! Please tell me she didn't just ask that!" Elaine said shaking her head in disgust. "I've never heard of borrowing someone else's driver's license. Isn't her picture on it?"

Also in amazement Ms. Veronica questioned, "Shaquanda, don't you know that borrowing a person's driver's license is illegal? Surely you are not expecting for someone to loan out their ID; anything can happen!"

"Dang! It ain't like she gonna rob a bank or something, she just wanna get in the club. I didn't think it was that serious." Shaquanda said, clearly annoyed.

"Do you guys have any morals?" Elaine asked in her usual snooty manner.

"I do," LaRita said sarcastically.

"Uh-un, oh no you didn't LaRita! Didn't you just buy some bootleg DVD's from that man outside the grocery store?" Shaquanda said unintentionally exposing LaRita's character.

"No morals *AND* no integrity? That figures." Elaine remarked.

"What's integrity, Tracy?" Ebony wanted to know.

"It's honesty, truthfulness, honor, and uprightness, Ebony," responded Tracy.

"Oh, so what if somebody don't buy bootleg copies, but they burn copies?" Ebony asked.

"It's the same thing. You are still stealing from those artists, actors, writers, or whomever," Tracy said.

"Okay Tracy, I get it," Ebony said.

"Dang! I didn't know it was so serious!" Shaquanda said pulling out another stick of gum.

"Shaquanda, integrity is very serious; it's your morals and values," Tracy replied.

"Okay, okay Tracy, I get it too," Shaquanda finally agreed.

Although the women weren't talking on the subject of the *Black Woman's Attitude*, at least they were talking. Now I had to create an environment where they would not only stay focused on the topic, but also feel safe to open up and get real in front of one another.

I decided to conduct these sessions as I do my usual WOMAN TALK so I started by *giving* a talk.

My Attitude

"Ladies, let me tell you a story," I said, as I kicked off my high heels and put on my flat shoes. The chairs were organized in a V shape around me so I positioned myself so I could see each of them clearly. "This story is called *My Attitude*," I began.

30

"Growing up I probably had one of the worst and rudest attitudes of all and the sad part was that I didn't know it. No one ever came straight out and said to me, 'Jerri you have a bad attitude.' Yeah, people hinted around from time to time about my attitude, but like a lot of women, I didn't catch the hint. It wasn't until I became an adult that I understood the effect my attitude had on me, the people around me, and my future. It was important for me to understand when my attitude became negative. I had to truly get real with myself and think back to the different events that had happened in my life." I paused and searched their faces as I went deeper.

"I was five years old when, what I have come to know, a spirit of self-hate attached itself to me. (A spirit can be an angel or a demon. Ephesians 6:11-13) Watching TV, one day back in the early 1960's, there seemed to be only two groups of black people on TV: light skinned and dark skinned. The light skinned people such as Lena Horne and Diahann Carroll, were considered, by many, to be beautiful black people. The dark skinned people such as Aunt Jemima and Buckwheat were considered, by many, to be ugly. At five years old when I looked at my dark skin color it was the color of the 'ugly' group and I hated it; so I processed in my young mind that I was ugly too. No one ever told me I was ugly, I just *felt* that way. For thirty-five years, I silently struggled with self-hate. I never told anyone how I felt."

"Ms. Jerri, you're so beautiful. How could you think you were ugly?" Ebony asked.

Before I could answer LaRita cut in and said, "Because she must've had low self-esteem."

"Low self-esteem, uh-un, she said she had self-hate," Shaquanda said.

"Shaquanda, what difference does it make? Self-hate, low self-esteem, they're both the same aren't they? Praise the Lord!" Niecey questioned.

Since these women had never attended WOMAN TALK, they were not aware that I usually give a talk first and then open the floor for questions and answers. However, I was already aware that these sessions were going to be different. Besides, I was glad the women had loosened up and began to interact.

Not addressing their comments I said, "We will discuss all of that in detail a bit later, but first I want to finish talking about my attitude. I think my experience can help you." I continued by talking about the deep dark secrets of my past, my future, and the affects it had on people around me.

"This is why I became an empowerment guide," I explained to the ladies, "to help women heal and be set free by exposing the pain, shame, and hidden traps of their past. So, the topic for the eight-weeks will be on, The Black Woman's Attitude *and* The Men Who Want To Love Us; Identifying the root cause behind the attitude."

Needless to say the topic came as a surprise to some of the ladies, mainly LaRita and Shaquanda. Although they were not aware of it, like many women, as they were talking their whole demeanor clearly came across as, "ATTITUDE!"

"I don't know where she got that topic from. Black women ain't the only ones with attitudes!" LaRita said to the other women, while rolling her eyes.

"That's right!" Shaquanda said backing her up with her hands on her hips. "White women, Hispanic women, Asian women, really *all* women have attitudes!"

32

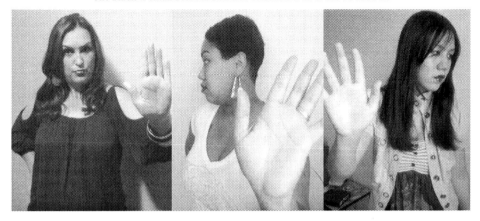

"That's true," I said addressing their comments. "But for these sessions I'm going to address, the *black* woman's attitude."

"Well, I ain't got no attitude!" LaRita said trying to stir up drama.

"Me neither!" Shaquanda joined in.

Elaine, who appeared to be disgusted every time LaRita or Shaquanda spoke, said in a sarcastic tone as she walked past them, "Sure you don't!" It was obvious Elaine felt they were beneath her.

As I wrapped up the evening's session I gave an overview of the format for the sessions, "We will start with prayer, listen to a talk based on the topic, and then I will open the floor for Q&A."

I stopped the women as they were leaving and said, "Oh, by the way ladies, your homework assignment for next week is to find the difference between self-hate and low self-esteem; if there is one."

•

Discussion Question:

Men: Do you think all women have attitudes? Do you think black women's attitudes are different from other women? How?

Women: Do you feel black women have a reputation of having an attitude? Do you feel black women are getting a bad rap? Do you think the black woman's attitude need to be addressed? Is there a difference between self-hate and low self-esteem, or are they the same?

33

Second Session

IDENTIFYING THE ROOT CAUSE BEHIND THE ATTITUDE

Self-Hate, Low Self-Esteem, And Its Effects

Although Tracy made it clear in the beginning that this would be an exclusive session for her clients, Niecey's mother arrived with her. They had been out all day shopping. Since she didn't have enough time to take her mother home before the session began, Niecey asked if it would be all right for her mother to sit in.

After our first session I wanted the women to stay more focused on the topics; so I started this talk by saying, "I will now like to address Ebony, LaRita, and Shaquanda's comment to me about self-hate from the last session. Because self-hate is such a serious issue that affects every aspect of our lives, as well as the people around us, I wanted to take some time and really explore its meaning. I know we, as women, like to get right to the *juicy stuff*, but in order to be set free from bondage and baggage we must change some things.

The way we begin is by first changing our mindset. That happens as we become empowered, and we become empowered through knowledge. I have a faith-based message, so it is important for me to use the Bible in my work. These scriptures explain just how much God values knowledge."

My people are destroyed from a lack of knowledge. Because you have rejected knowledge, I also reject you as my priests; because you have ignored the law of your God, I also will ignore your children.
Hosea 4:6 (NIV)

Choose my instruction instead of silver, knowledge rather than choice gold. Proverbs 8:10 (NIV)

I continued, "To help us understand how important knowledge is, the Bible tells us to choose **knowledge** rather than gold. If you noticed the Bible says, ***choice gold***, even up against the finest gold the Bible says choose **knowledge**."

Now with that being said, I opened the session with the homework assignment. LaRita, Ebony, and Shaquanda couldn't wait to comment on what they had read.

"Well I didn't have to look up *hate*; I think the word speaks for itself; a *strong dislike, anger, or hostility toward something or someone*," LaRita said.

"That's exactly right; and sometimes the hate can be against self and we don't even know it. It's one of those deep-seeded hidden traps that can keep us in bondage. In fact, many times it's not until we accept Jesus that it's revealed," I added.

"Ms. Jerri, I didn't realize that self-hate was so serious," Ebony said with a puzzled, yet serious look on her face.

I responded, "Self-hate, Ebony, means no self-love which is a very serious issue and a real problem because love is the foundation, or should I say, it is the glue that holds everything else together; without it, everything falls apart. Without self-love, we can't truly be happy or live our life's full potential. That's why we must be aware of hidden traps that can hold us in bondage."

"Ms. Jerri, even though the word 'attitude' was not one of our homework assignments, I looked it up too and was surprised when I read

> The word *attitude* describes a mindset, whether it be *positive* or *negative*.

the definition. I learned that 'Attitude' is not *bad* or *negative; 'Attitude* is a *state of mind, feeling, or the way in which we carry ourselves,'*" Shaquanda eagerly shared.

"That's true," I replied. "Yet so sad that we don't use the word *attitude* more in positive ways. In fact, it is depicted in society as a negative way in which most black women express themselves. The truth is, everyone has an attitude: black, white, yellow, and red; women and men. But, I want to address it the way "society" depicts the *black* woman's attitude.

There are so many of us with gifts and talents, but our attitudes are holding us back from greatness, fame, success, and even wealth. All those things mean nothing, if our attitude causes people to *not* want to be around or work with us. In order to move towards our great potential, we must get real with ourselves. We have to admit that we *do* have attitudes and there is something, or *some things* (roots), causing our attitudes to be bad or negative."

> Everything stems from something.

Driving home the point, I added, "There are people that have said things about me in the past, 'Jerri must not feel good about herself because she's walking around with a bad attitude.' Remember the self-hate I carried? Well, although I told no one, it was shown through my attitude."

Are you beginning to see that the warfare and deep-seeded attitude that offends us, is within us? But, more importantly we have the ability to change it. The Bible tells us:

[22]You were taught, with regard to your former way of life, to put off your old self, which is being corrupted by its deceitful desires; [23]to be made new in the attitude of your minds; [24]and to put on the new self, created to be like God in true righteousness and holiness.
Ephesians 4:22-24 (NIV)

•

Discussion Question:

Men: Do you feel knowledge is power? Does learning this knowledge about women help you understand us better? What about spirituality? Do you feel it's important?

Women: Do you feel spirituality has a place in helping heal and/or adjust your attitude? Why or why not?

Women Carrying Self-Hate

"**A**re women that are carrying self-hate dangerous? Do they have walls up?" I threw those questions out to the women to make a point.

Immediately Niecey answered, "Yes, because we refuse to be hurt again. Therefore, everyone is a threat! Since we don't know who to trust, walls are built as protection not to feel that same pain again. Praise the Lord!"

"I know that's right!" LaRita agreed and nodded vigorously. "That's exactly why I keep my walls up!"

"I felt the same way LaRita, until a wise woman shared an important point with me that I'll share with you," I replied. "The problem with walls is that the same way they can block hurt from getting through, they can also block love from getting through as well."

I continued, "Although it's a thin line between self-hate and low self-esteem, there is a difference. I believe women carrying self-hate are usually angry with themselves and their angry behaviors are displayed in different forms."

"I agree, when I was in school there was a girl who bullied, harassed, tormented, terrorized, and intimidated kids who showed weakness or fear. She seemed to despise the ones who appeared helpless. Once at a sleepover she confided in me that her older cousins bullied, harassed, tormented, terrorized, and intimidated her. She said that being younger, there was nothing she could do but feel helpless; so she began to bully others. But, deep down inside her anger was with her cousins, and with herself, for not being able to control what was happening to her," Ebony shared.

"The sad part about it is when people don't deal with their issues as a child, it continues on into their adult life. I see it every day on my job and can tell the ones who are carrying self-hate. They are usually, or most likely, the ones who are always bitter, angry, and negative. And the really sad part is many of these people are bosses and supervisor; so others feel the wrath of their self-hate. They are no different from the girl Ebony mentioned. They use their authority to bully, harass, torment, terrorize, and intimidate their employees or colleagues. If this is happening to you in the workplace, keep good documents and do what you have to do to protect yourself. I know I've had to stand up to a few of my bosses and co-workers. And don't underestimate prayer! Now I'm not the most spiritual person but, I've seen many positive results after I prayed to Jesus to bless the people who were abusive to me," Ms. Veronica admitted.

The room was silent and still, as each woman digested what was being said. I could see from their expressions that they were reflecting on their own experiences while processing this new information.

Ms. Veronica had hit on a very important but touchy subject: *Attitudes in the workplace*. This is a topic that definitely needs to be addressed in a book of its own. However, I will speak a little about that subject later, but, I wanted to continue with self-hate.

"I want to make this point clear, when we talk about self-hate and negative women, I'm not talking about women who have a bad day every now and then; no, I'm talking about the ones that *always* have a bad or negative attitude. She manages to find the negative in every situation. I agree with Ebony and Ms. Veronica, negative women (and men) are usually abusive in some form, either physically, emotionally, verbally, or mentally," I pointed out.

"There are many women walking around with unresolved deep-seeded hurts and pains. For some women, their hurts and pains are buried so deep that they don't realize they are still being controlled by them. Others realize the hurts and pains are there, but think they're covering them up by wearing a mask or pretending everything's okay. Then there are those who think they have dealt with their issues, until GOD reveals it to them HIMSELF or allows it to be revealed through another person or circumstance," I said.

"Ms. Jerri I know exactly what you mean," said Niecey. "One day while I was out shopping for my five- carat diamond ring, Praise the Lord! I saw a woman wearing a beautiful dress; I walked over to her and said, 'Your dress is so pretty!' Her response was, 'I know it's pretty, that's why I bought it. Do you think I would have bought it if it wasn't pretty?' Whoa! What was that about? I was just trying to pay her a compliment, Praise the Lord."

"Girl what did you say to her after she acted like that? I hope you told her where to go!" Shaquanda said trying to stir Niecey up.

"Well actually, with a big smile on my face, I said, 'GOD BLESS YOU!'" Niecey responded sincerely.

LaRita jumped in, "Now see, if that would've been me trying to pay that woman a compliment and she'd been all up in my face with that ignorant attitude of hers, baby trust me, it woulda been some drama UP IN THERE!"

"Before you were so rudely interrupted, Ms. Jerri," Elaine interjected, "You were describing negative people; please continue."

"I will but first I want to ask Niecey a question, how were you able to control your feelings to that woman's response? Now notice, I'm not asking how the woman made you feel because no one can control your feelings, only you have that authority. Only you have the power to choose how you want to feel about a situation. No one should ever give anyone else power or control over *their* feelings. It sounds like Niecey has gotten that figured out."

Niecey goes from bubbly to serious, "Well, if you only knew what I have gone through. I had to learn not to allow my feelings to get angry, offended, or even embarrassed based on other people. Besides, you never know what people are going through. She could've been dealing with some inner issues that she couldn't even accept a compliment. So I made a choice not to allow her *bad* attitude to ruin my day, or change my *happy* attitude. Praise the Lord."

"That's right Niecey. You make a great point," I said.

"Well, I don't get it. The way I was raised, if people get ignorant with you, you get ignorant with them," LaRita justfied.

"LaRita, I feel you on that, I grew up the same way; but, I've learned that it doesn't necessarily make it right. I now know the way I *react* to what people say or do to me is a choice. I don't have to play tit-for-tat. I'm proud that Niecey saw

> Growth is realizing what you've always done may not have been right. Maturity is being willing to change.

beyond the woman's attitude and saw her pain. In situations like that you could also say a silent prayer that God will heal the person's pain, whatever it maybe," I added.

"Now back to what I was saying Elaine. Another sign of women carrying self-hate are those who are usually never satisfied. I'm not talking

42

about people who are high achievers, striving to always be better; that's great! I'm talking about the ones who no matter what they do, or what someone does for them, they are just never satisfied," I stated.

"I have a question, what if you don't like somebody because they did you wrong? To people it might seem like you got an attitude or you're being negative, but what if you just can't forgive that person for what they did? Does that make you wrong?" LaRita asked sincerely.

"That's a good question LaRita, and it seems logical that people would think that way, but holding on to what someone has done to you is a form of pain, which in many cases manifests as a negative attitude; but hold on, I will be addressing the inability to forgive a little later." I said, shifting my focus back to negative attitudes.

"One of the ways you can recognize if you're a negative person is by paying attention to yourself. Pay attention to your interaction with other people, your tone, actions, and body movements; then, notice how they react. What is their demeanor? When they walk away from your presence, do they appear uplifted and encouraged or beat down and discouraged?" I gave the women something to think about.

"What's the big deal? It ain't like negativity can hurt you, can it?" Shaquanda asked sarcastically.

Finally, Tammy raised her head slightly, and in a low tone said, "That's what I was wondering. I'm just curious to know." It seemed that question had gotten her attention.

"Oh yes Tammy, it can! If not physically, it could hurt you mentally and even spiritually. Okay ladies try this," I challenged. "The next time you are around a negative person, notice how you feel about yourself, or your circumstances, *before* you are in their presence. Then, notice how you feel during and *after* you leave their presence. Negative people are draining and their negative energy can drain you and your positive energy."

The Bible tells us:

Do not be misled:
"Bad Company (association) corrupts good character."
1 Corinthians 15:33 (NIV)

If you know a negative person, then pray for them. Ask God to reveal it to them and teach him or her how to love the Lord, themselves, and others. If that person is someone you feel you can approach in love, you can briefly and in a non-judgmental way, tell that person how you feel when you are in his or her presence. Notice I said *briefly*; you do not want to get in a long discussion that could turn into a debate or an argument. Also notice, I didn't say tell that person how they made you feel. Remember, only you can control how you *choose* to feel, so take ownership. In the meantime, until they receive help, you may need to shorten or lessen your interactions. Remember you do not have to allow abuse from negative people."

•

Discussion Question:

Men: Have you ever been with a negative woman? What was it like? How did you feel? What's your view of a negative woman?

Women: Do you feel you are a negative person? Reflecting back, have you noticed people's demeanor changing in your presence? Were they encouraged or discouraged? If you feel you are a negative person, what steps can you take to change it?

Food For Thought

Positive Attitudes and Role Models

Before we go any further, I must take the time to acknowledge some of our positive role models. As we have now established, not *all* attitudes (state of mind) are negative and bad. In fact, I have found that the MAJORITY OF BLACK WOMEN'S ATTITUDES, WORK ETHICS, and MORALS ARE VERY POSITIVE. Some of our greatest examples include Oprah Winfrey, Maya Angelou, Coretta Scott King, and our own First Lady, MICHELLE OBAMA, just to name a few.

Educators

Principals

Attorneys

College Grads

Teachers

Women of GOD

Entrepreneurs

Black, Bald, & Beautiful
Cancer Survivors

Actors

Speakers

These are a few of our distinguished women who are making positive impacts. There are many, many more, from Judges, Doctors, Nurses, Military, Directors, and stay-at-home moms and grandmothers. I'm proud of all of us.

Now Let's Talk About Low Self-Esteem

"**C**an I share something that I think can cause low self-esteem?" Ms. Veronica asked. "Once I was visiting a friend, a white woman, and her children were running through the house and broke an expensive vase; glass shattered all over the floor. The first thing she did was run over and checked to see if her children were all right; then gave them a big hug."

Ebony interrupted, "Excuse me Ms. Veronica, did you say the first thing she did was check to see if her kids was all right? Shoot, if I had an expensive vase and my kids woulda been running in the house, well first of all, my kids know they ain't suppose to be running in the house anyway, but if they did, and broke my vase, and it was an expensive vase, Lord have mercy on'em, cause that's what they gonna need!"

"Ebony, just the way you responded, was the point that I was just getting ready to make!" Ms. Veronica proved her point.

"Anytime we make material things seem more important than our children, it could lead to the development of low self-esteem. Of course we know many of the obvious abuses that can cause low self-esteem: verbal, physical, mental, and sexual. These will be addressed later." I said.

"Ms. Jerri, you mentioned abuses that were obvious, but there are also abuses that are not so obvious but can cause low self-esteem, such as: weight, hair texture, education level, finances, or even skin color," Tracy concluded as I nodded in agreement.

Ms. Veronica spoke up, "What about what other people say about us? If we allow it, it could lower our self-esteem as well."

Tracy, now standing up said, "You said a key word Ms. Veronica and that is 'allow.' People can't say to us, what we don't allow. Well let me put it another way. People can say whatever they want; but, like Ms. Jerri and Niecey said, we have the choice in how we *allow* it to affect us, and I'm going to take it a step further, *OR* whether we chose to listen to it. There are some things I won't allow people to come to me with, or speak into my life."

"But Tracy, you said there are something's you won't allow people to come to you with or say to you, how can you stop them?" Ebony asked.

"Well remember, you have a choice. Me personally, I try to respect others, in the way I want them to respect me, and I'm very conscious to not gossip, speak harshly, or talk negative to people. So when someone comes to me in any of those ways, I immediately, *STOP THEM*, and in a loving way remind them that I don't bring those attitudes to them and I would appreciate them not bringing them to me.

I'm sorry Ms. Jerri, I wasn't trying to take over; I just wanted to address Ms. Veronica's comment, that what's even more important is what we think about ourselves, because it helps when we know we have choices."

"Oh no Tracy you're fine. I appreciate you bringing out that point because our choices are very important. I will talk a little bit more about it later, but right now I want to give an example of why it is so important how we think about ourselves," I responded.

Know Who You Are So Opinions of Others Don't Hinder Your Success

"I will share my own experience. I have two beautiful daughters, Tori and Ronyea. Tori, the oldest, grew up not thinking she was beautiful. Although she is absolutely gorgeous and very smart, she grew up with low self-esteem. As a child she adored my dark complexion and often stared at me in admiration because she thought I was beautiful.

One day while riding in the car, Tori, who was about six years old, looked at me and excitingly expressed, 'Mama, you're so pretty, I look just like you!' I looked at her and said in a harsh tone, 'You don't look nothing like me.' Sadly, I said that based on the self-hate I had about my dark skin; Tori was much lighter. However not understanding the self-hate I was dealing with, she perceived my words as, 'You don't look like me, *you're* ugly.' How many of us know that hurting people hurt people, even if it's unintentional.

Tori held on to my words. In addition to growing up not feeling good about herself; one day, in middle school, a few female classmates, obviously jealous, mockingly shouted to Tori, 'Your nose is big; You're so hairy; Ugh, you got gaps between your teeth!' Kids can be so cruel. These insults in Tori's mind were conformation, that she was ugly. There was also a time her teacher made a comment about her hips being big. From that day on, she began to wear oversized baggy clothes.

For years it was hard for Tori to see her true beauty, potential, and greatness. It wasn't until she was well into her twenty's, and after countless compliments about her beauty and intelligence, that she began to accept herself for who she was. She was close to thirty when she finally became comfortable wearing clothes that showed her 'big hips.'

Low self-esteem is a serious issue and reveals itself in different ways. I believe anyone who would intentionally try to make another person feel bad by putting them down is usually unhappy, jealous, and suffers themselves from some form of low self-esteem.

As parents, we have to learn who we are, our value, and our self-worth, so we can teach our children who they are, their value and their self-worth," I said.

Here are some signs of low self-esteem:
- Feelings of 'being stuck'
- Lack of motivation
- Self-Destructive
- Depression
- Insecurity
- Jealousy
- Feeling of Hopelessness
- Negative self-talk ("I can't," "I won't," "I'll never be able to")
- Disassociation from success or high self-esteem activities

"Now see that ain't me!" Shaquanda said defensively. "Everybody knows I ain't got low self-esteem. Plus don't nothing on that list sound like me."

"Ms. Jerri, do people with low self-esteem always look or seem down?" Ebony asked, obviously with a motive. "Now I ain't trying to talk about nobody or nothing but, like for instance Shaquanda, Ms. Ghetto Fabulous is what we call her, she is well over 250 pounds, but weight don't seem to matter to her. As she puts it, 'When I'm out on the dance floor, everybody be staring at me because I'm a BBB: big, black, and beautiful. Little skinny chicks ain't got nothing on me!'" Ebony concluded mocking Shaquanda.

"You got that right!" Shaquanda boasted. "Because I know I look good. Now I ain't trying to toot my own horn, but, *toot toot!*"

"Hmmm…" I had to choose my words carefully. "Well the truth is Ebony, yes, Shaquanda *could* be and probably *is* dealing with some much deeper issues as most of us are."

"Yeah but, I thank Shaquanda's issues go a little bit deeper," Ebony said with a snicker, "She's funny, I got to tell y'all some of the things she do.

Shaquanda, Ms. Ghetto Fabulous

Shaquanda is twenty-nine, has three kids: two sons, Jawan seventeen, and Jacobi sixteen, and even though Shaquanda won't admit it, she don't treat them with the love she do her thirteen year old daughter LaQuanda, Quanny is what we call her. Quanny is clearly the apple of Shaquanda's eye. Quanny is a big girl too, and just like her mama she is a Junior Ms. Ghetto Fabulous!"

"Ebony! Now, I know you ain't tryna talk," Shaquanda said in a humorous way.

"Girl I ain't talking bad about y'all, I'm just telling the truth and you know it," Ebony said again snickering as she continued. "Their pink updo hairstyles, pink booty shorts, pink shimmering lipgloss, fingernail and toenail polish, all matched to a "T." They both loved wearing stiletto heels and low cut tops showing their cleavage. They dressed like this even at the boy's basketball games.

"That's right, and we turn heads everywhere we go; all the men be looking at us. And as for the women, yeah they be hating, but I know they just jealous, they be wishing they had as much junk in they trunk as we do," Shaquanda proudly boasted.

"Umm-hmm, yeah right, in your head!" Ebony said as she rolled her eyes up. "But anyway, every time you looked around, Shaquanda was tricking some man into thinking that she was pregnant by him and needed money for an "abortion." Relieved they wouldn't have to pay child support for the next eighteen years, the men willingly gives her the money. Then while shopping and getting their hair and nails done, Shaquanda would laugh and tell Quanny how stupid men are. She says she's teaching her life lessons on how to *play the game, so she won't get played.*

Shaquanda loves her some Quanny, and she loved for the two of them to look good and would do just about anything to assure it, even using her bill money. Then when she can't pay her bills she'd go to different charities and ask for help. For the times help wasn't available, when bill collectors would call. She'd pass her cell phone to Quanny to answer and say, "My mama ain't here." Yep! That's right, she taught her daughter to lie.

Quanny is Shaquanda's best friend. She takes her everywhere with her, and they are truly a team, you should see them in a grocery store, they will pick through every package of bacon in the rack to find the leanness one. Oh, but then again I think a lot of black women do that. Shoot, I know I do, well anyway. They call themselves Divas, but everybody else calls them, '*Ghetto Fabulous Divas*'. And don't get it twisted, although Shaquanda likes to look good; make her mad, and she will cuss you smooth out, calling you everything but a child of God. She's ready to fight at the drop of a dime and she does it in front of Quanny, who finds it hilarious instead of embarrassing. Shaquanda doesn't seem to have respect for anyone especially men." Ebony said as she brought this story to an end.

Typically I would not have allowed Ebony's rag on Shaquanda, story to continue for so long. However, those two were close friends and I have often heard them talk that way to one another at the shop, all in fun. But seriously, I wanted to get Shaquanda to take a look in the mirror, and realize how serious what she does in front of her daughter was, so I asked the question:

How Do Our Daughters See Us Interact With Men?

Are we kind and respectful, or do they see us talking loud, being rude, nagging, complaining, cussing them out, and playing games? What about when we're on the phone talking to our friends, do our daughters hear us putting men down and degrading them? Do they hear us focusing on all the negative things we feel about men? We need to know that our daughters are watching and listening to us, and many of them will follow our example. Did you realize a mother with low self-esteem; will more than likely raise a daughter with low self-esteem.

•

Discussion Question:

Men: Have you met women who were very attractive, but had low self-esteem? Were you attracted to them? Which is more attractive to you: a woman who is beautiful, but has low self-esteem or a woman who may not be as attractive, in your eyesight, but is confident and knows her self-worth?

Women: Do you believe that childhood traumas, issues, or problems effect who we become as adults? Do you feel the life lessons Shaquanda's teaching her daughter is appropriate? What kind of woman/mother are you raising your daughter to become?

Light Skin vs. Dark Skin

It seems as if self-esteem and self-hate were only attached to dark skinned women. Many dark skinned women have been told that they are ugly no matter how beautiful they are. I remember an old saying, "If you're white you're right, if you're brown hang around, but if you're black GET TO THE BACK." I remember that area well. And what's sad is, even today we are still experiencing some of it. But also sad, was being a black girl and feeling that other black girls just like you, were better because their skin was a few shades lighter.

Even within our own race, black women have had to deal with issues about light and dark skin, and many of the issues start within the family. In the 40's, 50's, 60's, and early 70's, lighter skinned people were made to feel superior over darker skinned people.

"Oh how well I know. Elaine said thinking out loud as she reflected back. Somehow having a dark complexion had a negative stigma to it. My father had a very dark complexion and I have his skin color. My mother was very light complexioned and my three younger sister's complexion came from her. I hated the difference, and while my father will not admit it, he was harder on me then he was with my sisters.

He gave me chores, such as taking out the trash, washing the trash cans, feeding and cleaning up after the dog, cutting the grass, raking up the leaves, cleaning the toilet, and washing out the bathtub daily. My father who I felt adored my sisters, would only make them do the dishes and vacuum, and those chores were divided between the three of them. I couldn't help but to wonder why my father made such an obvious difference between my sisters and me. Was it because I was the oldest or was it because of the color of my skin? I silently struggled for years on the inside trying to make some sense of it," Elaine admitted.

I could relate to the pain in her voice. She was finally feeling comfortable enough to open up to the group that only one week before, she had looked at with such disgust.

Elaine continued, "Growing up in a small town where just about everyone knew everyone, the realization of what I felt in my own home was evident as I walked around town. People would make comments toward me such as: tar baby, spot, ju ju, greasy, nappy headed, smutty black, blue black, ashy black, black, blackie, darkie, smokey, black thing, or any name that would be derogatory or degrading. Some would even try to throw me a backhanded compliment like, 'You're pretty, to be dark.'

My sisters on the other hand were different. One was very tall, pale with freckles, and had very thin hair. Another was very short on the heavy side with very thick long bushy hair. The other had more of a caramel complexion, medium build with short kinky hair after my father. They were referred to as "the prettier ones."

While listening to Elaine speak, I was saddened that she had allowed negativity to block her from realizing her beauty. She was stunning.

 Her flawless smooth ebony colored skin, almond shape eyes, full lips, and high cheekbone structure, made her a sight to behold. Because Elaine's color was viewed in a negative way growing up, she never realized her beauty. In order to protect herself from the hurt of the harsh comments of others, Elaine learned early in life to put up a wall that comments couldn't pass through.

"Even my father made negative remarks about my skin color, often calling me 'Spook.' My mother never said anything negative about my color, but never stood up for me either. I wanted so badly to have the approval of both my father and mother that I became the best in everything I set out to do, but sadly I never got it. Even as an adult with a Ph.D, when people make comments about my skin color, positive or negative, I still feel like that little girl who was teased and called names," Elaine confessed.

Elaine was thirty-six years old, a very successful, strong, and independent black woman. She made her own money, owned her home, drove a Range Rover, and dressed only in designer clothes.

Elaine grew up in a very stern household. Her father was a workaholic. Although he was hardly at home, he was very dominant as the ruler and breadwinner of the home; his word was law.

He instilled in Elaine that the only way to have success in life is to graduate from college, work hard, and work her way to the top of corporate America; and that's exactly what she did. However, it left her with very little time for anything else, including fun and friends.

Although Elaine deep down disliked her father's harsh and stern way of running the household, she despised her mother for having such a weak, timid, easy going personality. Not seeing a healthy balance at home, Elaine was very successful, but very lonely and bitter.

She would not allow a man to get too close to her in fear that he may be like her father and she'd become like her mother. She made the choice not to marry nor have children. But, what Elaine didn't know was, although she didn't trust herself to choose the right man, she could have trusted Jesus.

Elaine has a standing appointment every Saturday with Tracy. Her appointments were always the first of the day. She preferred it so that she could get in and get out. There have been several occasions when Elaine has stayed at the shop longer to finish work she started on the shop's Wi-Fi, causing her to come in contact with some of Tracy's other clients. When this happens it's always an uncomfortable situation for Tracy. Being a workaholic, working long days, weekends, and much overtime, Elaine has very little tolerance for, as she sees it, *lazy, trifling, ghetto fabulous drama queens.*

Sadly, it wasn't that Elaine loved working so much as the reason that she was a workaholic; unbeknownst to her, she was trying to fill an empty space. SHE SAID SHE DOESN'T NEED A MAN, *but*, does she want one? Or was she just trying to convince herself? Hmmm…it was obvious Elaine was carrying deeper hurts and pains.

The Tables Turned

Dark skinned women weren't the only ones who had to endure harsh comments. In the late 70's the tables began to turn. All of a sudden, dark skin was in, light skinned women weren't as popular. They were being

called names like, high yellow, stuck up, sunshine, trying to be white, or get mad at a light skin person and wanna fight them because the people say, they think they're better. I have found that most light skinned people don't think that at all. Light or dark skin doesn't matter to most white people, to them, we're all just Black. Without feeling love from parents and being told that we are beautiful, valuable, and special, low self-esteem can develop.

•

Discussion Question:

Men: Have you chosen a woman based on her skin color? If so what was your reasoning for preferring one color over the other? Does skin color tell you a woman's character? Can you appreciate all skin colors?

Women: Have you judged someone based on their skin color? Have you felt judged because of your skin color? How did it make you feel? How did you handle it? Are you still dealing with skin color issues today?

Daddy's Little Girl

"It doesn't matter what shade you are when your daddy comes in your room in the middle of the night and gets in your bed." Niecey said. Out of nowhere, with a distant look in her eyes, she reflected on her past.

"I remember that dark, cold, December night well. It was two weeks before Christmas. I was only ten years old when I was awakened out of my sleep as my pink and white lace panties were being pulled off from behind. I tried to raise my body and turn my head, but all I could see in the darkness was the silhouette of who appeared to be my daddy. 'NO DADDY, NO!' I said as he climbed on my back.

His two hundred fifty pound body weight pinned my body down like a marshmallow, I could hardly breathe. 'Daddy no, please don't, again I said franticly. As he spread my legs I was confused, we had wrestled before and he had tickled me many times. But not pinning me down like that, and never with my panties off. So what is daddy doing, I thought. Then the worst pain I had ever felt, pierced me, as daddy penetrated my innocent little body with what felt like a log. I could feel my skin ripping and tearing as he forced his way through; the pain was excruciating. I didn't know what was happening. It hurt so badly. I had never felt anything like that before. I honestly thought I was going to die.

Barely able to speak, I pleaded with him to stop hurting me but he wouldn't; he kept on forcing his penis in and out of my tiny body. Helpless, frightened, and confused, his pain stricken little girl silently soaked her pillow with tears." The room was quiet and tense as she shared this lifelong secret.

"When daddy finished I wanted to jump up, run, and take a shower, I felt so dirty. But I couldn't move from being in so much pain. I was still lying on my stomach, when daddy leaned over and kissed the back of my neck then whispered in my ear, 'Don't tell your mother, or anyone. This is our little secret, my little princess.'

The next day, with my innocence stolen forever, I had so many questions racing through my mind. *Should I tell my mama? What if she doesn't believe me? What if it breaks up our family? What if mama thinks it's my fault? Why did daddy do this to me? What did I do wrong? Why didn't my mama protect me?* I was so ashamed.

That evening daddy came home with a big surprise for me. It was a new princess doll. I loved dolls and that evening we acted as if everything was normal. The more my daddy came into my room at night, the more dolls he bought me. The more this cycle continued I began to hate myself for it. I wasn't even sure why; maybe it was because I never told anyone, or because I was too ashamed and embarrassed, or maybe it was because I didn't think my mama would believe me. But one thing I do know, daddy had killed something inside of me. I had no idea the effect, years of constantly being raped by my dad would have on my life or my marriage years later."

Abuse and Betrayal Caused Her to Build Walls

Niecey was an only child and from the outside seemed to be the apple of her parent's eyes. Her father, in an attempt to cover up his misdeeds, catered to her every material need by buying her anything she wanted. He called her his little princess and her parents made sure she lived the life fit for a princess.

Niecey's abuse and betrayal had caused her to build walls; walls that presented itself as behavior problems as a teen. However, as a young adult she developed a "me me me" attitude. Yes, Niecey was all about Niecey.

Still dealing with inner pain, Niecey said, "It wasn't supposed to happen to me. We had a picture perfect family, a dad who was a good provider, and a mother who worked, but still came home every evening and cooked dinner. She made sure my dad and I had a hot meal. I was even a straight 'A' student.

We had a beautiful home in an upper class neighborhood. At age ten, besides all the princess dolls that could fit in my room, I had my own TV and phone line. My parents drove nice cars and our family was part of the elite at our church. Oh yes, we were faithful churchgoers! My parents wouldn't think of missing a church service. My dad was a Deacon at the church and my mother was a Deaconess. In fact, it was in that same church that I met a wonderful young man named Howard."

I Thought the Liquor Would Ease My Pain

"It was after the first few times my daddy raped me that I began to drink; I thought drinking would ease the pain." Niecey said reflecting back.

"Niecey, you were actually drinking liquor at ten years old?" Ebony asked with a surprised look on her face.

"Ebony, not only was I drinking I was getting drunk off E&J at age ten. I was deceiving myself, thinking it would take my pain away." Niecey replied.

"But at ten where did you get the liquor?" Ebony asked.

"Child PLEASE! My parent's kept liquor in the house. I'm sure daddy noticed it going down, but he never said anything. He could probably smell the liquor every time he climbed on me."

Shaquanda being curious asked, "Were you ever worried about getting pregnant?"

"No, and daddy wasn't either, you see, daddy never penetrated my vagina." Niecey said with a slightly embarrassed look on her face. "It was always anal."

Niecey Confronts Her Mother

Hearing Nicecy's confession her mother dropped her head in shame as tears streamed down her face.

"Niecey have you ever confronted your father or mother about what happened to you as a young girl?" I asked. I could tell Niecey needed some type of closure.

"No, because I never had the courage to." She responded.

"Is there anything you would like to ask your mother now? And mom, are you willing to allow her to?" I asked both of them. I felt in order for their healing to begin this was something that needed to happen. Since they had never talked about it, and since Niecey brought it up, her pain was at the surface and needed to be addressed. I felt this was the right time and the right place.

Niecey walked over to her mother and knelt in front of her. "Mama, did you know that daddy was coming in my room?"

Niecey's mother with her head still down spoke in a soft voice. "At first I didn't." She said, "During that time your father and I were not getting along very well. He had begun watching pornographic videos of different sex acts women were performing on men. One night he asked me to watch it with him. He said he wanted me to learn some things that he wanted to try, so I watched but was very uncomfortable. However, wanting to please my husband I tried some of the things I saw but didn't like it."

Her mother took a deep breath before continuing. "He said he wanted to try anal sex. The attempt was so painful I could hardly bear it and he hadn't even gotten his entire penis in, so I refused to try again. He became very upset telling me how I'm his wife and that I'm supposed to do whatever he says. Still I refused. Then he said, what I thought was a sick joke, 'If you won't do it, then I'll do it with Niecey.' I totally ignored that. I felt he was just trying to bluff me into doing what he wanted."

Raising her head slightly she looked at the women and said in a warning tone, "It never entered my mind that he would actually carry it out and hurt our little girl. He had never shown any signs of looking at our daughter in any inappropriate way, so even when he said it I didn't believe him. Since I don't drink I didn't notice the liquor going down, and because I had to be up so early in the mornings for work at the hospital, I usually went to sleep before the two of them."

Niecey studied her mother's face as her mother told the story she had carried for years.

"One night I woke up about midnight and my husband wasn't in our bed, I went in the den where he would sometimes fall asleep. When I didn't see him, I began walking down the hall toward the main bathroom and Niecey's room. As I passed the empty bathroom, I could hear a strange sound coming from Niecey's room; it sounded like Niecey was crying. My first thought was, 'Oh Lord, what did Niecey do for her daddy to be whooping her at this time of night?' But then I thought *that's strange because her dad had never whooped her before.*

As I got closer her agonizing cry sounded muffled, almost like something was over her mouth or she was crying with her face in the pillow or something. I put my hand on the doorknob getting ready to open it when I heard what appeared to be moaning sounds coming from her daddy. Immediately I felt a sinking feeling in the pit of my stomach.

It's that feeling most women get when something's not right.

Not sure I could handle what I might see if I'd opened that door, I simply backed away, went to my room, got in bed, and silently cried myself to sleep. I've never asked either of them what happened that night and I never got up through the night again to see. I don't really know when it began or when it stopped. I guess I had convinced myself that if I didn't see it I couldn't really say that it was happening. I know I was wrong and should have done something about it, but I was too ashamed and embarrassed to admit that something like that was happening in my home."

Wiping her tears she said, "You all just don't understand, like Niecey said, my husband was and still is a deacon in our church and I am a

64

deaconess. We had high positions. We were respected in the church and in our community. People looked up to us. We lived in a nice home and drove nice cars. So I reasoned in my mind that by not telling anyone, I was protecting my family.

But the truth is I should have protected my daughter. Hearing the pain that I have contributed to my daughter, I no longer care what people may think or say about me, it's time I try and help stop my daughter's pain, whatever it takes. I didn't realize when I came here that I would be telling something I've been holding in for so many years. But I'm glad I came." Then she turned to Niecey and with a tear stained face said, "If you want to, I will stand with you and confront your father. I am so very sorry Niecey. Will you PLEASE FORGIVE ME?"

With overwhelming emotions coming from both of them, they embraced. Niecey said, as tears streamed down her face, "Yes Mama, I FORGIVE YOU."

There wasn't a dry eye in the room. Niecey realized that whether she chose to confront her father or not, the choice she made that day to forgive her mother had set them both free. Yes, the truth can hurt, but it will also set you free. The room was dead silent. Niecey had gone deep and hit on some dark taboo issues. It was obvious she had awakened the women's feelings.

Niecey had set the bar by courageously taking off the mask and getting real. I wanted the women to think about the courage it took for Niecey and her mother to speak up. I also thought it would be a good time to **dismiss**.

•

Discussion Question:

Men: I didn't ask a question of you. I just want you to try and understand the heart, emotions, pain, and shame a woman goes through when she has been abused.

Women: Does reflecting on your past bring back hurtful memories? Are you holding secrets that could be keeping you in bondage and controlling your attitude? Have you ever used liquor to take away your pain? Did it work or just open the door to other problems? Do you feel Niecey did the right thing to confront her mother? Do you agree that Niecey forgiving her mother set them both free? Have you been unable to forgive someone for hurting you? If so, are you willing to forgive the person now? If you can relate to any part of Niecey's story, how did you deal with or have you dealt with your situation? Have you confronted your abuser? If you have not confronted your abuser, would you like to?

A Man Named Howard

Howard was thirty-five, six feet three inches tall, and good looking. He was raised by his father and mother in a Christian household. Although both had degrees, his mother agreed to put her career on hold to stay home and raise their three sons, while his father built his career.

Howard's parent instilled in their son's the importance of taking care of their families. They were taught to treat their wives with patience and respect, and above all to put God first. Howard's parents also instilled the importance of education. He and his younger brother listened and have both received M.B.A degrees.

However, his oldest brother Tyrone went the opposite direction. At an early age he chose to go down a different path that included joining a gang, robbing people, stealing cars, selling drugs, and pimping and beating women. Needless to say, Tyrone is now serving time in prison. Howard grew up witnessing Tyrone's dangerous life style, the disrespect he had for women, and his many encounters with the law.

Howard and his younger brother chose to accept Christ in their life in their early teens. Howard has strong spiritual values. He strives to maintain a positive image in the church and in the community. He is a very analytical person; Howard never makes a decision without first thinking about how it will affect the people around him. He is thoughtful, kind, and considerate of others.

When Howard first noticed Niecey at church, he was attracted to the way she worshipped and how much she seemed to love the Lord. He also noticed how she carried herself and in his mind was always properly dressed from head to toe! Never showing any cleavage or any part of her legs above the knee was very appealing to him.

After much prayer and consideration, he made up in his mind that she was the one for him. After a short courtship Howard proposed to Niecey, believing that when a man finds a wife, he has found a good thing and will have favor with the Lord.

Niecey Was Excited, But Concerned

Although Niecey was excited about becoming Howard's wife, she was concerned about the secret she was carrying and struggled with the decision of telling him before they got married. Niecey wanted so badly to be real with Howard and tell him the truth about her past, but she feared that if he knew how messed up she was, he wouldn't want to marry her. Besides, Niecey reasoned by telling herself, "I'm okay!"

Niecey, not thinking the abuse would have an effect on her mentally chose to keep her secret. She thought her past was behind her, but boy was she wrong. To fill the void of her past Niecey became a selfish, greedy, religious, shopaholic who controlled her household and husband. She spends all their money with no consideration for Howard.

Tracy once tried to explain, "That as a wife if you're not helping your husband get out of debt, you could be hurting him by causing him more debt." Niecey just disregarded the advice since she relates hurting with physical abuse.

Her response was, "What do you mean? I'm not hitting him!" She doesn't get it. She doesn't realize that abuse comes in different forms. Spending money that they don't have to spare or putting them deeper in debt *is* a form of hurting him.

Although Howard really wants children, at least one, although he would really like two, he knows the chances of him becoming a father are slim to none. Niecey has made it clear that she is not willing to stretch out her nice waistline, or as she put it, "*disfigure*" her body for a child.

Niecey could be considered a thick woman; however, she is shaped like a Coca-Cola® bottle. She has a large bust, a tiny waistline, and big hips. What stands out the most about her is her bubbly, yet straightforward personality. Niecey admits that she is too selfish to share her pampered life with anyone else. She feels a child might interfere with the life style she has grown accustomed to, thanks to Howard. Not being up front and honest about her past with her husband, had caused her to develop a selfish attitude to cover feelings of inadequacy and other emotions her abuse had created.

A True Man Of God

As a husband and true man of God, Howard fully understands his role in the relationship and will do whatever it takes to provide for his household. However, one day Howard confided in Mike, his barber and Tracy's business partner, about the despair he felt in his marriage.

"Man, would you believe that in the midst of a recession, Niecey just went out and bought herself a five-carat diamond ring? And what she doesn't realize is the recession is now affecting my job. I haven't told her yet, but there's talk going on around the company that there's going to be a major company layoff soon. I don't know if I'm going to have a job to pay the bills we already have! Now I got to get a second job just to pay for that ring she purchased, which she did without consulting with me first."

Howard was becoming discouraged thinking about the layoff and current financial hard times. He continued on, while Mike cut his hair, "And it's not just that, Niecey makes everything about her. It's always about her. She even controls when we have sex. Even though the Bible clearly says, since we are married, her body belongs to me and my body belongs to her. It also says neither of us should deny the other sex, unless it's agreed on for a specific reason, but she doesn't even care." Howard confessed to Mike.

Niecey's unwillingness to fulfill the duties of a wife in the home and in the bedroom is creating tension in the household. Howard is at his breaking point. He is frustrated with the way the relationship is going and tired of protecting Niecey from the truth about their finances. Although Howard really loves the Lord, and is trying to be patient and understanding with his wife, he now feels it is time to talk, or walk! No matter how nice or mild a person is, everyone has a breaking point and you can see Howard is clearly at his.

"Mike man, I want to love my wife, but every time she disrespects me by going over my head and controlling the relationship, it pushes me away a little more. Honestly, I don't know how much longer I can put up with this. There's been so many times where she'd come home claiming she was out shopping, but it was obvious she had been out drinking. In fact, she would be borderline drunk with no explanation!

I never thought divorce was an option, but I can't seem to communicate to her that she's pushing me away. Believe me man I'm not perfect, but I'm trying. Sometimes I wonder if Niecey really loves me, or just love what I do for her. And just think I chose her because she appeared to be a woman after God's own heart. Now, I question myself. Sometimes I just want to give up!"

"Howard, man wait before you do something you will regret. I know you love Niecey and I believe she loves you, just sit down with her and let her know how you're feeling. Pray and trust God, isn't that what you always tell me to do?" Mike advised.

After some encouragement from Mike, Howard realized his marriage is worth working on.

"Thanks man for the encouragement, I guess I took my focus off God when I started worrying about how I was going to pay all those bills. I even thought if only I could change Niecey to be more caring and loving everything would be fine. But now I realize I can't change one thing by worrying, and I certainly can't change Niecey, only Jesus can. I've got to trust Him to take care of my job situation, and Niecey. I'm back on the right track now; I'm not going anywhere. When I took my marriage vows it was for better or for worse. Maybe I'll find a part-time job that pays big money. Lord knows I'm going to need it," Howard confessed.

Howard's maturity toward his marriage along with his trust in God is what keeps him able to see past Niecey's attitude, and love her.

•

Discussion Question:

Men: Should Niecey have disclosed her secret to Howard before they got married? Can you understand Howard's frustration? Howard thought about leaving; do you think his maturity and love for the Lord help him make the decision to stay?

Women: Do you have a good man and you know you are taking him for granted? Do you find yourself withholding important information from your mate in fear that he may see you differently? Do you believe Niecey's disrespect to her husband is disrespect to God?

Third Session

THE SHAME BEHIND THE PAIN

I Didn't Want To Lose Either; I Lost Them Both

After our last session, I didn't want Niecey to feel she had made a bad choice by exposing her past or that she was out there all alone. So I began the third session with, "The Shame Behind the Pain."

Many of us are walking around smiling and going about our daily business as usual while carrying deep dark secrets. Yes, we look pretty on the outside, but inside there are scars and wounds that are a constant reminder of the pain we try to hide and the shame we hope no one ever finds out about.

I have talked to many women through WOMAN TALK, and about eighty percent admit they have secrets that they don't talk about. Secrets keep us in bondage and are baggage that we carry with us everywhere we go.

Once, a woman told me that she had been holding a secret for more than thirty years, a secret that happened when she was in her teens. She never told a soul, not even her mother or husband of twenty years.

> The shame behind the pain is why we don't tell.

It was at a WOMAN TALK session that I openly confessed to the group that I have had two abortions. I shared my story about my abortions because I wanted the women to know that I had sincerely repented and asked Jesus to forgive me for what I had done. Repent means to turn away from the sin and not do it again. Jesus said in His Word that when we sincerely repent, He remembers the sin no more.

Jesus took away my guilt by forgiving me and teaching me how to forgive myself. Immediately following the session, that same woman who was clearly amazed of my freedom, confessed the secret of her abortion she had as a teenager. She never thought she could be free, and although she'd ask Jesus to forgive her, years ago, she had not forgiven herself. She refused to forgive herself. She felt guilty and felt she deserves to be punished for what she did. As long as she held on to the guilt and allowed it to control her feelings, she wouldn't be able to accept Jesus' forgiveness. That day she was set free!

Lyric Revealed A Horrible Secret

"I would like to say something." Lyric said quietly. Lyric was one of the three ladies who missed the first two sessions. She'd been quietly sitting back observing. However, after listening to me tell about the lady who was set free and hearing about Niecey's breakthrough she stood up and said, "I didn't want to lose either of them but I ended up losing them both."

With tears in her eyes she cleared her throat and continued. "Being in denial cost me my child. I've always been weak behind men. I guess I was a fool for love. I had my first child by a married man named Dante'. Of course I knew he was married. I would spend the night at his house and we would have sex in their bed whenever his wife was out of town, which was often because of her job. We had a lot of fun. In the mornings I would wake him up with a pleasant surprise, if you know what I mean." She said with a slight grin on her face.

"Afterward I would cook him breakfast, then fill the bathtub with lots of bubbles and we would both squeeze in. In the tub, facing him with my legs across his, I would gently wash his body. I could tell he really enjoyed it; he always bragged about how I did things his wife wouldn't do.

Dante' was always telling me how much he liked being with me. I thought one day he would leave his wife for me. After I got pregnant, I just knew he would leave her then. After all I was giving him something that his wife hadn't given him, a child. Still he didn't leave her.

In fact, the day our daughter Harmony was born I sent him a text letting him know I was in labor before I left home. I was so disappointed he wasn't there with me; I never thought I would be in the hospital alone giving birth. I was excited when he called later that evening. Just hearing his voice made me feel better, until he said he felt I had planned the pregnancy in order to trap him.

Dante' went on to say he didn't want anything to do with me or my child and he wasn't even sure the child was his."

The ladies listened intensely as Lyric continued.

"I couldn't believe what I was hearing. This was supposed to be one of the happiest days in my life, but giving birth to my beautiful baby girl turned out to be one of the worst days ever. My heart felt like it had been ripped out and thrown in the trash like garbage. Before I could say anything he said, 'Don't ever call my cell phone or come to my house again. I don't want anything to do with either of you!' Then he hung up in my face.

I was devastated, hurt, confused, and embarrassed. I was in disbelief. I loved that man's dirty underwear, and for him to just throw me away like trash after he was finished with me..."

I could tell by the heads nodding as Lyric spoke that several of the women could relate to her story.

"But looking back what was even more hurtful was after he had a DNA test done on our daughter and it came back 99.9% that he was the father, he immediately signed over his rights. He meant *he wanted nothing to do with us.* I know this is going to sound crazy, but still I couldn't see life without him!" Lyric said, dropping her head in shame.

"I didn't even think about my newborn baby who needed me more than ever. In fact, I didn't even bond with Harmony. I couldn't get past the hurt and pain I was feeling from Dante'. I was mentally sick behind that man and I just wanted it to stop," Lyric said.

I Just Wanted to Get Rid of the Pain

"One night while partying with a group of people I barely knew, I was introduced to crack cocaine. Hoping to feel better about my situation, and thinking I was just getting rid of my pain, I became addicted. Not long after that I hooked up with the shady dealer, Quentin. It seemed I had gone from bad to worse because over the next few years that's how my life went.

Now, don't get me wrong, I wasn't your walk up and down the street dirty crack head. Oh, no! I drove a Lexus, my make-up was always flawless, and I got my hair done every two weeks as well as a manicure and a pedicure. I've always been a sharp dresser and very intelligent. I graduated at the top of my college class. For years I was a functioning crack head on the inside, on the outside I was a 'DIVA.' I even went to work every day. That was until a week before Thanksgiving. That night Quentin and I got into an argument over my little girl, Harmony; then things got worse."

The women seemed very interested in Lyric's story, but couldn't imagine it getting any worse. She continued, "We were getting high in our usual spot, the last row of our apartment complex next to the big green dumpster, when my mother called my cell phone and said my little girl was complaining about her private hurting. Harmony had just turned three at that time. My mother said when she looked at her vagina it appeared to be swollen and she wanted to know what had happened to her.

Well since we all lived together the only person I'd leave her with when I go to work or on one of my binges other then my mother, was Quentin. So I asked him if he'd been touching my child. He got all upset and started cussing me out. Then he got out of the car, opened the trunk, got the crowbar, and start breaking out all the windows in my car, glass was flying everywhere. Glass stuck in different parts of my body, cutting my face, arms, and hands. It was a good thing I had my hair braided and weaved because the glass would have cut my head. He also beat out all the lights.

He told me to get in the back seat. I had no idea why he wanted me to get in the back, I was so scared. When I opened the car door I wanted to scream but it was past midnight and there was no one around to hear me. I thought about running but I was afraid he would catch me and hit me or something, so I just got in the back seat.

I'd never seen Quentin like that before, in such a rage. I sat there shaking in fear watching as he stabbed holes in all four of my car tires. Then he got in the back with me, his eyes were very wide and fixed; it was eerie. Without saying a word, he began beating me with that same steel crowbar. I couldn't believe what was happening. Enormous pain pierced my petite body with each forceful blow to my head, back, legs, and arms.

It seemed as if it was never going to end. Blood gushed from my head as I pleaded with him to stop. I was in disbelief as blow after blow struck my whole body.

I thought it couldn't get any worse but as I lay there barely conscious, Quentin raped and then sodomized me with that same bloody crowbar. When he finished he told me he would do whatever he wanted to do with Harmony, and I better not ever accuse him of touching my little girl again. He promised the next time it would be worse. He then got out of *my* car, and left me there in the back of the apartment's parking lot to die!"

As I looked around the room at the women's faces they were clearly touched by Lyric's story. There was no judgment or attitudes, just compassion.

Lyric continued, "I laid there literally clinging to life for three long days. I was unable to move, and frequently slipped in and out of consciousness, I guess since the car was so far in the back with all the windows busted out, people assumed it was a junk car and unfortunately there were no scheduled trash pickups on those days. If my neighbor's two little boys playing ball nearby hadn't heard me moan, I would not have survived another day, I was told.

My mother was horrified when she saw me; she was crying and instantly wanted to know who had done this to me. My voice was barely recognizable when I lied and said I didn't know the person who did it. I'm sure she knew the truth because Quentin had also not been seen in three days.

I was in the hospital for eight agonizing days. The doctors were surprised I survived. The withdrawals from crack alone had me praying to go home. After numerous test, IV's, x-rays, antibiotics, and blood work, I was discharged. Not one time in eight days did Quentin come to see me."

A tear rolled down Tracy's cheek as she imagined what Lyric had gone through.

I Was In Denial

"Over the next few weeks my mom took care of me and Harmony. I know what I'm about to say next is going to be hard to believe, but like Ms. Jerri and the other ladies, I no longer want to live in shame; I want to be healed; I want to be free. As soon as I got better I called Quentin and asked him to come home. He did and we never talked about that situation again, nor did I question him whenever Harmony complained about her vagina hurting.

In fact, I just ignored her complaints completely. Even my mother ignored her and never brought it up again. I don't know if my mother's silence was out of fear for me, or if she was just trying to stay out of my business, but none of us in the household ever talked about my little girl or that time in the car. We simply went back to our life as we knew it."

The women thinking that was the end to Lyric's story, were speechless. No one knew what to say. But her story wasn't over as she continued on.

"A few weeks later someone called child protective services on suspicion of child abuse. After questioning all of us, including Harmony who was not able to articulate exactly what happened to her, did apparently act out some inappropriate behavior that raised concern. I was told Quentin would have to leave the apartment or they were going to take my little girl from me.

Earlier that day I had gotten extremely high on crack, since I had to make a decision. I told the social worker I love my little girl with all my heart and I don't want to lose her; but I also love my man and didn't want to lose him, so I *wasn't* going to put him out. Without fully understanding what I was doing, I signed over my rights and never saw my little girl again. Oh God! What did I do?! Well I guess you could say I picked my man over my child, because I just didn't want to lose him."

•

Discussion Question:

Men: Do you have a theory of the kind of men that would treat a woman the way Quentin treated Lyric? Do you wonder what makes women stay? Have you ever walked in Quentin's shoes and are now ready to repent and ask for God's forgiveness?

Women: Do you feel *any* man is better than *no* man? Have you ever made unthinkable sacrifices for a man? Was it worth it?

I Was Messed Up

Over the next four years I sunk deeper and deeper into drugs, trying to cover up the pain of giving away Harmony. I was so messed up that one time when I went to buy some crack, it was actually small broken up pieces of sheet rock. It took me a minute to realize that the person who sold it to me was long gone. You heard right, *sheet rock*, the material used to build walls.

Two years ago I gave birth to a son, Quentin Jr. Having another child made Quentin and me happy but it still didn't stop us from getting high. However, what eventually stopped me was just one month after giving birth to Jr., Quentin, the man I loved and gave my daughter up for, was shot and killed while making a drug deal. I didn't want to lose either of them, my daughter or my man; I ended up losing them both.

Oh, how I miss my little girl. Now that I'm clean, I want so badly to get her back. I think about her every day. I still don't know who called protective services on me. I really think it was my neighbor who I haven't spoken to in years. I can't stand her; I can't even look at her. I feel the rage coming up just thinking about her. It's because of her that I lost my daughter."

Lyric broke down crying uncontrollably in Tracy's arms. She has since accepted Jesus in her life but finding forgiveness for her neighbor is a real struggle. "I HATE HER Tracy! I HATE HER and I will NEVER FORGIVE HER!" Lyric sobbed. Tracy trying to console Lyric, with tears in her own eyes said, "Lyric there's something I need to tell you." Lyric, still sobbing in Tracy arms, raised her head to look at Tracy.

"Lyric, it was me who called child protective services. It was me who turned you in. I never meant to hurt you, but I had to protect Harmony. I had no idea you would sign over your rights. I was told that if you would be willing to put your man out, your little girl would not be taken away." Tracy confessed.

Lyric, pulling away shouted, "TRACY HOW COULD YOU!? You were supposed to be my friend." Lyric said in disbelief. "When I confided in you I thought you cared, yet it was *you* who turned me in and caused me to lose Harmony."

Lyric's eyes showed hurt and anger. "Tracy, I can't believe it was you who stabbed me in the back. All this time I was blaming, and hating my neighbor. I will never forgive you for that!" Lyric said bitterly.

The look on everyone's face was perplexed. Although they sympathized with Lyric, they applauded Tracy for her actions.

"I do care Lyric," Tracy insisted. "That's why I called. I cared enough to protect your little girl. I didn't know all this time you were blaming and hating your neighbor, but someone had to call."

The session was beginning to get out of control. Lyric was crying and screaming, while Tracy and the other women tried to explain that Tracy had no choice. I didn't want to allow the enemy, Satan, to use this situation to tear their relationship completely apart. I also didn't want the other women to have fear and doubt about being open and honest in the sessions. I immediately called for the women's attention.

"Ladies, let's all pray," I said, taking charge of the room. Soon after, the atmosphere was calm and we continued on with the session. I decided to outline a few things I wanted the women to understand.

1. Healing and being set free, like anything else, is a choice.

2. Accept responsibility for your actions. Lyric has blamed everyone for losing her little girl, except herself when the choice was hers to smoke crack, sign over her rights, choosing Quentin over Harmony.

3. Be willing to forgive; I didn't say forget. It may not be easy, and it probably won't happen overnight, but be truly willing. Speaking of forgiveness, I'd like to share some scriptures.

But if you do not forgive others their sins, your Father will not forgive your sins. Matthew 6:15 (NIV)

When they kept on questioning him, he straightened up and said to them, "Let any one of you who is without sin be the first to throw a stone at her." John 8:7 (NIV)

Ladies, I want to thank you for showing love to Lyric as she shared her story. I'm sure it wasn't easy exposing such deep issues not knowing if people are going to judge you. The truth is, there is not one of us who has not made bad choices in life. On the other hand, Tracy committed no sin; she did what she had to do. The principle of forgiving is what I hope Lyric understands, I also wanted her to realize her worth.

Know Who You Are

So I said to Lyric, stop expecting for a man to know who you are, when you don't even know who you are. And please stop jumping from one relationship to another expecting that things will be different, without first taking time out to find out who you are. Think about it, and then look back at some of your past relationships. If you will be honest, you will probably notice similarities in your situations, just with a different guy.

Until you take the time to find out who you are, you will continue to find yourself in similar situations. But be encouraged, the Bible tells us that, "All things work together for our good." I asked Lyric if she believed this was true.

"Well I guess it is true." Lyric said this time in a much calmer tone. "I still miss my little girl, and promise I will search for her when she is older. In the mean-time, I've been clean for a year and now have met a new man Bryant who is good to me and my son. He knows about my past and even wants to marry me with all my baggage."

"Girl that's good, are you going to marry him?" LaRita asked.

"I don't know; I may consider it down the road. However, Ms. Jerri is right; I have to know my worth. So I've decided I'm going to explain to Bryant that as much as I like him, for once in my life instead of rushing into another relationship, I want to take some time to get to know me. For my sake and his, I need to allow Jesus to heal me and make me whole. And if he's still interested later, I would love to marry him."

I'm so proud of Lyric! She got the point and has learned valuable lessons about herself. Before she can love a man, she has to love herself first. And despite what she said about not forgiving Tracy, she did forgive her.

Many women are like what Lyric used to be. We let our whole lives revolve around a man. Even when they do us wrong, we continue to hang in there before we realize we don't need *just any* man in our life. Jesus can fill the void of affection until the right man presents himself.

•

Discussion Question:

Men: Would you respect a woman who would put you on hold to sincerely get her life right with Jesus?

Women: Are you willing to take some time and get to know Jesus and yourself? Do you trust that Jesus can fill the void of affection until the right man presents himself?

Living With Guilt And Shame

Seeing Lyric's grief, guilt, and pain, I decided to share the story of a woman named Mrs. Leola. While their situations are very different, the grief, guilt, and pain are the same.

Mrs. Leola is woman of God. She is 64 years old, a college professor who is happily married to a wonderful man, and has two wonderful, grown children. However, Mrs. Leola lives with the guilt, pain, and shame, and constant reminder of giving her first born child away. Other than her parents, no one ever knew. Now, before you judge her, what if I told you that Mrs. Leola didn't want to give her child away, but she had no choice since she was only sixteen? Well, that's what happened.

Mrs. Leola was an only child from an upper class family. Her life had been planned out for her. She was supposed to graduate from one of the finest universities; get married to her peer; have two children, and follow in her parent's footsteps, becoming a college professor. She did just that!

However, not before meeting a boy at age fifteen, having sex, and getting pregnant. Although she and the baby's father were only fifteen, like most teens their age, they felt they were in love. They wanted to get married and raise their child, but Mrs. Leola's parents wouldn't hear of such a thing. By the time they found out, it was too late for her parents to demand an abortion. They felt if people found out that their daughter was pregnant and had a baby, it would ruin the family's reputation. So they sent her away until she gave birth. She returned home as if nothing happened, but the shame and guilt she carried caused her to be distant

> Pain can sometimes present itself as *distant,* or an *attitude.*

and standoffish. Most people perceived her to have an attitude.

Even as an adult, Mrs. Leola never shared her secret with her family. All those years she held that shame and guilt in her heart. It wasn't until after a student in a similar situation expressed her helplessness that Mrs. Leola realized what happened to her as a teen wasn't her fault.

Knowing now that there are other women and teens that this has happened, or is happening to (living in bondage), she chose to share her story with me and allows me to share it with others. Mrs. Leola finally faced her past and no longer carries the shame of people finding out she gave her first born child away.

Although they were happily married, her courage to be open with her husband shed light on her distant attitude and brought them closer. Her husband confessed he had always felt something had happened in her past, but since she never mentioned it, he never asked.

Mrs. Leola now has full support from her husband and children. However, unlike Lyric, who plans to find her daughter when she gets older, Mrs. Leola has no information on her child. She never even knew if she gave birth to a boy or girl.

Giving up your child is probably one of the worst feelings a mother can feel. Not a day goes by that she doesn't think of her child, but she no longer lives in bondage. Mrs. Leola has learned to change the things she can change, and give God the things she cannot. That attitude has freed her, and hopefully her story will set someone else free.

•

Discussion Question:

Men: Do you understand the emotional bond of a mother and her child?

Women: Are you living with the guilt of something you had no control over? Do you believe God will forgive you if you ask?

Me And My Sister's Secret

The women were starting to open up, and little by little the masks were coming off. "Well since we're getting real and everything, I guess I'll go next. I just hope y'all ready to hear my story, me and my sisters had a secret." Shaquanda said in a surprisingly calm tone.

"I finally got the courage to tell a woman I learned to trust. This was a secret me and my sisters have lived with for years. We promised that we would never tell a soul because we didn't want people to judge, shun, blame, or look down on us. We experienced enough of that as young girls when we told people our mama was dead. It's amazing how mean people treat the innocent. People can be so cruel!" Shaquanda said as her whole demeanor changed to serious.

The women were surprised to see that underneath all the ghetto-ness and loud talking, was a person in a lot of pain.

"It started immediately after our mama died and to this day I probably would not have mentioned it if a woman would not have shared her story with me first." Shaquanda went on to explain.

"The woman's name was Maggie. She had just moved into the house next door. She seemed nice. Often times after my father left the house, I would go over to Maggie's to borrow things like sugar, eggs, a cup of oil, things like that. Maggie was cool and not much older than me. Sometimes

88

I would stay and visit a little bit before I had to get back home. Maggie, who was twenty-three, had three children; two boys, twelve and eleven; and a girl, ten. I liked Maggie, we had something in common. Although I was only seventeen, I too had three children, two boys, five and four; and a baby girl, twelve months. I knew why I had my babies so young but I wondered why she had her babies so young; so I asked her. I will admit, I was not prepared for her answer or openness.

Maggie's whole demeanor changed as she began telling me, that her father had raped her repeatedly, and as a result, she now has three kids by him. OH MY GOD! I couldn't believe what I was hearing. Her eyes became filled with tears. I could understand the pain she was feeling, and it wasn't until she said to me, 'You will never know how it feels; the hurt, pain, and shame of having children by your own father; or, the filth and discuss I felt every time he touched me.' That day, I broke years of silence. Sobbingly I said, 'I do know how it feels. You see, My Children and I Have the Same Father.'

My Children and I Have the Same Father

I thought me and my sisters were the only ones that had happen to. I went on to tell her how after our mama died. The night of her funeral, while me and my sisters were still mourning, our father called us in his bedroom and said, 'Your mother is no longer here to take care of me, so now y'all are going to have to take her place.'

I was nine years old, Yolaunda was eight, and the twins Teauna and Tawana were seven. We didn't understand what daddy meant by 'take care of him' until the next night when he came into my room.

It made me sick to my stomach every time my daddy had sex with me. Wanting to spare my sisters of the pain and shame I felt, I told daddy that

I, would take mama's place, but he made it clear, he wanted us all! He took turns raping us for years. Once we started our menstrual cycle, we begin giving birth." As she looked at each of the women not knowing if they would judge her, Shaquanda said, "Yes me and my sister's secret was, our father is also our children's father."

There was a silence in the room; Shaquanda clearly was nervous and very uneasy telling her story. She kept rubbing her hands back and forth while trying to hold back the tears as she continued her story.

"Over a course of nineteen years by my father, there have been four miscarriages, three stillbirths, and eleven children born between me and my sisters. Yolaunda and Tawana have two, Teauna has four, and y'all know I have three," she said.

With tears streaming down her face, Ebony walked over and put her arms around her friend. "Shaquanda, I didn't know. We have been friends for years why didn't you tell me that your father was your kid's father?"

"Think about it Ebony, if your own father was also your kids father, would you tell that?" She asked looking her straight in the face.

"Is that why most of y'all kids have some form of birth defects?" Ebony asked sincerely.

"I'm not sure because not all birth defects come from incest." Shaquanda replied with a look of despair.

"You know you could have told me, I would not have judged you. I can imagine how you feel," Ebony said.

"Ebony, I know you mean well but, if you have not gone through anything like this, you truly can't imagine the disgust and shame many women in this situation feel." Niecey said trying to help Ebony understand the pain of incest from a father.

"Or the feelings we carry every time we look at our kids who are now suffering." As a tears rolled down her face Shaquanda continued, "My sisters hate our father for what he did to us, but it really didn't affect me." She said obviously trying to convince herself she hasn't been affected.

"Shaquanda, you don't think what happened to you and your sisters has any effect on how you view and treat men?" I asked, hoping to get Shaquanda to honestly evaluate her feelings towards her father.

"Well I didn't think it did, but thinking about the question I guess I did hate him, and now I realize I took the hatred for my father out on the men in my life including my two sons. And just think, all this time I was allowing that hate to control me," Shaquanda said. Then she dropped her head and said in a low tone, "I know this may sound crazy, and I can't believe I'm about to say this myself, but, all these years I've been angry with my mama, angry that she died and left us to deal with all of this."

You could clearly see the deep-rooted anguish she'd been carrying. I said to Shaquanda as I embraced her, "Your mother loved her littler girls soooo much. But, she had no choice, she died, and holding on to that anger, is stopping you from fully living. Shaquanda," I said again this time looking into her eyes, "*you must forgive* your mother, EVEN IN DEATH, and forgive yourself for holding the anger towards her, so that you can heal and move

> Forgiveness is not for the other person, it's for *you*.

on." Shaquanda stood there for a moment, then took a deep breath; she hadn't shed a tear all while she was telling her story. It wasn't until she said… "*R. I. P. Mama, I FORGIVE YOU,*" that she broke down. As proud as we were of her, she wasn't finished, to everyone's surprise she then said, "Despite all the hurtful things my father has done, I want to forgive him too."

"And you can Shaquanda, because the choice is yours. You had no control over what happened to you in the past. However, by forgiving him it gives you the power to take control of your future," I honorably interjected.

"Looking back, I wish we had the courage that Maggie had when she turned her father in for incest, to this day her father is still sitting in prison. At that time being young girls, we didn't know we had that right. I've been told it's not too late, and as an adult I've often thought about it. My father is a very old man now, lonely, unhappy, and in very poor health. None of his family will have anything to do with him. Over the years me and my sisters have had different attitudes on how to deal with and cover up what our father did to us. Yolaunda married a good man who adopted her children. Teauna began prostituting. Tawana is now divorced and seems very angry with men. Me, to cover my pain and shame, I became *Ms. Ghetto Fabulous.* I've never been married, I *wanted to* allow a man to love me, but I didn't know how. Now I want to learn how."

Shaquanda had finally gotten her breakthrough; she forgave herself, and both, her mother and father. I know it wasn't easy for Shaquanda to tell her story. I was so proud of her courage, I'm sure her mother would have been too.

●

Discussion Question:

Men: Could you patiently love a woman who's been through some form of devastation?

Women: Do you know of someone who has gone through some kind of tragedy? Did you reach out to that person? Do you feel it is important to forgive someone who has died?

Your Stepfather Don't Mean No Harm; It's The Alcohol

Vanessa, another one of Tracy's weekday clients attending WOMAN TALK, spoke up and said, "I have been sitting here listening to all the women share their stories, determined not to say anything. However, like Ms. Jerri said, maybe if fathers and mothers realize the impact of being parents have on their children, maybe they would make different choices. It made me think about my mother and stepfather, but especially my mother, the woman whom I looked to, to protect me from abuse.

Abuse is not always sexual. Abuse can also be mental. Like you were Lyric, my mother was in denial," Vanessa said. Then standing with her arms crossed she recalled her mother's words, *'Your stepfather don't mean no harm, it's the alcohol.'*

That's what she told my sisters and me every time our stepfather woke us up in the middle of the night to cuss us out for no reason. It was normal in our house to get liquor bottles, beer bottles or cans thrown at us at any given time. If only people knew what went on behind closed doors. I'd like to share with you the abuse my two older sisters and I went through at the hands of our stepfather for nearly ten years under the name of **alcohol.**

My mother and stepfather met and married nearly ten years ago, which is about how long he has been an alcoholic. Hmmm… let's see, if they were married ten years ago, and he's been an alcoholic for ten years; did she knowingly marry an alcoholic? Well, you do the math.

> Sistas, are we really that desperate for a man?

Talk about living in a dysfunctional household. When my stepfather was not drinking he was one of the nicest, kindest people you could know; that's probably how he got my mother. But, there was something evil that took over him when he began to drink alcohol. My sisters and I still don't know how to process in our minds the difference between the good and evil; and we never knew which one was going to show up.

You see, along with all the other things our stepfather would do when he was under the influence of alcohol, such as cussing us out, throwing things at us, and embarrassing us in front of our friends, we had to watch helplessly as he beat on our mother. Why did she put up with it? I don't understand.

I never knew anyone like my stepfather. Monday through Friday he would get up no matter how late he stayed up, or should I say kept us up the night before harassing us with meaningless conversation, and go to work.

Now personally, I never knew what he did for a living. He said he was self-employed, and I guess he did make some money here and there because on the days he made money he would come home with a small bottle of gin. But still, the weekdays were nothing like the weekends. There's a song we use to play called, *Living For The Weekend*. Yes, that was my stepfather's song and he took it literally because by five o'clock every Friday evening he would be sitting on the couch with a fifth of gin. It was as if he literally lived for the weekend.

Now I guess the good, if there is any good that came out of this, was that he didn't drink and drive. He always stayed home. Besides, whenever he ran out of gin, he wouldn't have to leave the house, my mother kept extra bottles hidden in the cabinet over the stove. So I guess the good that came from that was, with him drinking in the house, the rest of the world was safe. But for us, him being home was a nightmare.

Yes, the weekends at our house were a living hell, especially when he would talk to us all night long. If he thought we weren't listening or if we fell asleep, he would get mad and wake us up by throwing anything he could get his hands on while cussing us out. Then talk another two or three hours about how ungrateful we were. We always had to get up early so we needed to get sleep; but unless he passed out first, the whole house had to stay up.

Living with an alcoholic stepfather, for me, was torture. And my poor mother, she always looked so tired from carrying the household load. Everything, from working a full-time job, supporting the whole household, making sure the bills were paid including both car notes, the insurance, and all our cell phones. She would then come home and cook a hot meal. Most teens don't want to do chores but as my sister and I got older we wanted to cook, do laundry, or something just to take some of the load off our mother. Of course our stepfather would not allow it; he wanted our mother to do all the cooking, and takes care of all his needs; and she did it without ever complaining.

Ms. Jerri around the shop you are always saying, 'People will treat you how you allow them to.' You're right because although our stepfather insisted our mother treat him like a king, he treated her like a servant. Oh yes, and after everything else that our mother had done all day, when our stepfather finally finished nagging us girls and went to bed, she still had to have sex with him.

However, we still couldn't get any sleep because all the moaning and groaning sounds of them having sex, not only grossed us out, it kept us up! Eventually, being so exhausted, my sisters would fall off to sleep. But as fatigued as I was, I couldn't sleep until those sounds stopped.

And my poor mother, I wondered if him being drunk had any effect on his ability to have sex, because it seemed like it took forever. I couldn't tell if my mother's groaning was pleasure or agony. Watching the clock I wondered, *when will it be over*? Once my sisters and I asked our mother why she put up with his abuse, but all she said is, 'Your stepfather don't mean no harm, it's the alcohol.'"

The entire time Vanessa was speaking I was scanning the room. It seemed a few of the women could relate as they nodded their heads several times in agreement.

Vanessa continued, "I have never understood how the very thing a person hates is, many times, what they end up doing, or being with someone who does it. For instance, I hated the fact that my stepfather was an alcoholic; so what did I do? You won't believe my story.

When Will It Be Over?

"*When will it be over?* Is all I could think about everytime my husband and I have sex," Vanessa said. "I could have used the term 'making love' but it seems he only wants to touch me when he's drunk, and at that point, believe me, it's not making love, it's just sex.

On my wedding day ten years ago, I vowed to not withhold my body from my husband, and I have kept that vow. However, to be honest, although I never turn him down, the thought of him climbing on top of me with the smell of alcohol reeking from his breath is becoming more difficult for me to endure. Every time he kisses me, or should I say, slobbers in my mouth, I feel like I want to vomit. In fact, because of him being drunk, it usually takes a lot longer for him to get an erection, if he can at all that night.

Sometimes even my foreplay with him is not enough. After a while, I become tired. But, I vowed for better or for worse so I keep the foreplay going with him as long as I can and most of the times it works; finally, we are able to have sex. However, after the sex is over and he's passed out, many times still on top of me, I have to struggle to get his weight off me so I can get up and..."

Vanessa paused, embarrassed, and hesitant to go on.

"What's wrong, Vanessa?" Tracy asked.

"There's a secret I've been holding for over a year. One that I wish I could talk to my mother about since my stepfather was an alcoholic, but my mother has never been open with us and I'm not sure she would be comfortable talking about it. Every time after my husband and I have sex and I go to wash up, I notice that mixed in with his semen is blood. *Where does the blood come from I wonder?* It is surely not coming from me; it has been more than five years since I've had a hysterectomy.

I'd also like to clear up a myth; women who have had hysterectomies still want to have sex **and** enjoy it very much. A hysterectomy mainly removes the uterus, which holds a baby; the cervix, clitoris, vagina, and vaginal walls are still there. In fact many men, if any at all, wouldn't know the difference. 'If a woman is sexual by nature or has a high sex drive before the hysterectomy, she will still have those same desires; and if she is not very sexual or has a low sex drive then she will probably be the same,' my doctor said.

Me personally, I do have a high sex drive and would love for my husband and I to be intimate more often, without him being drunk, or without having to wonder where the blood comes from. I've asked my husband time and time again to go see a doctor; I've even offered to go with him. But he refuses, so like my mother I continue to stay, hoping one day he will change. And just like my mother I get up every day and go to work, then come home every night and cook a hot meal. However, there is one difference between me and my mother, 'I HAVE AN ATTITUDE'"

•

Discussion Question:

Men: Have you ever made choices or did things you regret under the influence of alcohol? Do you agree that excessive drinking could affect your ability to having sex? Is the alcohol worth it?

Women: Did you, or do you know someone who married someone like their parent? Was the outcome Good or Bad?

My Mother's Addiction To Drugs
"Mother?" Well, I Beg To Differ

After Vanessa finished speaking, the mood in the room was somber. I noticed Ebony with her hands up covering her face so I walked over and kneeled in front of her. Rubbing her eyes she looked up at me and said, "I've never been married so I don't know what it's like living with an alcoholic husband, but if Vanessa thought living with an alcoholic father was bad, then imagine your mother addicted to drugs."

Ebony began to tell her story, "For as far back as I can remember we have lived with my dear great-grandmother, who we call 'Big Mama.' Now when I say *we*, I mean me, my five brothers, and MY MAMA. I know this might be a bit much so let me explain."

Ebony stood up, "Big Mama thought she couldn't have any kids but at the age of thirty-five, she finally had her first and only child, my grandma Odessa. Big Mama was so happy when she had my grandma that she vowed to give her everything she wanted. She sacrificed, suffered, and worked really hard to provide for her. Grandma Odessa never heard the words *NO, STOP,* or *DON'T DO THAT!* As a result she never learned responsibility and was allowed to do whatever she wanted.

Grandma Odessa was thirteen when she started using drugs. At fifteen she gave birth to twins, my mama Michelle, and her brother Milton. Two months later, Grandma Odessa died from a drug overdose.

Big Mama was heartbroken. She couldn't believe her only child was gone forever. On the day of Grandma Odessa's funeral, Big Mama promised to raise my Mama and Uncle Milton as if they were her own.

When Uncle Milton was nine years old he was hit by a pickup truck when he ran into the street to get his ball. He was in a coma for seventy-one days before he passed away. Thinking my mama had experienced enough loss in her short life, Big Mama, just like she did with Grandma Odessa, allowed my mama to do whatever she wanted. We would later all suffer because of it." said Ebony.

The women really listened as Ebony spoke. "Some people believe in generational curses. I don't know if they're true or not, all I know is just like my Grandma Odessa, my mama started using drugs when she was young and by the time she was fifteen she had me too. But then again, I don't think that generational curse stuff is true because I'm not on drugs. I mean yeah, I smoke a little weed and yeah I did have my oldest child when I was fifteen, but that don't mean nothing, DO IT?"

Ebony continued, "Well anyway, 'Beauty is in the eyes of the beholder,' is what people say. In fact, I've been told that back in the day, my mama was considered beautiful. I never got to see her true beauty because whenever I looked at her all I saw was a drug addict."

One day as a little girl, about nine, Big Mama picked me and three of my brothers up from school two hours after finding out my mama never showed up for us. We never locked our door because my mama was always losing her key. So when she pulled up at the house, while Big

100

Mama was getting her purse and some bags, we kids got out of the car and ran straight in. As a child, I was not prepared for what I saw. Inside the house, right in the middle of the living room, was my mama lying on the floor. She was naked from the waist down and her legs were wide open with blood on them. As I stood there in shock, my brothers started crying and screaming hysterically as they draped themselves across mama's lifeless body. I was frantically trying to figure out what had happened to her, who could have done that to her, and why was she naked from the waist down and bleeding?

Hearing our screams, Big Mama rushed in and swiftly ushered us off to her bedroom. We were in her room for about fifteen minutes, but it seemed like hours. Although I was so afraid and wanted to know what was going on out there with my mama, I knew I couldn't fall apart, I had to be strong because I had to comfort my younger brothers. I was relieved when Big Mama came into the room and said my mama was not dead, and the blood we saw, well, I learned that day what it meant for a woman to be on her period. It seemed mama had a man over who she was doing drugs with. After she passed out, he raped her and left her like that.

It was so embarrassing seeing my mama that way, but I had no idea that was only the beginning of embarrassing moments I would later encounter behind my mama.

By the time I was in middle school, my mama was known as the neighborhood junky. It was very embarrassing when the kids would point and laugh at her. She was no longer a mama to me, but a ninety-five pound woman, whose hair was always matted, uncombed, and all over her head. Her teeth, well the ones she had left (she hadn't been to a dentist in years), were chipped, brown and rotten. Her clothes were dirty and torn.

She always smelled like she hadn't showered in weeks, and she constantly walked the streets night and day in search of her next fix. Every night when we went to bed, we hoped that mama would be safe where ever she was, and since we couldn't lock our front door we had to hope that we would be safe too.

By senior high, most of the kids had stopped pointing and laughing when they saw my mama. Maybe out of respect for me and my brothers, or pity; I don't know which. They would just walk by her hesitating to make eye contact so that she wouldn't ask them for money. To be honest, me, and my brothers, would also walk by her as if she was a stranger, for that same reason. But, that didn't stop the shame of her calling our name and cussing us out if we didn't give her any money."

Ebony no longer sounded like the naive woman we had met at the first session. She sounded like someone whose childhood had been stolen. I could hear the hurt in her voice from the pain she'd been carrying all this time.

She Caused So Much Heartache

"It's hard to like someone who has caused you so much heartache. I can't tell you how embarrassing it was the many times we got ready to check out at the grocery store, but couldn't buy any food because mama had stolen all Big Mama's money from her purse. And I can't count how many times I have seen Big Mama crying as she cleaned the bloody wounds, black eyes, busted lips, and knots on mama's head. My mama would often stagger in the house in the middle of the night after being beat up.

Did you know you can get beat in the face so much, that you no longer look like yourself? I could see Big Mama's heart breaking every time mama went on one of her rampages going through the house like a mad woman. She would yell, cuss, and beat up on all of us, including Big Mama, even when we had given her all the money we had. Oh, and you can't imagine the fear I felt every time drug dealers came to our house looking for my mama. When they couldn't find her they would threaten Big Mama about the debts mama owed. Sure enough, Big Mama would give them everything she had to protect mama and us. I know this sounds bad to say about your own mama but I couldn't stand her. I used to wish she would just go away. Big Mama nearly lost our house trying to pay off all of mama's drug debts."

My Trifling Mama

"My mama was never a mother to me. When I graduated from high school, oh sure, I knew my mama wasn't going to come even though she said she would be there. Surely, after all those years, you would think I wouldn't set myself up for more disappointments. She did not show up for any of my school activities, birthdays, nor the birth of my first child, so you would think I wouldn't set myself up to be hurt, but deep down I was still hoping that for once, my mama would do something she said she was going to do. I couldn't enjoy the ceremony because I was focusing on the audience. I stared at each individual hoping that my mama was somewhere in the crowd, but she wasn't.

It made me sad to see all the happy parents. It wasn't fair. What was it about me? What had I done so bad that God would choose her to be my mama? I'll admit I grew up a very mad and angry child with a very bad attitude. My mama not being there on one of the most important days of my life really hurt. I was the first ever to graduate from high school. If she only knew the struggles I had to go through just to finish school, especially with two kids.

Big Mama is the reason I graduated. I promised her I would. But my trifling mama, ooh, as I sat there, on my graduation day, all the anger, pain, and hatred I felt for her was beginning to surface. With an attitude, I continued to look around still not wanting to accept the fact that my mama was not there. Scanning the audience, the one person I did see, looking proud as a peacock, smiling from ear to ear, was my dear sweet loving Big Mama, and instantly I was alright. Even though mama didn't show up for my graduation, I made it."

The women felt Ebony's pain and understood her anger.

"Although I was the only one to finish school, I keep thinking about what people call generational curses and I sometimes wonder if I could be under it. Because looking over my life I can see some of the same things grandma Odessa, and my mama did, that I'm doing. We all had a baby at fifteen, we all have used drugs, and as much as I didn't want to be like my mama, me and my brothers all had different daddies just like my kids, and just like my mama, I'm raising them on welfare and food stamps." Ebony confessed.

Tracy speaks up, "Ebony, I believe generational curses exist, now, I can't tell you whether or not you are under one but what I can tell you is, if you are, be encouraged because generational curses can be broken."

"Ebony, I didn't know your situation. What happened to the rest of your family?" Lyric was curious to know.

Ebony replies, "Well, my dear Big Mama is still living and we just celebrated her eighty-fifth birthday. Three of us have moved out of the house but she is still raising great-grandchildren. Three of my brothers still live there with some of their kids, and one baby's mama.

Then Ebony, with a cold stare said, "And as for my mama, well, six months after my high school graduation my mama was arrested on a drug charge. That day was a bittersweet because there was sadness for my mama having to go to jail, but it would end the madness of us worrying about her in the streets, or so we thought. But, Big Mama couldn't bear the thought of mama in jail, so she got an attorney who found a loop hole in the system and it wasn't long before mama was out.

To this day she's still walking the streets and cussing us out when we don't give her money. It's been years now and I still haven't been able to forgive her for all she has taken us through." Ebony concluded.

Sometimes we repeat the mistakes of our parents even when we don't want to but we do so because it's what's familiar to us. As a speaker and guide, I've seen this happen many times so I understood exactly where Ebony was coming from.

"Have you truly accepted Jesus Christ in your life?" I asked Ebony. "You know it is a lot easier to forgive once you have accepted Jesus and understand the power of forgiveness. All the anger, hurt, resentment, and disappointment you feel for your mother is hurting you more than you know Ebony. Once you sincerely forgive your mother, you then will be set free and able to move forward." I told her.

Niecey walked over to Ebony, grabbed her hand, and nodded in agreement.

Ebony didn't shed a tear the whole time she told her story. In fact she still appeared to have an attitude. Then to everyone's surprise she said,

"You're right Ms. Jerri, I'm tired of holding on to this pain. I'm ready to forgive her." Ebony had gotten her breakthrough.

The session was going good. The women were courageously revealing their past. Since most of the stories were pretty heavy I thought it would be a good time to take a break.

•

Discussion Question:

Men: Now that you know more about Ebony, do you still see her as a trifling woman with an attitude, or a woman who had not dealt with the pain of her past?

Woman: Have you ever faced heartache caused by a parent? If so, how did you deal with it or are you still dealing with it?

Fourth Session

STOP BLAMING YOURSELF IT'S NOT YOUR FAULT!

Molested By My Uncle

"Tracy I bet you didn't know your clients were this messed up, huh?" Lyric asked her as the women were returning from the break.

"Well, Lyric, we all have things we've gone through in the past," Tracy responded.

"Yeah right Tracy, like you've gone through some things in your past. You've always been our voice of reason, what have you been through?" LaRita asked. Tracy paused; it was a question none of the women had ever asked her before. As a professional Tracy felt it wasn't fitting for her to bother her clients with her personal problems; but now she had been asked.

Reflecting back at her life she said, "My earliest memories of being at my grandmother's house was being molested by my uncle, my grandmother's baby brother. Baby Brother is what everybody called him." Tracy said, as tears welled in her eyes.

"Going to grandma's house was always fun. My grandmother had five children, and when my mother, aunts, and uncles all brought their children over, we had so much fun. It was the place to be, until the day something happened that changed my life. I can remember it as if it was yesterday; I was four years old.

We were having a cookout that day. Although all the adults were outside in the back yard, the kids were running back and forth; our parents kept yelling for us to stop running in and out of our grandmother's house. I have found that adults' attention spans can be very short when they're doing something they enjoy, and when the whole family got together it was a lot of laughing, singing, and playing games.

Eventually everyone was in the backyard, except for me, I had to use the bathroom. Baby Brother, my grandmother's seventeen year old brother was in the house too. You might be wondering why my nearly fifty year old grandmother at that time had a seventeen year old brother, well when my grandmother was thirty-three, her mother who was going through the change of life, got pregnant, and had another baby. Sadly, right after giving birth there were complications, before her mother passed away, she promised her that she would care for her baby brother as her own.

Now, back to my story, Baby Brother was coming out of the bathroom, and was attempting to zip up his pants; seeing me in the house alone he called me into the bathroom with him and shut the door. Then he unzipped his pants and pulled out something that I hadn't seen before; it was a part of his body that was long and hard. Then he told me to put it in my mouth. 'Don't bite it,' he said. 'Just lick it like you do a Popsicle and I'll give you some candy later.'

So I did, until we heard a door slam. I guess he knew someone was coming because he hurried and snatched it out of my mouth, put it back in his pants, and zipped his pants up. I didn't think anything of it, until he said to me right before he opened the door, 'Don't tell anybody what you did because if YOU do, YOU are going to get in trouble.' Then he opened the bathroom door and we both walked out.

> Perpetrators want the victims to think it's their fault.
> **IT IS NOT YOUR FAULT!**

(If you notice he said, 'WHAT YOU DID.' This is typical of a perpetrator.)

After we walked out I saw one of my cousins getting something from the refrigerator, so I guess that's who had come in and slammed the door.

My Uncle stole my innocence that day; he exposed me to something my innocent mind didn't understand nor was able to process. That wasn't the last time, or the only sexual act Baby Brother had me perform. Most of the time, the molesting happened in my own home when he would babysit me and my 18-month-old brother, while my mother went on dates. I guess my mother didn't pay attention to how my little brother screamed, cried, and clang to her for dear life every time she left us with him; but thank God my aunt did. She noticed it because it was the same way her son, who was a toddler, acted when Baby Brother babysat him.

> Parents PLEASE pay attention to your children's unusual behavior.

One day my mother and aunt confronted Baby Brother and my grandmother about what they suspected; of course he denied it. But the really sad part was not only did my grandmother not believe that her baby brother would molest his own relatives, she was so upset that her daughters would even accuse him of such a thing, that she wouldn't speak to them for nearly a year. It split our family apart and things were never the same.

With all the attention on the molesting of my little brother and cousin, no one ever asked me if Baby Brother had molested me, and I never said anything. I was molested several more times by non-family members as a young child. I often wondered what made me a target; it was as if there was a sign on me saying, 'I've already been molested, so you can molest me too.' Maybe it was at that young age that I lost my self-worth."

Tracy had surprised the whole group. Even though the women didn't really know each other all that well, they all thought they knew Tracy. But, then why would they think they knew her? Their relationship with Tracy had always been based on them telling her *their* problems.

•

Discussion Question:

Men: Can you see how the event of a woman's past can affect her future?

Women: No one bothered to ask Tracy if she had been molested; could that have been when her feeling of unimportance developed? Have you ever felt unimportant?

I Wanted My Marriage To Work BUT, His Mama!!!

T racy had stunned all the women with her shocking revelation. "Tracy we didn't know," Niecey said. "You seem so happy."

"I am now, but you have no idea what all I've gone through." Tracy replied as she continued.

"I am so grateful for these WOMAN TALK sessions; they are even helping me see some things clearly. Looking back I can see the pattern of how my life would unfold. Not feeling important as a child I felt I didn't matter, and I now believe subconsciously I carried that into my adult life.

I tried to make my marriage work. When I took my marriage vows, 'For better or for worse,' I had no idea how bad the *worse* would get. Although he never put his hands on me, for years I felt beat down."

"Tracy?" LaRita called out. "You said years, but I thought you and DeJuan was only married a short time. Didn't he leave you right after the twins were born?"

"Yes, but I'm not talking about him," Tracy replied.

"Well *who* are you talking about then? I thought DeJuan was your ex-husband?" Shaquanda asked.

"DeJuan is my ex-husband but he wasn't my *first* husband; Todd was." Tracy answered in a somber tone.

Surprised to hear Tracy had been married before to another abusive man all the women looked at Tracy with their mouths open.

"Tracy, I've been coming to you for several years now and I have never heard you talk about or even mention this first husband," said Ms. Veronica.

"That's because she ain't never mentioned nothing about this Todd man. I mean it's funny how you can be around a person for so long and still don't know them." LaRita said sarcastically.

"Oh LaRita, why are you making such a big deal out of it? Everyone has a past." Ms. Veronica snapped back. "I'm sure there are things about you that no one knows about. After all, people only tell you what they want to know. Now be quiet and let Tracy finish telling us about this first husband of hers. Go on Tracy," Ms. Veronica said.

"Well, we got married two weeks after our high school graduation. People tried to tell us we were too young to get married, but we didn't listen nor did we care about what anyone said. We were so in love. We dated all through high school so it wasn't like we were strangers, and besides we felt we knew what was best for us. Looking back, oh how I wish I had listened to their wise advice," Tracy admitted.

"Tracy, were you pregnant? Is that the reason why ya'll got married?" Shaquanda asked.

"No! I was not pregnant! We got married because we wanted to. It was just the two of us, oh yeah…and his mama. We moved in with her because she said it would be best. Although I didn't really like the idea at first, it seemed it was best because we had no responsibilities; we didn't even have to pay any bills. We both only worked part-time about fifteen or twenty hours a week, therefore, we spent a lot of time lying around and having sex; after all, we *were* newlyweds. That summer was wonderful; we didn't have a care in the world. It was a lot of fun.

Then came the real world. His mama started to complain about us lying around the house all day and not helping her with any of the bills. She would talk about me loud enough to make sure I heard her. She said things like: 'I don't like the way she clean.' 'I can't understand why her mama didn't teach her how to cook while she was growing up.'

She even said I was lazy and trifling and anything else she could think of that was negative. She tried to make me look bad to my husband and it worked, because soon he started to join her with his complaints of things I wasn't doing right.

The two of them would have a good time sitting around the kitchen table pointing out all my flaws, even though I would be sitting at the table too. I felt like I didn't matter. What his mama didn't know was I wasn't lazy or trifling I worked all through high school to help *my* mother pay bills. And actually I did know how to cook, I just tried to stay out of her kitchen since she was constantly making comments about how she couldn't stand people coming in her kitchen cooking. Since it was just the three of us in the house and my husband didn't cook, I figured she must have been talking about me. Besides, she made sure her son had a hot meal every day and night. And she made it clear that when it came to cooking, no one could please her son better than she could.

It Was Always My Fault

As much as his mama gossiped about me on the phone to her friends and put me down in front of my husband, never once did she say anything negative about her son. What hurt the most was my husband never stood up for me or took responsibility for anything he did. No matter what, it was always my fault.

I remember one time his mama let us use her car to go to an early movie across town. On the way back I asked Todd if we could stop by and see my mother and brother since I hadn't seen them in a while, and we were in the area. It was a good day. I really enjoyed myself at the movies and the visit with my family.

On the way back to his mama's house I noticed the gas hand was close to empty. I told Todd we needed to stop and put gas in his mama's car since we had been driving it all day. But he wouldn't hear of it, Todd said he was tired and didn't feel like pumping gas.

I knew his mama, like anyone else, would be upset if her car had half a tank of gas when she loaned it and it was returned empty. Therefore, I told Todd if he would just stop to get gas, I would get out and pump. He said, 'I don't feel like stopping, period! My mama can get some gas in the morning.'"

The women were surprised as they listened to Tracy talk about her first husband.

"I didn't feel good about it." Tracy said, "But what was I supposed to do? I tried. Sure enough when we got in that night his mama asked for her car keys because she wanted to run to the store. And oh boy, a few minutes later when she walked back through that door, you talk about a black woman with an attitude! She yelled for us to come into the living room. I knew she was serious then because you know black folks don't go in their living room unless it's serious.

Standing in front of us with her hands on her hips she asked us why her car was on empty. I couldn't believe Todd's response. After he had taken a seat in a chair across the room, making quick eye contact with her, my husband cowardly said, 'Mama you know it wasn't me,' as if to say *you raised me better than that*. Then he said, 'Well, see after the movie Tracy wanted to go by her mama's house…'

It seemed all she heard was, 'Tracy wanted' because she began chewing me out like I was a stepchild or something. She called me everything but a child of God. She said I must be out of my mind if I thought she was going to put gas in her car for me to stop by every Tom, Dick and Harry's house, I didn't even know what she meant by that, I didn't know a Tom, Dick, or Harry. She went on about how she let us use her car to go to the movies, not rip and run all up and down the streets.

I understood her anger, but my husband just sat there while his mama chewed me out. He never once took responsibility for not putting gas in the car or explained to her that I tried to get him to do so. He just sat there allowing his mama to think it was *all my* fault. Even after I gave her money to fill her tank, she said with the money in her hand, 'It still don't matter because the fact is I wanted to go to the store tonight and now I can't because there's no gas in my car.'

If only you can image the hurt I felt in my heart that night. It wasn't from his mama, I was used to that, but I was hoping for once my husband would step up and defend me. I didn't want to cause any problems between Todd and his mama; for once I just wished he would be on my side.

Living with Todd's mama was becoming unbearable. By the fall we both had full-time jobs. So we decided, well *I guess* I should say, I decided and then talked to him about it, that since we had to work anyway we might as well get our own place.

Not realizing the load we were taking on, that fall we also started college. Oh how I wish we had listened to the wise advice people gave us. But we didn't and it didn't take long before school, work, and trying to take care of a family, took its toll on the both of us.

Especially him; he was tired, cranky, and angry all the time. He acted as if he couldn't stand me. The more frustrated he became, the more he would take it out on me. He constantly called me stupid and worthless. He would say he hated he ever married me, and he should've listened to his mama. Wow, I had no clue his mama told him not to marry me. His nagging and complaining went on for four long years. The entire time I was attending both college and beauty/barber school, I endured his abuse and no one ever knew.

I was determined to make my marriage work so I didn't talk to anyone about my situation. I didn't want to hear, 'I told you so.' Now I realize that was my pride.

> If only we can learn to put our pride aside.

Todd was miserable, the responsibility was too much for him to bear so he dropped out of college, and never returned. He also decided he no longer wanted to honor the vows 'For better or for worse.' One evening when I got home, he had packed up all his things and moved back with his mama, or so he said.

Later I found out that he didn't actually move back in with his mama, but with a woman he had been cheating with off and on throughout our marriage. His mama knew about the other woman all along," Tracy revealed.

"Tracy what I want to know is, what made you stay in that relationship so long?" Shaquanda asked sincerely.

"That's funny you should ask. I have asked myself that same question, and there are only two reasons I came up with. One, as I mentioned, was the vow I took on my wedding day. The other, well, growing up not feeling important I didn't learn to value myself.

I believe when people don't learn to value themselves they stay in situations a lot longer even when it's unhealthy because it's familiar, and to make a change means doing something about it, something different. Many times a woman may try and reason *if I do something, like make known my feelings, he might leave or put me out, then where would I go?* Or *I don't want anyone to know we're having problems.* Or at her lowest point she may reason *what difference does it make that I'm unhappy he's not going to change, because I'm not that important.* So she stays, or worse, ends up in another relationship where we feel unimportant. At least that's what I did."

•

Discussion Question:

Man: Should Tracy's husband have stood up to his mother and defended her when his mother was wrong? Do you feel you could stand up to your mother if you knew she was wrong? Have you ever let someone take the blame in a similar situation?

Woman: Do you feel Tracy's mother-in-law contributed to the downfall of her marriage? Have you ever felt that everything that goes wrong is your fault? Do you agree that when a woman feels unimportant she has the tendency stay longer?

From One Bad Relationship To Another

Tracy is a thirty year old mother of two year old twin girls. She and their father DeJuan divorced when the twins were just six months old. Tracy is also a born again believer and lovingly uses every opportunity to encourage her clients spiritually. Although Tracy listens to her clients day after day talk about their problems, they didn't seem to think Tracy, being human, had problems too.

They also found out that Tracy is still dealing with issues with her ex-husband DeJuan. Tracy's ex is so low on the man pole. He is what sistas would consider a scrub, trifling, lazy, worthless and good-for-nothing. Let's get real, I bet right now there's someone you know like that running through your mind. In order for a person to change, they have to want to change, cry out to God, and be willing to allow Jesus to do a healing in them, or they will always be the same.

Tracy has always been a hard worker and very ambitious. Being the oldest she has also suffered and sacrificed the most. Her mother received no help or child support from Tracy's father who was unemployed and living with his mama. Because of it, Tracy carried guilt she shouldn't have had to take on as a child, or give all the money she worked for to help her mother financially.

Tracy's mother married her brother's father, but never married Tracy's father; adding to her feelings of unimportance. However, she divorced him a few years later. Tracy's single mom had a hard time paying the bills; even with paying a little on each bill, every paycheck

119

would be spent before she even got it. Which meant, by her senior year, Tracy didn't get the things like her peers: a new prom dress, senior pictures, class ring, et cetera.

At fifteen, Tracy began working after school in an ice cream shop giving most of her money toward helping her mother pay bills. You may be thinking, *if Tracy hadn't given her money to her mother, she could have purchased many of her senior items herself*; that's true, instead she made the sacrifice.

Growing up Tracy watched how her mother interacted with the men in her life. She saw her jumping in and out of relationships, taking care of men, and supporting them. The men always moved into their house and either laid around all day or they did so called work out hustling only getting a dollar or two here and there. Either way, it was obvious to Tracy that those men were not bringing any money into the house. Tracy also knew that much of her mother's hardship was because of the men her mother had chosen; or should I say, "So-called men," that moved into their house and allowed her mother to support them.

After seeing that lifestyle, Tracy decided she wanted a better life for herself. And although her first marriage did not turn out the way she'd hope, she worked even harder, putting herself through college, and with the help of a few grants, Tracy graduated on President's Honor Roll and the Dean's List with a Business Degree. She simultaneously attended a barber/beauty college and graduated at the top of her class there as well. That's where she met Mike, and together they purchased "GET REAL Beauty-n-Cutz."

As hard as Tracy tried to have a better life, different from her mother's; she ended up marrying another man much like her father. By the time Tracy met her second husband DeJuan she already had a successful career, was a homeowner, and drove a Mercedes; now, she wanted to have a family. After knowing DeJuan for four weeks, they met while he was serving as a volunteer security guard at a mega church; she thought she had met the man of her dreams.

They married and *he* moved in with her (Hmmm, sound familiar?) The fact that he did not have a steady job wasn't too much of a concern to Tracy. She thought he was just going through a rough period in his life and things would get better (Red flag!); but they didn't. Tracy found out after they were already married that not keeping a job was not a period he was going through, it was a pattern. Just weeks into the marriage, it became obvious to Tracy

Pay attention to RED FLAGS

that she was in a bad situation. Not wanting to end up like her mother, in and out of relationships, Tracy tried everything she could to make her marriage work.

"After I got pregnant, I hoped my marriage would grow stronger, but it didn't," Tracy said. "In fact, it progressively got worse. During the nine months of my pregnancy our relationship was on again, off again, on again. I did not realize you could not take an immature, childlike man and turn him into a mature responsible adult. It was becoming too much to bear." Tracy pouring out her heart continued.

"The day before our twins were born, DeJuan was arrested for past due traffic tickets. He took what little money we had left in our bank account and bailed himself out of jail. So just six days after giving birth, I had to go back to work, doing hair, in order to pay the bills since DeJuan didn't have a job. Six days after that, he walked out on me and the twins for good."

I Stood On HIS Promises

Tracy began to realize that it was no longer about the men she was attracting, but, it was something about her, and that she needed to get herself together.

"I was truly leading while bleeding. Not knowing what else to do, I cried out to Jesus for a healthy, happy marriage. I asked Him to show me my mistakes and to heal me. Then I stood on His promises that as long as I did my part by being faithful to my husband and God, that He would take care of my situation. I trusted Jesus and thought HE would straighten up DeJuan and restore our marriage. Sometimes it's not in the way we think it's going to be. But, Jesus is true to His Word."

Tracy's life stories had been so full of gloom that the look on the women's faces as I scanned the room clearly read: *see I knew there were no good men out there.* But Tracy's story wasn't over; there was still hope. So she continued on.

Her "Boaz"

"DeJuan never came back. However, three months after our divorce I met the man of my dreams, Derrick. He is wonderful and a true man of God. Derrick has been a widower for the past three years. His wife died in a car accident shortly after giving birth to their daughter, whom he was raising as a single father. Derrick and I both made the choice to start our relationship doing things God's way." Tracy said, as she looked at the women whose faces were starting to show relief.

"We also made the choice not to have sex until after we were married, and we were very mindful not to go to each other's houses for late night dinners or spend isolated time alone with each other. Instead, we used our courtship time mostly in groups, with family, on the phone, texting, and by email, getting to know and love each other's character within and becoming best friends."

Tracy is so happy she did things God's way. She and Derrick were married eight months after they met. They agreed that since Tracy really enjoys doing hair, she would continue. However, she would cut her five day a week workload to three days a week, giving her more time to spend with her family as a wife and a mother.

"Tracy I love you and Derrick's story. One thing I have noticed about you is you're always pleasant. I wonder if black women were more pleasant would it make it easier for men to approach us." Ms. Veronica inquired.

"Yeah!" Ebony said, "Because my brothers say usually when they approach black women they act like they got an attitude. My brothers say black women are too mean and that most of the black women they be trying to holla at, act like they don't want to be bothered, or that they are too good for a brother. They say, and women be wondering why they can't get a man. Oh yeah, and my bothers say black women are too picky and their standards are way too high. To be honest I kinda agree with them; just look at Elaine. I mean I'm not trying to be rude or anything but...Elaine, don't you think you could get a man if you lowered your standards a little bit?"

"I can't believe I'm even entertaining this question. However Ebony, first let me say, I have worked very hard to get where I am. It is my high standards that will keep the riffraff out of my life. Why should I lower my standards just to allow *any* man who can't appreciate me, tear down what I've worked so hard to build up?" Elaine intelligently replied.

"I agree with Elaine, the answer is not for women to lower our standards," I said. "However, our standards must be attainable and our requirements should be equivalent to what we *are willing* OR *not willing* to accept. For example you stop by the his place unannounced and expect for it to look immaculate and yet when he brings you home from a date, he can't even come in and use your bathroom because your place looks like a pigsty.

You want him to be romantic, yet you don't like to be touched. He has to have plenty of money and be a good budgeter, and yet you spend money like it grows on trees. He must be enthusiastic about what you do in life, but when he talks about what he does, you seem bored or disinterested. You admire the fact that he doesn't drink, smoke, cuss, or frequent the clubs; yet you do them all. What I'm saying is make sure your standards are realistic, and then you will draw the right man to you. Now I will say this, even with high standards and self-esteem you still need to be approachable."

"I think that's what my brothers were trying to say, Ms. Jerri, black women need to stop having attitudes when my brothers approach them. I mean I'm just saying," Ebony concluded.

"Naw now Ebony, there's a big difference between women with attitudes and women who are confident and know what *they want* AND *don't want*," Ms. Veronica said.

Ebony, I know your brothers, TRUST ME, I'm sure it's the latter one. I mean I'm just saying," Shaquanda sarcastically smirked.

Discussion Question:

Men: Do you find it hard to approach black women? When you meet a woman with high standers, does it matter to you that she also possesses the same standers? Is there a difference to you between women with attitudes and women who are confident and know what they want? Are you open to dating a woman who has been married and divorce, twice?

Woman: Like Tracy, do you believe it's possible your life can turn around? Like Tracy, do you believe a change in your life began with a change in you? Also like Tracy, do you believe sincerely doing things God's way makes a difference?

Life Made Her Hard

"**D**ang Tracy! I didn't know you been through so much. I'm surprise you ain't got no attitude towards men with all they done put you through!" LaRita said as she stood up. "Well, you're a better woman than me, because child I got to tell y'all what this dude took me through. And y'all know me, baby I had to set it off up in there!"

Just as LaRita began to speak, Shaquanda jumped up, waving her hand excitingly, and said, "Ooh… LaRita, please let me tell them about you, I know your story like the back of my hand and I'm gonna keep it real, okay!"

"Okay Shaquanda, dang! Tell it then!" LaRita said rolling her eyes as she sat back down.

"Okay. I'm going to try and act professional. Meet LaRita, or should I say, 'Ms. Drama Queen.' She can't keep a job because her attitude is too bad. LaRita is very attractive, and men are drawn to her; that is, until she opens her mouth! Once that happens the only thing the men hear is drama. But, for real though, underneath all the drama is a person dealing with a lot of pain. Wait! Let me first back up and tell y'all how her pain began.

LaRita ran away from home at fifteen and vowed never to return. Since that time she has been on her own. LaRita is twenty-seven, doesn't have any children and doesn't really know the whereabouts of any of her six brothers and sisters.

Both her parents were drug dealers and are now incarcerated. No one in the family could afford to take in all seven of their kids, so they were split up and sent to live with relatives in different states.

LaRita, who was ten at the time, ended up with mean old Aunt Bessie, an alcoholic who was verbally abusive to her. From the time LaRita arrived she was told by her aunt that her mama and daddy were nothing. She constantly reminded LaRita she didn't believe she would be nothing or have nothing, and often told her no one wanted her. This was told to LaRita daily.

She was also told that people didn't like her and after five years of hearing this LaRita began to believe her aunt. Her attitude soon became, 'well, if people don't like me, then I don't like people.' She has lived by that code for more than ten years.

After running away LaRita ended up in Dallas, Texas but wasn't very successful in the workplace. She was always starting a new job because she was either let go because of her bad attitude, or she would quit jobs. She said her bosses and the customer's had bad attitudes and she didn't want to 'catch a case fooling with them'. Well if you ask me I would bet it was LaRita with the bad attitude. But anyway, she needed to work to pay her bills. LaRita wasn't very successful with her love relationships either. I don't know if it's the type of men she picked, the drama she kept up, or simply that she just talk too much. One day LaRita met a man who she thought she would be with for the rest of her life. He was tall, dark, handsome, and he seemed to be educated.

After two weeks of them knowing each other they began shacking up. That's when she discovered that he didn't have a job, and the car she thought he had was stolen. Well, according to LaRita, 'it really wasn't stolen; it was his baby's mama's car. And see what had happen was, when she found out that he wanted to be with me instead of her, she gone come calling the police telling them that her car was stolen and stuff.'

LaRita found out about this when the police came to her job asking her questions about her man and the stolen car he had been driving. LaRita lied and told the police that she didn't know anything about that man, or the car.

Upset, immediately after the police left her job, LaRita asked if she could take a break. She left work and went to her apartment to confront her man about lying and having his baby's mama send the police to her job. Of course he lied, and then began to sweet-talk her about how he didn't know that his baby's mama reported the car stolen and that she had said he could borrow the car for awhile.

Then he told her his baby's mama was just mad because he won't come back and live with her and he was just using her car to try to get a job. And like a fool in love, LaRita believed him.

A few weeks later LaRita, who was stressed out from dealing with the drama of her man, his baby's mama, and as she says, 'them rude customers who be getting on my last nerve,' again left work on her break and went home to discover that her man was nowhere to be found. All his clothes were gone and he had taken the rent money that was in a shoe box. She also noticed that her TV, iPod, and laptop were gone too. Immediately, LaRita called over to his baby's mama's house and he answered the phone. Before she could get a word out he yelled, 'STOP STALKING ME! I DON'T WANT YOU!' then hung up in her face."

Hearing that, Ebony stood up with her hands on her hips and said, "Oh no he didn't!"

"Oh *yes* he did!" Shaquanda answered back. "But wait you won't believe this. In shock she calls back but this time his baby's mama answered his phone. She shouted, 'Look Trick, HE SAID HE DON'T WANT YOU!' then she hung up in LaRita's face."

"Oh no she didn't!" Ebony said, becoming agitated over hearing this new information concerning her home girl. "LaRita how come you didn't call me? You know it would've been on and poppin'!"

"Ebony, you're six months pregnant. What were you going to do?" Niecey asked.

"Y'all wait now, let me finish telling the story," Shaqaunda said. "Furious, LaRita rushes over to their house, and began banging and kicking on the door. She was cussing and yelling for her man, oh I'm sorry the man she thought was hers, to give her rent money and the rest of her stuff back. But of course, they never opened the door. They just left LaRita standing outside acting like a fool. She finally got tired and left mad, hurt, and devastated."

All while Shaquanda was telling the story, LaRita was making comments like: "Lord, they better be glad they didn't open that door," and "Woo if I could've just got to them, Ebony... trust me, it would've been on."

"But wait, y'all ain't heard the worst!" Shaquanda said waving her hands animatedly. "The next day LaRita goes to work and her boss confronts her about leaving work those two days on her break. He said he had to let her go because of the complaints he's been getting concerning her customer service skills. In other words, the customers were saying that she had a bad attitude."

Ebony joined in, "I can't believe LaRita's boss let her go because people said she had a bad attitude, I've been to her job lots of times and she didn't act like she had an attitude to me. In fact most of the time LaRita didn't even interact with the customers; she would just be sitting over in the corner watching her customers while they stood in line. So I wouldn't call that an attitude, *rude* maybe, but not necessarily an attitude," Ebony said.

LaRita, trying to defend her actions said, "Well I would be on my break all those times."

"Please y'all let me get back to the story," Shaquanda said as she continued. "Anyway whatever the case, LaRita had no money for her rent, was jobless, and man less. She felt everything had been taken from her. Now, she's on the defense and the rage that has always lived within her dark shadows, has surfaced as a protection."

Her Mouth

"LaRita's attitude is she's not to allow herself to be vulnerable again no matter what! And she ain't scared to fight, cuss, or threaten anyone that stands in her way. Trying to protect herself; she put up a wall, determined that no other man will hurt her, because she was going to check him out first.

So when John, one of Mike's clients, noticed LaRita at the shop and tried to step to her, she acted like she was an employer and he was trying to fill out an application. Immediately she started running off at the mouth, telling him all her business and then had the nerve to start asking him all of his. All he said was hi! Without taking a breath, this was her response:

130

'Hi I'm LaRita. Now I don't know if you're trying to get at me or what but if you are let me keep it real and tell you this: I don't talk to nobody that's married got a girlfriend baby mama drama or live with they mama. And I certainly don't talk to nobody that's broke. Now, I'm not saying I'm a gold digger but I'm not gone mess with no broke.... Well, you know the rest. Although you don't look like you broke judging by the suit and shoes you have on, but then again I don't know you and for all I know those clothes could've been boosted; because the last dude I messed with look like he had it all together too but come to find out he didn't even have a job or a car. I don't even know what kinda car you drive or if you even have a car. Do you have a car? If so what kind is it because I ain't finna be seen riding in nobody's hooty! Because...'

Well, John musta had enough of her attitude, because he jumped in and interrupted LaRita by saying, 'Excuse me,' then he turned and walked away. He actually left her standing there with her hand up, and mouth open. And you don't think it had nothing to do with her mouth? Hmmm... well, whatever the case, LaRita can't seem to keep a man, maybe it's because she talks too much!

And LaRita can somehow manage to cause drama everywhere she goes, even when she goes to get her hair done, Tracy was even surprised when she came in the shop talking all loud and upset over a parking space.

LaRita actually believed that because she looked over at a parking space in the parking lot while she was going the opposite way, that the space should be hers. So when this little old lady who was on the right side parked there, LaRita got all upset saying she took her parking space. Just drama! But anyway, back to John; if you ask me, John from what I had

131

heard, is a good catch." Shaquanda said as she finished her story and was getting ready to sit down.

"How would you know that's he's a good catch?" Ms. Veronica asked.

Shaquanda didn't miss a beat. "Well, see what had happen was, one Saturday morning while I was waiting for Mike to cut my sons' hair, I overheard him and John talking."

"You mean you were ear hustling," LaRita said, exposing Shaquanda's intent.

"Whatever! The point is, men gossip just like women do!"

•

Discussion Question:

Men: Have you ever been turned off by a woman who talked too much? What do you think about a woman who tells all her business the first time you meet? Have you lied to keep a relationship?

Women: Have a man ever told you a lie that you believed to be true? Have you gotten into it with another woman over his lies? Do you talk too much? Have you ever told all your business to a man you just met for the first time, and then wondered why he didn't call you back?

Suave, Charming, And Debonair

Shaquanda talk about John's qualities, and the conversation she overheard between him and Mike that Saturday morning at the shop.

"John is in his early forty's, good looking, and suave. His caramel color complexion complimented his bald head. He is truly a man's man.

He used to be a womanizer. He changed women like he changed his socks; there was practically a different woman every day. John felt for him to look good and be successful he had to have a 'Trophy Woman.' To him, a trophy woman had to have looks that were drop dead gorgeous, long flowing hair, perfect body measurements 36-24-36, and flawless skin. Having a degree and being a successful accountant at one of the largest accounting firms made him that much more appealing to the ladies.

In the past John wasn't as concerned about what was on the inside of women. He could care less about their mind, feelings, and thoughts; he was only interested in their outer appearance. John was not interested in settling down, getting married or having a family; but then why would he? He was living what he considered, *the good life.* He knew there were enough desperate women out there so glad just to have a piece of a man, that he could have a different woman in his bed each night with no commitment.

John led the women on by telling them he really liked them, but that he wanted to take the relationship slow so that he could "get to know them better." Really, that was just John's way of being assured that the women wouldn't be able to lock him in to anything. Because he did not want any children he made sure to protect himself during sex. It was all just fun and games to him. But as John began to mature, he was beginning to take a closer look at his life and how empty it really was.

Now that John is getting himself together he has become a good catch and is even interested in getting married. John is ready to treat a woman like a woman. But the problem is most women take John's kindness for weakness, because he's not hitting on them and no longer degrading them.

Even though he doesn't have any children of his own, he is now open to dating women who has children. John is looking for true love, but is finding too many women are not being real and are still playing games.

John is a stickler for being on time. For years like clockwork every Saturday morning he's waiting at the door when Mike arrives at the shop. He even gives Mike a hard time about being five minutes late. John is not only very time conscious, he's neat, organized, and into health and fitness. He's up every morning at 5 a.m. and workout two hours at the gym before going to work.

His Impression of Black Women

Now open to dating black women, John gets real serious about some issues he has. He explains to Mike what happened in the relation between him and Shelly, the first black woman he dated.

John told Mike how he really wanted to like Shelly but she was so insecure about her weight, which he had *no* complaints about, and he thought she was beautiful just the way she was. She tired him out talking and complaining about her weight all the time. He couldn't even put his arms around her waist without her pushing him away saying, "I don't want you to feel my rolls."

134

As much as John wanted to like Shelly he let her go. He said he got tired of trying to reassure her of her beauty and self-worth. Mike agrees with John, even commenting on how an insecure woman not only gets on a man's nerves, but it's a turn off.

Did you notice what John said? He had no complains about Shelly's size; it was her own insecurity that allowed her to sabotage the relationship. We can't look for anyone to confirm our value and self-worth; we have to know it.

John was maturing; even Mike noticed the change in him. Being open to dating a black woman for who she is and not her size or shape impressed Mike.

"Man I can't believe I'm hearing this kind of talk coming from you. You were the main one who had to have a trophy woman on your arms and most of the time she was a white woman!" Mike said.

"Right...right...yes I did and I still like Caucasian women, Asian women, Hispanic women; I guess you could say I like all women. I realized it wasn't the race of the woman, but my motive for choosing her is why I began to examine myself," John replied.

"But man, for as long as I have known you, I've never known you to date a black woman, so seeing you with Shelly was surprising to me. Was there a reason why you chose not to date black women in the past?" Mike questioned.

"To be honest I love and respect my mother and two sisters very much, but it was seeing the way they treated black men in their life that turned me away from black women.

My mother wore the pants and was the breadwinner in her relationships. Her last man was willing and wanted to be a strong man but didn't get a chance to because if he didn't move or jump when she told him to, she would just take over. My mother didn't allow her men to be men."

As much as John loves his mom, he felt she was very strong, controlling, domineering, overbearing, bossy, and ran her men. As for his sisters, one played mind games with her man; while the other played two or three different men at a time.

"Growing up seeing that, I thought all black women were the same and would never allow myself to get to know them as individuals. However, lately as I began reflecting back over my life, I realized the main thing I disliked about what my mother stood for, a strong black woman, is now what I admire. She is a strong black woman who raised her children as a single mom.

My values are beginning to change, and now I'm ready to love that special woman no matter what her race is. In fact, I now can appreciate a strong black woman, especially a black woman who's confident and knows who she is. I'm looking for someone who will not compete with me but who will complete me; someone who is strong but still allows me to be the man. See I don't want her to walk behind me and I sure don't want her to walk in front of me! I just want her to walk beside me; walk *with* me."

"Man! John, you have changed. But it's a good thing though," Mike said proudly.

"Right...right, yes I have. In fact, I think I've found the one I want to be my wife," John confessed.

"Man! Are you for real? Well congratulations. Tell me about her," Mike insisted.

"I saw her about two months ago. Although she is totally the opposite of the women I usually date, it was something about her that caught my attention right from the start. I mean her caramel complexion, sassy hair style, and thick physique; all that topped with her strong confidence, was and *is* very sexy to me."

"Man! You really have changed. Hey, I'm impressed and also surprised," said a shocked Mike.

"Yes, I am too. I never thought I would date a black woman and I sure wouldn't have considered marrying one. Like I said, she is the opposite of the women I'm used to dating. However, to me she is more beautiful than any other woman I've dated in the past. I believe she has the ability to complement me, encourage me, restore me, lift me, strengthen me, be real with me, pray for me, respect me, admire me, look out for me, enjoy me, and bring joy to me. To sum it up I believe she will complete me," John concluded.

"So it sounds like to me that John likes somebody," Shaquanda said with a curious look in her eyes.

"I wonder who it could be," said Ms. Veronica.

"LaRita, didn't he try to step to you a few months ago?" Ebony asked.

"Oh, we all know it ain't LaRita, because she don't even…, fit the description," Shaquanda said as she casually laughed.

"Dang! Shaquanda, I thought we were supposed to be home girls," LaRita said slightly irritated.

"We are, but I said I was gonna keep it real. Anyway whoever she is, she most definitely got John's nose wide open. Listen to his spoken word," Shaquanda concluded.

Jerri Lynn

A Trophy Woman

Women were just trophies to me, with good looks and bodies,
All the brothers envied me.

I had to have the best, be better than all the rest,
Is what I thought was success.

But one day I realized that I was missing the prize,
That a good woman comes in all shapes and sizes.

It's not the color of her skin,
Or the package she comes in.

It's the attitude she shows. When she's confident and knows,
Who she really is.

I thank God HE showed Mercy on someone like me,
I no longer treat women like trophies, But as human beings.

•

Discussion Question:

Men: Have you ever dated a trophy woman? Have you ever been in a relationship were you had to constantly reassure your woman? Have you ever been in a relationship where the woman was domineering? How did you feel?

Women: Have you ever dated a man who you felt was only interested in your outer appearance? Have you ever been a trophy woman and knew it? Do you feel a man is weak if he's not hitting or degrading you?
Are you a woman who is constantly complaining about your weight? Do you need to be reassured of your beauty and self-worth? Be honest, are you domineering? How do you think the black males in your life view black women?

138

Gang Raped:
Breaking The Silence

Although LaRita's story was serious, it was pretty humorous listening to Shaquanda tell it. Suddenly Elaine who had been sitting back, showing no emotions, approached me and said, "Ms. Jerri, I need to go."

"What's wrong Elaine, are you alright?" I asked.

"Yes, I just have to get out of here," Elaine replied.

As I walked her to the door, I could see that Elaine was trying hard to fight back tears. "Elaine you can't run away from your past," I told her.

"Ms. Jerri you don't understand, I'm not like these women. I can't just sit here and talk about my business." She repeated, "Ms. Jerri, I have to go."

As the tears start to roll down her face, I gave her a hug and whispered in her ear, "Elaine it's okay. You have to let it out and allow yourself to be healed."

Not able to hold it in any longer she yelled out loud, "I was gang raped!"

All the women stopped and began staring at her in amazement. Elaine, standing by the door looked like she wanted to run out, but instead, summoned the courage to put away her pride, take off the mask, and break her silence. With a tear stained face and her head raised, she walked back towards the group, and began to tell her story.

"I was only fourteen years old that summer afternoon when I decided to go outside and hang out with some friends. In the neighborhood where I grew up, everybody knew everybody. It was one of those neighborhoods where during the day hardly anyone locked their doors because kids were always going in and out of each other's house.

Usually everyday one of the boys would bring their boom box out and have it blasting loud. Before you knew it kids would be dancing up and down the street. Most parents didn't really worry or care about their kids hanging out in the neighborhood as long as they had finished their chores and were in the house before the streetlights came on.

Even though I didn't get to hang out as much as my sisters, summertime in my neighborhood was still fun; until that day everything changed, well, for me anyway," Elaine said, drawing in a breath as she was about to become transparent.

"They were not strangers; I knew every one of them. The boys were fourteen to seventeen years old, all whom I had grown up with. They were classmates, my friend's brothers, and who I considered to be my friends. Therefore, I had no reason to be concerned when they called me over to the side of one of the boys' house. Immediately the boys surrounded me asking me to 'give them some.'

At first, I thought they were just joking; but it soon became very apparent to me that this was no joke, when the boys started touching my breasts and pulling at my shorts. Then Stanly, my classmate, suggested to Jeremy that they take me into his house through the back door and into his room. I should have screamed but I thought, *surely, this is not really happening to me, I'm just having a bad nightmare*. However, it was broad daylight, the street was full with kids playing, and my sisters were just a few houses down visiting their friends.

140

But it was true; my nightmare was becoming a harsh reality. That nice sunny Tuesday afternoon I was about to be raped. As I lay there on that dirty old hardwood floor, they didn't want to put me on the bed in fear that the squeaking old bed would make too much noise.

With my blouse open and my bra pulled up exposing my bare breast, I was naked from the waist down. I lay there in horror, looking up at the ceiling while four of the boys, Kenny, Will, Jason and his twin brother Josh pulled my arms and legs in four different directions. They had my legs spread so wide it literally felt like my body was going to split in half.

Lying there it was almost like an out-of-body experience. It was as if my inner self had risen up from my body and I watched as one by one those seven boys climbed on top of me. I could feel their roughness tearing inside and around the opening of my vagina. The pain seemed unbearable but still I didn't scream. In fact, I think by the time Stanley and James, the third or fourth boy climbed on me, my body went numb. That was probably a good thing because all of a sudden Jeremy's bedroom door opened, and in walked another boy.

I thought my heart was going to stop, *how much could my body take,* I wondered. But when I saw who it was I thought *what a relief, finally someone is going to help me.* I just knew my terrifying ordeal was over; after all, he was my best friend's older brother, Walter. He had always been like a big brother to me. I have spent the night many times at their house and he had never shown any signs of disrespect. So I just knew he would help me. But he didn't help me; in fact, he joined in becoming number eight.

Confused, everything I thought I knew and the trust I had in people was shattered. I don't think words can illustrate all the things those boys did to me during those horrific two hours. The boys rotated holding my arms and legs apart. While James was ejaculating in my vagina, Jeremy was ejaculating in my mouth. Will, whose father was a minister, didn't want my vagina so he flipped me over.

Everything you can imagine, they did to me. I can still smell the funk from Kenny, who had obviously not showered in days; and feel the sweat that dripped from Stanley's wet body to mine. The musty armpits of Jason and Josh who had been playing basketball outside on that hot day; and the stench of Jeremy's anus as he straddled my face are forever stitched in my mind. I can still remember the taste of the stale thick semen as it went down my throat, and the odor of funk, mustiness, and bad breath that filled the room.

As I lay there, I could tell Jeremy's mother was somewhere in the house, maybe the living room or a front bedroom because although the sound of the television was quite loud where she was, I could faintly hear several times her yell to the boys to stop all that racket. Maybe she thought the boys were playing video games, wrestling, or something, but if only she have come to his room."

Elaine sharing her story had an impact on all the women in the group. They realized they had misjudged her pain as a snooty, uppity attitude. The women were showing growth, Elaine continued.

"When it was all over, the boys didn't even think enough of me to give me a towel to wipe off. As I was zipping up my shorts, Jeremy's mother came and opened his bedroom door irritated from all the noise. Seeing all those boys and me, all she said as she closed the door back was, 'boy I told you not to have those little fast hot tail girls in your room, and open up your window, it sinks in there.' Wow! I couldn't believe her. I wanted to yell out, 'Your son and his friend's just raped me!' But what good would it have done, she probably would've just thought it was my fault.

As I was leaving out the back door, the same way they brought me in, I passed his window. I could hear the boys laughing and making jokes about what they had just done to me. They were saying things like: I wanted it, I enjoyed it, and that I was already a hoe. The truth is, before that day, I was a virgin."

The Longest Walk Home

"Walking home, I was barely able to move because of the intense pain, and burning, I felt between my legs. My vagina felt like it was literally going to drop out of my body. I tried to walk as straight as I could so I wouldn't draw attention to myself or to the dried up semen that had turned cloudy white on my legs or the semen stains on my denim shorts. My breasts were sore and throbbing from all the pulling, squeezing, and sucking the boys had done to them.

All kinds of thoughts were running through my mind. Then my mind started to play tricks with me. I felt like everybody was staring, pointing and laughing at me, saying, 'I know what you just did; you're nasty!' But when I looked around everyone was going about their usual business; I realized that was how I felt.

It seemed the closer I got to my house, (Just a few doors down) the farther away my house seemed. All I wanted to do was just get in my house, get passed my mother, take a shower, and get in the bed; which is exactly what I did. Later that day my mother came in my room and asked me why I was in bed in the middle of the day.

Oh, how I wanted my mother to realize that something was wrong with her little girl. I wanted her to come put her arms around me and tell me everything will be all right, but she didn't. She didn't pay attention that her daughter's behavior was unusual. It was a bright sunny hot day and I was lying in the bed with the covers over me, and the shades pulled down.

As I lay there, trying to decide what to do; to tell or not to tell. I remembered a girl who had been raped and when she told, the other kids blamed her, made fun of her, and were even angry at her for telling. They said they could tell she wanted it by the way she dressed. Therefore, I don't know if it was because I was ashamed, afraid, or embarrassed, but I tried to just block that day out of my mind and never told anyone, until now. And I never understood why people blame the victim?

As an adult, I realize now, that what those boys did to me was not my fault. I was a victim of a brutal criminal assault, and that those boys deserved to have been punished for what they did to me. They *stole* my innocence. That day, I became an 'Angry Black Woman with an Attitude.'

And since I didn't have a balance to show me what love from a man was, not even from by father, I grew up having an attitude toward all men. I even had anger toward my mother for not noticing that day that something had happened to me, I have even been angry with myself all these years for not telling," Elaine bravely admitted as she gave a sigh, this time from the relief of the weight she had been carrying.

I elected to share some of the gorier details about Elaine's story. It's time we stop minimizing the seriousness of theses violent crimes. The words molestation, rape, and incest are becoming so common we begin to see them as just that, words. But maybe by allowing ourselves to go there with the victims, to think what they thought, to smell what they smelled, and to imagine the pain that they felt, then just maybe we will **STOP** blaming the survivors!

The atmosphere had become pretty heavy. The women, at least most of them, had taken off their masks. With so much pain in the room, I thought we would break session and dismiss. But, before I could say those words, Tammy, who had been sitting quietly over in the corner throughout all the sessions, raised her hand. Finally Tammy had something to say.

•

Discussion Question:

Men: Do you think women set themselves up to be raped by the way they dress?

Women: Do you feel Elaine being gang raped was her fault? Do you feel society has become desensitized to rapes, molestations, and other sex crimes?

DEPRESSION, A Silent Killer

One day at the shop when Tracy pulled back Tammy's hair in an attempt to comb through it, she was overcome by what she saw. The bruises on the side of her face as well as knots throughout her head were undeniable. Tracy confronted her about it, but Tammy insisted they were caused by rocks that her three year old son Jackson, had thrown and accidently hit her with. Stunned, Tracy took Tammy to the side and lovingly but point blank asked her if her man was hitting her.

Embarrassed, Tammy denied several times that her man was hitting her, but finally, she broke down and confessed that not only has her man been beating her, she found a letter under a pillow that Taylor, her twelve year old daughter, was writing to a friend, that stated, *"My mother's live-in boyfriend be coming in my room at night touching me while my mother is at work."*

Tracy, still baffled, told Tammy, who was sobbing uncontrollably, that she has to call the police and get that man out of her house. As Tracy attempted to lead her to the back to make the call, Tammy stopped her and said, "But that's not all. I've noticed that lately when I've been giving Jackson a bath he's been holding onto his clothes not wanting me to take them off screaming, "NO, NO!" Then, when I finally get him in the tub and make him sit down in the water, he would cry and fight to get out. At first I thought the water would be to hot so I started making sure the water was lukewarm, even cooler; but, it didn't matter. Each time I got the same reaction. When my man first moved in Jackson really liked him, now I've noticed that in his presence he seems frightened and withdrawn. Tracy, I don't want to admit it, but I think... I think... he's been molesting my son too!

"Oh, Lord No!" Tracy said as she caught the collapsing Tammy in her arms. "Tammy, you have to protect your children. You must call the police, put that man out, and get your children some help!" Then looking her straight in her eyes Tracy said to Tammy, "As much as I like you, if you don't report this, I will."

Although Tracy's heart went out to Tammy, she still had a business to run, as well as other clients to attend to, so she beckoned for me to come over and lead Tammy into the salvation prayer.

But, Tammy refused to pray or accept Jesus into her life. She also refused to allow me to pray for her. She said she wasn't ready yet and that some day she would get around to it. Then she said, as she was walking out the door, "Don't y'all worry about me. Really, I'll be all right! My man won't hurt me; he loves me!" Again Tammy refused help.

Tracy was right, Tammy needed more than just encouragement, she needed someone who could help her take off the mask, go deep into her past, and indentify the root cause behind her attitude. It was my hope that attending WOMAN TALK would help her. I just hoped it was not too late.

That afternoon when Tammy returned home, although she did not really want to, and was very nervous and scared, she realized she had exposed a very important situation and that now she was forced to do something about it. So to give her courage (in her mind), she seduced her man into drinking a whole bottle of Vodka with her. Her plan worked, he went to the bedroom and passed out. Tammy then called the police and her man was arrested. However, Tammy did not anticipate, that when the police arrived her demeanor would appear unstable; crying uncontrollable, stumbling around, and words slurring. (CPS) Child Protective Services, was also called out and her children were taken as well; for the time being.

She Was Severely Depressed

After an investigation and trial, her man was sent back to prison. With her children gone, and her man, again Tammy began spiraling downhill. Most of us knew some of her background (women talk at beauty shops) and were concerned as she became more withdrawn. Tammy refused to allow her family to help her, or seek professional help, but she had been attending all the WOMAN TALK sessions. Although she rarely spoke, I was hopeful that something said would spark in her, and maybe it did because, one particular session, to everyone's surprise, Tammy was ready to share her story. As she stood there, head down, voice low, and quivering, she spoke.

Tammy Shares Her Story

"From birth to age eleven, I lived with both my parents. I came from a large family, and I was directly in the middle with six older siblings and six younger ones. Ruth, my mother, was a stay-at-home mom, it was hard for her to divide her time between thirteen children. Trying to give each child individual and special attention was an ongoing task for her. But being a true middle child, I often struggled to find my place in the family, so eventually I became withdrawn and quiet.

My daddy noticed that I was distant so he made every effort to make me feel special even giving me his undivided attention. It was clear I was a daddy's girl. Mama was jealous of me and daddy's relationship and made it known by focusing and catering to the other twelve children. The lack of mama's affection and attention didn't faze me one bit; my attitude was, I enjoyed being a daddy's girl! It didn't matter how late it was or how tired daddy would be, he always came home from work and made time to hear how, his favorite girl's (at least in my mind) day went.

As much as they tried to put up a happy front I was awakened many nights to the loud voices of my parents arguing. They weren't aware that I had been listening. My daddy had a mild tempered, fun-loving personality, he hardly raised his voice. So on the nights when I would wake up and hear them arguing, I couldn't make out everything he was saying. However, mama on the other hand had more of a serious, strong, take care of business, *I don't have time to play*, attitude, so I could hear everything she said. She was upset, saying something about being sick of him and his gambling debt.

Being too young to fully understand what was going on between my parents, when daddy moved out, I was heartbroken and I blamed mama. I felt she had taken from me the one person who really loved me. I felt her putting him out is what changed our lives and lifestyle.

Mama made it clear she was going to get a divorce. Her choice caused her to have to work two full-time jobs just to pay the bills. My older siblings thirteen to nineteen all had to get after school jobs as well. They cut yards, babysat; whatever they could do to help mama make ends meet. This left me with the total responsibility of taking care of the house. Which included all the chores, preparing all the meals, and caring for my younger siblings: Twin brothers, Ajay and Alex seven, sisters, Olivia, six, Rose, five, Hannah, four, and baby sister Kayla, two. Even working two jobs, 3pm-11pm and 11pm-7am mama still didn't have money for daycare, so she kept Hannah and Kayla during the day while we were in school. Or should I say, Hannah and Kayla kept themselves, because mama slept all day. I had no time to socialize after school or participate in any after school activities because I had to rush home to care for my younger siblings. I hated it; I felt it was too much responsibility for a young child. I felt the choice my mother made to get a divorce, was selfish, because it also affected us as children."

The women listened intently. Literally at the edge of their seats with their necks extended even farther trying to hear the details of the horror they had only heard bits and pieces of what Tammy had gone through, at the hands of her father. Tammy never raised her head. She couldn't bear to look the women in the face because of the shame she was getting ready to reveal as she continued.

"With so much responsibility, my blame and anger towards my mama turned into hatred and resentment. But, being a kid, the only ones I could take my revenge out on were my younger siblings; and that's exactly what I did. My behavior was silently out of control. I say silently because when mama and my older sister and brothers were at home everything seemed fine. She was unaware that her six youngest children were holding a secret.

However, when they would leave, the younger children felt my wrath. My anger had caused me to become an abuser. I would intimidate and manipulate them to do whatever I wanted. I even forced them to steal, lie, and scheme. But, I did something even worse."

Ms. Veronica cut in, "Tammy, there's nothing you can do so bad, that God won't forgive you if you ask Him."

150

Suddenly, Tammy, who was bending over holding her stomach, began sobbing uncontrollably, "You're wrong Ms. Veronica. God won't forgive me for what I did, and I don't deserve to be forgiven, that's why I won't ask."

The women all gathered around Tammy trying to convince her how much God loves her, when she said, "I forced my younger siblings to perform oral sex on me, drink water from the toilet and clean the bathroom floor by licking it; and this took place on a regular basis."

The women were speechless.

"But that's not the worst," Tammy said sobbing. But then my daddy, whom I loved and thought loved me, did the unthinkable.

•

Discussion Question:

Men: Did you realize the impact divorce has on children?

Women: Did you realize there is such a thing as putting too much responsibility on a child? Have you noticed any strange behavior from your children, especially fear, worry, or nightmares?

My Daddy Did The
UNTHINKABLE

"Growing up people thought I had an attitude because I was distant. Well what do you think your attitude would be if two months after your daddy moved out? One nice sunny day he came by for a visit and your life changed forever?

It was a typical Sunday afternoon, we had just returned home from church. With mama working two jobs and my older siblings working part-time after school, Sundays were the only day of the week that we all spent together. I always looked forward to Sundays because it was the day that daddy came for his visit.

It was the Sunday after the Thanksgiving Holiday, and we had all enjoyed spending the last three days together. (Mama had asked that everyone take off during that time so we could spend it together) It was fun, us all being together; the only person that was missing was daddy, but now we were getting ready to see him too. On that particular day my siblings and I were all busy doing different things around the house. My older sisters Jan and Aubrey were in the kitchen with mama doing their chores and helping mama cook. My older brothers Paul, Greg, Wylie, and Xavier, were in their room watching TV, and most of us younger children were outside playing in the yard when daddy passed us and went inside the house. But it was something about him that seemed unusual. First, I noticed he had on a jacket even though it was a warm sunny day. Generally if we were outside when he came he would always stop and talk or play with us for a while, before he entered the house. However, this day he walked right past us with a strange look on his face as if he didn't even see us. Not thinking too much about it we continued to play.

It wasn't long before daddy called us all into the living room, he said he had a surprise for us. As we each lined the couch and chairs in anticipation of the big surprise, Mama, still in her church dress with house shoes and apron on, came in and sat on the arm of the chair my oldest sister, Jan was sitting in, next to the kitchen. Mama had just bent down and picked up Kayla who wanted to sit on the arm of the chair alongside her. With everyone in position we waited for the big surprise.

Daddy made sure we were all paying close attention to him when he walked over to mama, pulled out a gun, and at point blank range, shot her in the head. He then grabbed a knife from the kitchen counter and begins stabbing her.

In a split second right before my eyes, my innocence was stolen, and my life was changed forever. I can still picture my siblings and me running and screaming in horror in different directions.

I, and the ones closer to the front door, ran to the porch; but daddy's rampage wasn't over. After hearing several more shots fired in the house, daddy also ran out on the porch where he fired several more rounds before my oldest brother Paul, nineteen, who was also shot, was able to wrestle daddy down, taking the gun from him."

Tammy paused for a moment as she wiped her eyes and blew her nose. The pain and guilt she carried was hard to watch, so I asked her if she'd rather not finish. Sobbing she said, "I have to," then she took a breath and continued. "I can still see the image of blood everywhere. When daddy's shooting rampage was all over," again she took a breath, "laying dead was mama, on the floor right by the kitchen; my baby sister Kayla, laying next to mama; Greg was found in the hallway toward the bedrooms with Ajay underneath him, I guess he was try to protect him; poor Wylie, he never moved, maybe it was the shock of seeing his mama killed right before his eyes, because he was still sitting in the living room chair in the corner by the TV when he was shot in the head; outside more were dead, Jan was laying backwards on the front porch with her eyes open; Aubrey and Rose was laying face down in the front yard, both had been shot in the back while running.

What a sad day that was. On that day, hatred destroyed my entire family. Also sad, was the way people treated my surviving siblings and me after that happened. We did nothing wrong, my daddy made a choice that day that affected all of us, and instead of people showing us love, most treated us like we were freaks.

After that day life was never the same, Paul being the oldest wanted to keep us together. Since mama and daddy owned the house we were able to stay in it. And although grateful to have a place to stay, living in that house was a constant reminder of that tragic day. For a long time I couldn't even go into the kitchen without feeling that I had to step over mama.

Mentally, a few of my siblings never recovered. Some turned to alcohol and drugs trying to erase the pain of that day. Me, I just wanted to put the past behind me.

•

Discussion Question:

Men: Have you are someone you know, ever been so angry over a divorce that you *thought* about doing something unthinkable? What stopped you?

Women: Have you survived a tragedy? How did you get through it?

I Thought It Was Behind Me

"**W**hen I was twenty years old, I married Richard, a good man. Although I worked, I didn't have to; Richard was a good provider and allowed to use my money how I pleased.

Richard and I really wanted children, but were told it could not happen because of the large fibroid tumors growing in my uterus. However, one year after our wedding date, I gave birth to beautiful, Taylor; seven years later to our pleasant surprise, Jackson arrived. During my pregnancy with Jackson, Richard and I made the choice that I would become a stay-at-home mom to our two children." Tammy stood silent for a moment as she reflected back on the good times she had with Richard.

Tammy seemed to have had it all; she had a really good marriage, a husband who loved the Lord, and her unconditionally, and two beautiful children. She appeared so happy. And yet, I couldn't help but to notice that sometimes at the shop while waiting to get her hair done, she would have a deep faraway disturbed look of sadness in her eyes. I have often startled her when I've walk up and touched her, inquiring if everything was alright. She'd look at me and smile, then say, "Oh yes Ms. Jerri, everything is great!"

The entire eight years Tammy and Richard were married Richard seemed to really adore her; he was a great father to the children as well. Unfortunately, at a 4th of July picnic celebration on the lake, Richard drowned. Jackson was just two months old.

From Jail To Living In Hell

Tammy was devastated over the lost of Richard and for a few years seemed to be on a downhill spiral; but, she finally began to get it together. She got a job and things were going well for her and the children. However, being single for more than three years, Tammy was beginning to lose hope that she would ever find love and happiness again. So when a friend, who was on her way to visit her boyfriend in prison, invited Tammy to come along for the ride, thinking nothing of it, she agreed. Little did she know that ride would change her life forever.

While at the prison Tammy was introduced to another inmate, due to be released in three months. The two of them seemed to hit it off well. She really enjoyed her visit and at the end gave him her phone number and address to keep in touch. Tammy and the man began writing everyday; it was as if they were having a love affair through their letters. So of course when he was released with nowhere else to go, he moved in with Tammy; who was thrilled to have him there. Unfortunately, the thrill did not last long.

Right from the start, Tammy, who worked the 11pm-7am shift at a 24-hour diner, began noticing when she would get home in the mornings there seemed to be a strange feeling between her man, and Taylor. She mentioned to her man the strange feeling she was getting but he convinced her that it was all in her head, then he pat her on the butt and insisted she have a drink with him.

Tammy longed for that picture perfect life she had with Richard. She tried to put up a front to everyone on the outside that her new relationship was just that. However, behind closed doors Tammy's man was verbally abusive and was slowly beating her spirits down. (Did you catch that, *slowly?*) He often called her stupid, worthless, and the B word. Although he didn't have a job, he constantly reminded her of the many women who would be privileged to have him.

> Learn to love yourself so that nothing can creep up on you.

Tammy's man was very controlling and insecure. Although he wouldn't allow her to cut her thick long curly hair, he wouldn't allow her to wear it down either because it gave Tammy a natural sexy exotic look that only added to his insecurities; he insisted that she only wear it pulled back into a bun. He dictated the clothes she wore and the style. Also, she was not allowed to wear makeup; only lipstick on special occasions, because he felt other men would notice and find her attractive.

Tammy began drinking daily with her man. Soon she realized that the alcohol not only helped her cope with the abuse, it masked that strange feeling she was having about him and Taylor. In three short months, Tammy's life had flipped upside down.

Tammy's synopsis was quite different from the others. She seemed to be crying out for help. Oh how I wanted to help her, even when she came to her hair appointments, just from her demeanor everyone there could tell that there was something wrong. Several times Tracy and I have both offered her resources, to get help, but Tammy was in denial. She had convinced herself that her man really loved her even though he was abusive to her. She was hiding behind a mask trying to pretend that everything was ok but, it was obvious she was becoming more and more depressed. If only she would allow someone to help her. Tammy was hanging on to life by a string, while silently trying to deal with the pain of a broken heart.

You see, even though Tammy had begun drinking every day, still deep down she was concerned about Taylor and Jackson. They had both become very rebellious, distant, and fearful, wanting nothing to do with her man. But in denial, Tammy was only fooling herself thinking her situation would one day get better. But why would it, when nothing changed? Tammy's attempts to keep up her front was failing, deep down she knew that people could see through it.

"Ms. Jerri," Tammy says continuing to talk as her tears again began to flow. Can't you see it? Can't all y'all see that I'm being punished for what I've done? My daddy, who I thought loved me, *KILLED MY MAMA*. My husband who adored me, *DROWNED*. My children who love me have been taken from me, because I allowed a man in my house that *MOLESTED THEM*. And y'all want me to believe that God loves me?

Well, on that fatal day, back when I was eleven years old, I stopped believing, and became a black woman with an attitude toward everybody, including God.

It has been years since that day. Daddy died a few years ago in prison. We found out the reason daddy killed mama and my siblings, was he didn't want to pay her child support for all his children."

Stolen innocence, the victims? *All of them.* After Tammy finished telling her story, there wasn't a dry eye in the room. I, along with the other women tried again to convince Tammy, who was sobbing uncontrollably, that none of that was her fault. And that through all she has gone through Jesus still loves her. Tammy refused to believe it. The sorrow in the room was overwhelming, I had to **dismiss.**

•

Discussion Question:

Men: Do you, or know men who says they love their children. But, hate their children's mama? Who do you think suffers from your actions (mentally, emotionally and/or physically)? Can you now understand what you are doing to your children?

Women: Where do you think Tammy's issues stemmed from? Tammy felt God wouldn't forgive her. Do you feel there's any sin that God won't forgive, if you asked? Do you think the tragedy that happen to Tammy's family was her fault?

Food For Thought

Divorce, And Its Effect On Our Children Caught In The Middle

Marriage is not a game.
people think it is. So what
marriage playing games,
charades, hide-and-seek, I
stones, tug-o-war, and one
good at, keep-a-way. The origin

The problem is too many
do we do? We enter into
such as, a tit-for-tat,
spy, pay back, sticks and
that we as women are really
of games is competitiveness.

The problem with competitiveness is that you and the opposing player are on opposite sides. Hmmm, Let's stop for a moment and let that *marinate*.

When I was a child, I spoke as a child, I act like a child, I thought as a child: but when I became a man, I PUT AWAY CHILDISH THINGS.
1 Corinthians 13:11 (KJV)

Jesus knew their thoughts and said to them, "Every kingdom divided against itself will be ruined, and every city or household divided against itself WILL NOT STAND.
Matthew 12:25 (NIV)

If a house is divided against itself, that house CAN NOT STAND.
Mark 3:25 (NIV)

Divorce is the outcome of a house divided. We can already see that marriage is for mature people who are on the same side. Not, for immature people who play games. However, once the choice to get a divorce has been made, it's time we focus on what's most important, the effect it has on our children who are caught in the middle.

Grow up and stop playing games. IT IS NOT ALL ABOUT YOU! Mature people find ways to work things out for the *love* of their *children*. They don't play games, or hurt the children they say they love.

Although both fathers and mothers claim to love their children, most often they allow the bitterness, anger, and hatred, they feel for the other parent to control and many times consume them. When that happens, many times it's a door opener for the devil to step in and plant evil thoughts in their minds. The main tool he uses is pride, and rejection.

Where is the love you claim you have for your children? Do you not understand that to take revenge, or be vindictive, towards the other parent causes pain and hurt to your children?

When a parent does not pay child support for his or her child, you make your children suffer. (Now don't get me wrong, single parents, *mostly women*. Have been taking care of children, with no help from the non-custodial-parent for years, and has done just fine) But I'm making a point to the (NCP) who don't want to pay, is it that you want to see them fall? Why don't you spend time with your children? Oh! I know because she won't let you see them, hummm. And to be honest, I know there are women out there who play games and are not allowing men to see their children. But try explaining that to a young adult who has spent their whole childhood waiting, hoping, and praying that one day their parent will love them enough to come see them.

Or better yet, what about you parents who comes and pick your children up when you really don't want to, but to spite the other parent you do. Then, mistreat the children, or even worse, take the children and drop them off at somebody else's house (that may not be safe). All because you really don't want to be bothered, but want to spite the other parent.

WHAT PART OF THIS DO YOU NOT UNDERSTAND! YOU ARE HURTING YOUR CHILDREN, THE SAME CHILDREN YOU SAY YOU LOVE. GROW UP AND STOP PLAYING GAMES. IT IS NOT ALL ABOUT YOU! Mature PEOPLE find ways to work things out for the LOVE of their children. They DON'T PLAY GAMES, OR HURT THE ONES THEY SAY THEY LOVE.

Fifth Session

WOMEN CAN ACT JUST AS SCANDALOUS AS MEN

Exposing Raw Truth About Some Women

Scandalous Acts Of Women: The Raw And Naked Truth

It was the fifth session, in the previous sessions many of the problems that the women seemed to had came mostly from men. I didn't want the women to relate all hurt, pain, and abuse to ONLY men because the truth is, it can come from ANYONE.

Not many people are willing to talk about this topic. Why, because it could be considered taboo. In fact, it was suggested to me that I should stay away from this touchy unpopular topic because it could raise feelings, denials, and issues that many women are just not ready to deal with. For many women their first induction to hurt, pain, and abuse come from their first line of contact, (other women) namely mother, stepmothers, grandmothers, sisters, aunts, neighbors, child care providers, teachers, and even spiritual advisers. Women who were in positions to encourage, up build, and protect, often times were the abusers.

It is understandable that no one wants to blow the whistle or expose the evilness or wrong doings of people that they still love or care for. It is in our nature to want to think good about everyone. However, I feel that in order to be set free, we have to face the fact that there are women who commit scandalous acts out there. Yes, that's right I said *scandalous,* and no I'm not going to apologize for using this description or sugar coat its meaning. Thought it was just the men? Hmmm....

As a speaker and guide I have heard the pain in the voices of women who have suffered at the hands of *scandalous acts of women.* I feel it is an injustice to them to act like these women don't exist. Being human, I will

163

admit, I was a little angry at the women who had caused the hurt. And my initial motive for this chapter was to shame these women for the pain they have caused. But as I began to write, Jesus showed me His love for all mankind. Although it does not excuse the conduct, I began to understand the concept that "Hurting people, hurt people." I was also able to do for them what Jesus has done for

> It was by allowing Jesus to heal my hurt and pain that I was able to stop causing hurt and pain.

me, to look beyond their faults and see their needs. Light expels darkness and there is no sin that is so deep that Jesus is not deeper. However, we must be accountable. Therefore, I began my talk by sharing stories of *"SCANDALOUS ACTS."* In these stories I will be exposing some raw and naked truths of these women; and even more importantly, identify the root cause of how they might have become scandalous.

Meet No Boundary Mona

Mona is the oldest of her six siblings: five brothers and a sister. She lived with both her mother Helen stay-at-home mom, and father Joe a hard worker, who works very long hour days. They seemed to love and adore each other dearly. When Mona was about nine, one day her mother said to her, "Mona, your father's food is in the oven, when he comes home from work, make sure he gets it. I've got to go run some errands. I will be back later." She then walked out the door and down the street, it was be more than ten years before Helen's family saw her again.

Joe was a good man. When Helen walked out on them, he stepped up as their father and mother. I'm sure his heart was broken because it was rumored that Helen left them to be with another man. Nevertheless, Joe would always encourage them to pray for their mother asking God to protect her and one day bring her back home to them.

Over the years Joe did a good job raising the children, well, all accept for Mona. By the time Mona was in middle school, she had begun displaying an angry, destructive, careless, and rebellious attitude. She was disrespectful- cussing, fighting, stealing, ditching school, drinking, getting high, staying out all night, and having carefree sex. At fifteen, Mona organized and participated in an orgy. She was fearless. It didn't seem to matter what anyone said or tried to do to help. Teachers, counselors, family members, authority figures; it didn't matter. Her rude mouth and careless attitude kept her in trouble.

Mona had put up a wall, and nothing or no one was able to get through. What happened to Mona? What was this deep dark hurt that had hardened Mona's heart? Whatever it was, she now has no boundaries.

> Women with no boundaries are even more dangerous than women with self-hate because they will do *anything*.

Mona carried her careless no-boundaries attitude into her adult life. Before graduating from high school, Mona had given birth to a daughter and over the next five years she became the mother of two more daughters. She never married nor had a relationship with any of her daughter's fathers.

By her mid twenties, Mona had begun living with a man named Fred. Although Fred had his hands full dealing with Mona's no boundary, out of control behavior, he seemed to care a great deal for her and her three girls, treating them as his own since biologically he was unable to father any children.

Just when it seemed that Mona had found true love and was settling down, she did the unthinkable. One morning Mona got up out of the bed with Fred, kissed him and her girls, and left for what was supposed to be a weekend get away to Las Vegas with a couple of her home girls. However, within an hour of them arriving Mona met a man twenty-five years her senior and they became inseparable. And by the end of the weekend, they were married. She returned home to Mississippi and acted as if nothing had happen. That night she had sex with Fred, and never said a word about it.

For about a month Mona lived a double life, going back and forth between both men. She told her husband she was trying to get a transfer to St. Louis, where he lived so she could live with him, but was having a hard time finding a replacement for her job. While telling Fred she had gotten a new job that requires her to travel out of state several times a month, when actually she had taken a three week leave from her job, as a home health aide. But with time running out, one day after Mona had just finished having sex with her husband, still lying in the bed with him, she realized she could not keep up the lie about her job so, (she came up with a plan) she lied and told him that she was being put on a special live-in assignment for several months and they wouldn't be able to have much contact.

Seeing the surprised and confused look on his face, Mona had to think quick, so she gave him a big kiss, then said, "But don't worry, I'll try and sneak away as often as I can," then rolled over on top of him as she initiated round two before leaving.

Having only known Mona a few days before they got married and still not aware that she even had children, her new husband didn't have time to

166

think much about it because of the immediate foreplay that distracted his mind. (Mona knew what she was doing.)

Two weeks had passed without Mona's husband hearing from her. After talking with his job and explaining the situation of his new wife's transfer, he founded out that he could be transferred to Mississippi. Not knowing where Mona worked, he decided to call her cell phone to inform her of the exciting news. That particular morning Mona had just gotten out the bed and was taking a shower, (to go on her same job as a home health aide) so Fred answered her cell phone and the two men told each other everything.

I know you are curious to know what happened. Well, to this day she is still married to her husband who did not move to Mississippi, and she's still living with Fred. Somehow she and the two men came to an agreement.

Rendezvous Weekends

There's an old saying: a leopard don't change its spots and Mona's no-boundary behavior, didn't just stop there. Her next endeavor was unexpected, but it was just like Mona to somehow take advantage of the situation.

Mona's only sister, DD, was married to Terry. DD was more of a homebody, the same with Fred; partying was just not their thing. On the other hand, Mona and Terry live for the weekends. When the weekends came, drinking and partying was at the top of their list. So it wasn't surprising to anyone that the two of them spent most of their weekends together. Neither DD nor Fred thought much about it because usually the two would end up drunk and passed out on the couch, chair, or floor at either of their houses. When that happened DD or Fred would just put a

167

blanket over them and call the other's mate to let them know they were all right. Well, one night Mona and Terry got drunk and instead of going home, they ended up in a parking garage in the back seat of Terry's car. That was the night they crossed the line. Realizing they had stronger feelings for each other, more than in-laws, they allowed their burning desires to take over, and that was the beginning of a five-year "lust" affair.

Lying, scheming, and deceitfulness became a way of life for the two. What started out as innocent, fun weekends turned into rendezvous weekends. They had convinced each other that their affair was DD and Fred's fault for not giving them the love they wanted. But, Mona and Terry's fun was about to turn into a nightmare. When Mona became pregnant with Terry's child, they both panicked. Fearing their lifestyle was about to be exposed, Mona came up with a plan and convinced Terry, whose heart by that time had become hardened as well, to do with her the unthinkable.

The plan was to kill both DD and Fred by adding poison to their food a little at a time. Mona and Terry, with no regard to human life, was about to carry out their plan in a few days until Mona went to the emergency room complaining of sharp pains in her lower abdomen. After a thorough examination and x-ray Mona was told that she had a tubal pregnancy that would have to be aborted. With such a close "wake up call" it seemed that Terry, against Mona's wishes, finally came to his senses and made a choice to end the affair.

What caused Mona to commit those scandalous acts? Maybe it was the anger she felt from the abandonment of her mother or the fact that she never got a chance to establish a bond with her. Or feel the love she wanted and needed from her mother. As for where Mona's careless and

168

destructive behavior came from, well, that probably began to develop at age four; the first time Mona was molested by her fourteen year old female babysitter.

All while I was speaking, I couldn't help but to notice LaRita, who appeared to be very uneasy. After I finished telling the story, I asked her if there was anything she wanted to say.

"No!" She said with what appeared to be an attitude. So I continued on to my next story.

•

Discussion Question:

Men: Do you believe a person can be controlled by their pain and make unwise decisions? Do you believe there is hope for that person?

Women: Despite Mona's scandalous behavior, can you see her pain?

Women Who Abuse Men

W e often see headlines of men who abuse women; well, did you know there are also women who abuse men? In both cases, IT'S WRONG.

Take Melody for instance, she is five feet, one inch, and weighs about 130 pounds, and is in her early forty's. She is married to Mark who is six feet, two inches tall, and weighs 220 pounds, and is in his mid forty's. They have been married for fourteen years and have three teenage children, Mark Jr., sixteen, Mary, fourteen, and Milton, thirteen. At first sight they seem to be the model family. Melody and Mark both have good jobs and live in an upper class gated community. Their children are all honor roll students. It seems they have it all.

But, there's a secret in the Wilson household. Although Melody is a good mother strict, but reasonable, she is very abusive to her husband. Well maybe I should stop here and go back a little bit. You see Melody and Mark met through a co-worker when Mark was married to another woman. They began an affair that led to the breakup of Mark's former marriage. Oh, you are wondering how his wife found out about their affair? Melody told her. She also told her that she was going to "take her man" and proceeded to do just that. In fact, it became a mission for Melody.

After Melody and Mark married, she always felt her mission was accomplished. She had "won" the game. But, did she really? See, Melody could not get out of her mind the things that she and Mark did *while* he was married and living at home with his first wife. She often remembered the many romantic trips they took together. While she and Mark would lay in bed arm in arm, she'd listen to him tell his wife how his so called "business trip" was going. She often reflected on the many phone messages from Mark's wife expressing how lonely she felt when he was away, and asking if he could arrange his business deal so that they could spend holidays and special times together. All while Mark spent every holiday wining and dining Melody.

Melody's obsession with their past was causing her to despise Mark. She felt she couldn't trust him. If he did it with her, maybe he would do it to her (Hmm, that's a thought ladies). Although Mark appeared to love Melody and there were no signs of infidelity, all Melody could see when she looked at him was a lying cheater, whom she had begun to despise.

At first, she became verbally abusive, belittling him in front of his family, friends, or anyone. She would cuss him out like he was her child who stole something, and everything he said or did was wrong. For instance, Mark could say something like, "Whatever my baby wants, I'll make sure she get." (Ladies, now don't that sound good). However, Melody would immediately say, "Yeah right, that's the same thing I heard you tell your first wife."

Although Melody cheated with Mark and didn't seem to have any remorse for what she did to his first wife, she just couldn't get pass all the deceit, lies, and plots Mark used on his first wife with no remorse.

And although Melody stayed married to Mark for the sake of the children, she has made his life, and hers, a living hell with her bad attitude. Melody thought she had won by taking another woman's husband, but did she really? Was her few years of romance, worth a lifetime of mental and emotional torment? Don't fool yourself.

"You WILL reap what you sow."

The bible says…

The one who sows to please his sinful nature, from that nature will reap destruction; the one who sows to please the Spirit, from the Spirit will reap eternal life.
Galatians 6:8

•

Discussion Question:

Men: Do you know couples who have cheated with each other then ended up marrying? Was their outcome similar to this story? Do you realize the way you treated your former wife, your present wife remembers?

Women: Do you feel that abuse by a woman is just as wrong as abuse by a man? Have you done a scandalous act and afterward regretted it? Did you repent and vow not to do it again?

Stepmoms:
"I Want The Man, NOT His Kids!"

With so many divorces these days, blended families are becoming more and more common. However, the attitude of a mom, even a step mom, can make the difference between a happy home and one that is filled with *turmoil, hurts,* and *pains.* I want to share with you Margret's story. I just hope when you see a man that you are interested in, you won't be like her. Once she sets her eyes on a man, her mind starts calculating what she needs to do to get him.

"When Margret see a man the first thing she thinks about is, 'Oohwee, he sure is fine. I can already picture him in my family portrait.' And that's exactly what she thought when she saw Tony in the grocery store. 'Let's see now, it'd be him, me, my two daughters; nine and seven, and my four year old son. I can just see it now, picture perfect! Accept, there's a slight problem, he has two kids. A boy, Jamal, ten, and a girl, Jeopardy who is also seven; which he has full custody of because their trifling mama didn't take care of them.

Tony made it very clear, that he and his kids Jamal, and Jeopardy, are a package deal. But if their own mama didn't want them, what makes him think I do? If she weren't so trifling, he wouldn't had to take her to court and fight for full custody. So believe me, I talk about how trifling she is to him and his kids every time I get mad. Oooh… she makes me sick! I don't even know her and I can't stand her trifling behind, because now I'm stuck with her kids. I want the man, not, his kids!'

All while Margret and Tony were dating, which wasn't very long, she pretended that she liked his children. She pretended that she cared for them just as she did her own, but it was all a lie. Of course he couldn't see it. He was blinded by what she was 'putting it on him.' Sistas, you know what I'm talking about because some of you got your husbands the same way; manipulating him with sex, then *clink clink*, y'all married. You got your man and a daddy for your children. You got what you wanted, well almost. Oh, that's right, you want the man, not his kids.

Once Margret was married to him, she no longer had to pretend. She then let the witch in her come out, and got away with it. Why? Because by this time she had manipulated his mind into believing that she really did care about his kids. Now if you notice I said, his kids. They've been married going on nine years and yet she still refers to them as 'his' kids, not 'our' children, like she says when she talks about her own.

It seemed the longer she and Tony was married, the worse she treated his children. What kind of man was Tony to allow his children to be mistreated? When his children did something that Margret didn't like, she would put them in a very small, dark, damp, smelly closet in the back of the house where she kept the broom, mop, and trash. They literally had to stand there for hours since there wasn't any room to sit. She would make them stay in their room (a room they shared) for an entire day reading the Bible. She wouldn't allow them to come out to eat or use the bathroom. She told them God don't like ugly and He didn't like them. Without

174

warning she would hit them in the mouth; kick, punch, and hit them in the stomach, chest, arm, knees, legs, and in the middle of their back as hard as she could. Even in public if his children did something she felt was inappropriate, she would make them come sit next to her then grab the skin of their thigh or buttocks and twist as hard as she could and dare them to make a sound."

"Where was Tony when all this was happening is what I'd like to know?" LaRita asked furiously.

"Well I don't think it really mattered. Margret had gotten so good at manipulating her husband until after she finished her cruel acts against his children, she would tell their daddy what they did, and usually made it sound a whole lot worse. Then he would turn around and whoop them.

As bad as it is to hit any child in the mouth period, you would at least think that child must have said or done something harsh. Something like cussed at her or someone, or stole something; nope, none of that. She would hit them in the mouth if they forgot the say, 'yes ma'am' or 'no ma'am'. She would also make her stepchildren do all the household chores while her children got to play.

I learned about this information after talking to Jamal and Jeopardy who had grown up and moved out. If I had I known about the situation, it would have been my duty, and yours, to report the abuse. It might help protect a child who maybe going through something like this now.

In addition to the many other cruel things he had to endure, Jamal vividly recalled, the many large family holidays in which he, alone, was made to clean up after everyone. It included clearing the dining room table and washing all the dishes, pots, and utensils by hand. He had to break the remaining foods down into many containers, and then find room in the refrigerator for all of it. (And y'all know at holiday time, *"black folks"* refrigerators be packed, so I'm sure that was a job all by itself). He had to clean the stove and counter tops with bleach making sure no chitterling juice was left behind. He recalled being in the kitchen for hours while everyone else was playing games, watching TV, or sleeping.

He mentioned one particular Thanksgiving, that after dinner, everyone went bowling; everyone except for him. He had to stay behind and clean up. In frustration trying to get rid of the chitterling smell, he used too much bleach and almost passed out. If it had not been for one of Margret's relatives who came back to the house to retrieve something he had left, well…I hate to think about what could have happened. He also had to sweep and mop the kitchen floor, then take out the trash. And like after most big events, outside trash cans were full so Jamal had to jump up and down in the cans, to make a little more room for the trash. He did this so he wouldn't get in trouble if the neighborhood's cat got in it.

Now, if you're one of those mamas who still don't get the point, and you are wondering what was so cruel about him doing his chores; the cruelty is in making him clean up after *everybody*, by himself, which took hours, while everyone else relaxed, watched TV, and played games. It may not have hurt him physically, but what about his mental state of mind? What does that tell him about his self-worth and his value? Mentally abusing a child is still, ABUSE. Remember John, his impression of women, came from his mother. A solution could have been for at least three or four people to pitch in together; it probably wouldn't have taken but about fifteen or twenty minutes to complete. Then, EVERYONE could relax, watch TV, play games, and enjoy the rest of the evening.

But, what brought me to tears was when Jamal said, 'As bad as our stepmom treated Jeopardy and me, what hurt worse was when she would talk bad and negatively about us to everyone who would listen. And she always referred to us as her *step* kids or *his kids*. Like all children, we longed for a mother's love and since we could not be with our biological mother we had hopes that one day Margret would love us as her own. But she never did.'

Ebony, in frustration, raised her hand and said, "Ms. Jerri, I just can't see how a step mom, or any mom for that matter, can hurt a child like that. They ought to be ashamed of themselves!"

"If you noticed, I put this story under the title 'Scandalous.' Now, if any of you have done or is doing these or similar things to a child, and if you will be honest and admit that some of the things you did to your man's children would be considered appalling if he did the same things to yours, then you are no different than the women in the previous chapters.

I know you already know the meaning of appalling, however, sometimes seeing something literally with our eyes helps us to understand it and its impact. Therefore, I looked up the meaning in the thesaurus and appalling means: *awful, terrible, dreadful, horrendous, inexcusable, unspeakable, atrocious, abysmal, horrifying, shocking, disgusting, upsetting, sickening, outrageous,* and guess what, <u>*Scandalous.*</u>

You can destroy great potential if you don't know the damage you could be causing. This is not just for step moms; it goes for mothers, fathers, grandparents, foster parents, and anyone who has guardianship or influence over a child. LET'S STOP HURTING OUR CHILDREN!"

Again Ebony spoke and said, "And I bet they call they self a Christian. Ooooooh!"

"Ebony, just because people call themselves a Christian, doesn't make it so. The Bible says in 1 John 1:6, *if we claim to have fellowship with Him yet walk in the darkness, we lie and do not live by the truth.* Also in Matthew 7:16, it says, *'you can tell a tree by the fruit it bears.'* An apple tree produces apples. Just as a pear tree produces pears. Those really living their lives as Christians should line up with the word of God and others will see its fruit," Tracy added.

Tracy was right on point. However, I didn't want to leave it there. I wanted to offer hope to anyone whose life might *not* have been producing the right fruit, by letting them know that Jesus loves them, He just despises the act. So if you can identify with this story and really want to live Christ-like, you can make it right. This may be hard to do but, put away your pride; sincerely apologize to the ones you hurt; acknowledge your wrong; if possible, try to recompense with that child; repent and ask God to forgive you; and vow to never hurt another child. Remember, it is not about you; it's about that child and helping him or her to *heal* and be set *free*.

LaRita spoke up. "Ms Jerri, I'm with Ebony on this one, now I know you want to see the good in everybody and stuff and that sounds good saying that Jesus will forgive them and stuff but, from what I understand, Jesus will help those who want to be helped, and ask for forgiveness. Well it's obvious by the kinda stuff we see happening on the news everyday to kids that all these people ain't running to Jesus for help and asking for His forgiveness. So for those ruthless, vindictive, spiteful step moms out there who intentionally hurt innocent kids, I think they need to be exposed; especially the so-call 'Christians.' They could be the reason some kids don't want to know God. "

"I will admit, LaRita, you do have a point," I replied. "However, I have to say this- not all stepmoms are bad. In fact, I believe most stepmoms are kind, loving, and caring. So to them I would like to give a big…"

THANK YOU to the Step "MOMS" Who Really CARE

"I personally know several stepmoms who has stepped up to the plate on behalf of 'their' children, even when the birth moms wouldn't; possibly even saving them from her. These stepmoms go way beyond the call of duty even many times paying child support on behalf of their husband. I won't use the word stepchild in this part, because a good step mom doesn't use the word step, she just sees the children as theirs. I believe these women don't get enough recognition. So, on behalf of the children who are blessed to have you all as their moms, we want to say, THANK YOU! We applaud you for being wonderful, loving, caring moms."

"Excuse me Ms. Jerri," Ebony said, waving her hand to get my attention. "Another type of woman that I think is scandalous is a woman who makes a man think he's her baby's daddy, because he has money or she's trying to keep him, when all along she know her child don't belong to that man. That's just wrong."

"That's right Shaquanda," LaRita shouted.

"What you saying my name for, LaRita? I don't just go around telling men that they my kid's daddy," Shaquanda shouted back defensively.

"Oh yeah, you just make men *think* you're pregnant by them to get their money," LaRita added.

"Yeah, but that's different!" Shaquanda said.

LaRita ended with, "No, that's scandalous."

•

Discussion Question:

Men: Were you raised in a stepfamily? If so, what was your experience? Are you a stepparent? If so, what is your relationship like with the child? What do you think he or she would say? Honestly have you known that your children were being abused (Let's be honest and call it what it is) by their stepmom (YOUR WIFE) and you just didn't say anything, nor protect them?

Women: Honestly, have you ever wanted a man, but not his children? I know this takes a lot of courage but, will you admit it if you have ever taken the anger or spite you feel for their mother out on his children? Have you repented, or would you like to now, ask Jesus for forgivingness and if possible ask that child?

I Survived My Mother's Hate

A S I attempted to give my next talk, another one of Tracy's weekday clients Evelyn raised her hand to ask a question. She hadn't attended the first two sessions and sat quietly through the third and fourth sessions. "Ms. Jerri, you talked about a stepmom who abused her stepchildren, but can I talk about a mother who abused her own child? I feel it's important because I didn't have a group like WOMAN TALK to help me through my situation. I also feel there are people who need to know, they're not crazy, nor are they alone."

"Sure!" I said as I beckoned for her to come to the center of the room and address the ladies.

As she came forward she said, "I survived my mother's hate."

The women had no idea what she was going to say, but she certainly had their attention.

"When people first see me, right off the bat, they usually judge me. Some have said I act uppity; others have said I look like I've got an attitude. Then there are those who just stare with a confused look on their face trying to figure out if I'm black or white. The truth is; I'm both. The facial expressions that people misunderstand for an attitude, is the pain in my heart from years of abuse. But, I thank God because each day I overcome the abuse a little more and more.

I was the baby of the family; I had two older sisters. For most children who are the baby of their family, a lot of attention is centered around them. Not me. Soon after my mother and father married, my father was sent off to war. Years passed, while my dad was still away at war and maybe thinking he would never return or just being lonely, my mother met and became pregnant by another man.

My mother is white, I'm talking blonde hair, blue eyes white, and although my dad is black, the man she got pregnant by was white; therefore my oldest sister is white. My sister Eve looks identical to my mother, including her very thin fine blonde hair. Soon after her birth my dad returned home, and while very angry and resentful toward my mother and her white child, they decided to keep the marriage together.

However, my dad could not forgive my mother's infidelity. His unreasonable thinking made him feel the only way to get back at her was to go out and have an affair with a black woman. He did, and it also produced a baby girl, Alicia, whom my dad later gained full custody of and brought home to be raised by him and my mother. Even with all the infidelity, still my parents chose to stay together, however their marriage and relationship was full of turmoil.

He resented her daughter and she resented his; they both became very protective of their own little girls. In the midst of their madness, somehow my parents felt a solution to their problem would be to have a baby together. So one year later, they had me. It seemed having me didn't change the sick mental rivalry games my mother and dad would play. In fact, as we got older their games became more interesting.

Born To Be Hurt

Mother absolutely adored Eve, and felt she had to protect her from the bitterness of my dad. Whenever Eve would get in trouble at school mother would make excuses for her actions. If she didn't feel like doing her chores mother would do them for her before dad came home from work.

182

She would take her shopping and buy her the prettiest dresses I'd ever seen.

On the other hand, Alicia was dad's first-born child and the apple of his eye. He just adored her and also felt he had to protect her from the vindictive jealous ways mother would display. Alicia, had a dark complexion and short kinky hair and looked just like dad and in his eyes, she could do no wrong. Dad gave her any and everything she wanted and more. He would even take her to the beauty shop every six weeks to get her hair braided. I loved all her styles and the colors of her beads.

With mother adoring Eve, and dad adoring Alicia, the question in my mind was who adored me? It didn't take me long to realize the answer was, *no one*. It seemed mother nor dad wanted to have anything to do with me. (Maybe they felt to share some of their love with me, would take away from all the love each of them had for their own special daughter) I was an innocent child, a victim, caught in the middle.

Growing up my life was very difficult; like I said, when Eve didn't do her chores, mother would do them for her. When Alicia didn't want to do her chores, well whenever dad was around, Alicia just didn't have to do them. However, when I forgot to do my chores, I was beat severely by either my mother or my dad, and many times by both.

Often, after mother would beat me, when dad got home she would tell him about the situation except she would leave out the part that she had already beaten me. It was as if she got some sick joy out of watching me get beat. It seemed like it gave her some sort of pleasure. In fact she would tell him about every little thing I did. She would even making up lies about me talking back, or eating something without her permission. So my dad, who never once asked me if it were true or not, would just start beating me.

I couldn't understand why my parents hated me so much. Could it be because I looked different? Oh how I wished I was dark like Alicia because maybe then my dad would adore me too, or if I was white like Eve, maybe my mother would buy me pretty dresses and adore me as well.

But me, my skin tone is pale, my hair is thick, wavy, reddish brown and very long past my waist, which as a little girl I hated, because my mother hated it. I remember my mother being very angry every time she combed my hair; she would pull and snatch my hair so hard, that I thought she was going to one day break my neck. She said I was tender headed, but who could tell mother was so rough, I had to sit and endure the pain, because if I moved or made a sound, it would just give her a reason to beat me with the back of the brush. Even my sister's didn't want much to do with me. I don't think they hated me like mother and dad did, I just think with each parent giving them their own individual protection, love, and attention, they just didn't have time for me. There was just nowhere for me to fit in.

We lived in a pretty diverse community. In the neighborhood and at school, my two sisters each had their own set of friends that they could relate to. Me, even at school was a loner; it was hard to make friends because being mixed wasn't as popular then as it is now. Eve was all white and Alicia was all black, I was different. But even still I was afraid to make friends in fear that they might ask to come over to my house or for my phone number. I wasn't allowed to talk on the phone. The one time I tried it, dad caught me. He immediately snatched the phone from me and pushed the button to hang it up, then beat me senseless with it. I was twelve years old when that happened. Before you ask, I wasn't on the phone with a boy, it was a classmate who was calling to invite me to her birthday party; the only time someone invited me to anything.

I have other relatives: cousins, aunts, and uncles, but because my mother spoke so badly about me at every opportunity, none of my relatives would even talk to me.

I could hear her on the phone telling them that I was crazy, lazy, ugly, dumb, stupid, retarded, annoying, a troublemaker, and anything else she could think of to keep them from wanting to have anything to do with me. It worked, because I was shunned by all of them.

In fact, she talked bad about me so much that I began to believe it myself, even though I was a straight A student (I had to be; I got beat for anything less). Mother and dad felt anything less would make them look bad. Who could I relate to? I had no identity.

I Didn't Know If I Would Survive

My mother despised me and made sure I knew it. Eve and Alicia's rooms were both right off the living room, or should I say, my room because the living room is where I slept. Our house only had three bedrooms, one for my mother and dad and since Eve and Alicia wanted their own rooms, and each of my parents saw that they got it. Every night I would take down my covers from the top shelf of the hall closet. Mother said the couch was for visitors to sit on not for me to sleep on, so I slept on the floor. Oh it didn't make me sad to sleep on the floor but what did make me sad was almost every night I could hear mother and Eve laughing and talking in her room with the door shut.

When I was younger I used to think that after she left Eve's room she was going to come in the living room and do the same with me, but she

185

never did. Mother acted as if I didn't exist. She acted as if Alicia didn't exist either, but Alicia didn't really care; she had dad and he made up for the things mother didn't do for her.

I had a very sad, empty and lonely life. One that I hoped no other child would ever have to experience. Sometimes I wanted to just stand in the middle of the floor and scream out, 'Does anybody care about me?' But, I'm sure no one would have cared, and besides, that would just be another reason for me to get beat. Loneliness is a horrible feeling and can lead to serious issues. No one was meant to be alone. Even God said, 'It's not good for man to be alone...'

I Survived By Pretending

Growing up there were many times when I thought I was going to lose my mind. I survived by pretending I was a princess and that my real parents were royalty, the king and queen of a whole country and they asked the people I lived with and called mother and dad to care for me until they returned. And when they come back for me, they were going to take me home to my room filled with everything I wanted. In the mean time, my job was to take care of Buddy, my invisible dog.

Isn't it funny the things God will use to get us through tough situations? When I became a teenager, about fifteen, I noticed that a boy at church named Christopher, had been noticing me. He and I would take every chance we'd get to talk, which was only about five or ten minutes right outside the restroom door before my mother would come looking for me. One day Christopher said he loved me. *Wow!* I was so excited. Somebody loved me! No one had ever told me they loved me, I couldn't wait until we got home. I said to my mother with a big smile on my face,

'Mother guess what? A boy at the church named Christopher said he loved me!'

My joy and excitement immediately turned to confusion and bitterness as the evil vindictive look on mother's face turned to stone. Mother looked right in my face and said, 'He's lying to you. That boy doesn't love you. Nobody does. You're not loveable nor deserve to be loved.'

Oh God, how could she be so cruel I wondered. From that day on, I gave up on the hope of anyone ever loving me. After I graduated from high school I moved out and married the first man that came along. Immediately I got pregnant with twin boys. Remembering my mother's words, I *did not* expect to be loved however; I did expect to be beaten. That's all I knew, and I got just what I expected. My husband's beatings were way worse than my parents' had ever been. He would literally pick me up (I have always been very petite) and throw me across the room. He would grab hold of my long hair and swing me around real fast, literally lifting my legs off the ground, than just let me go. I would fly into different things. Once I landed so hard against a shelf that it fell over on me, pinning me under all the books. As I laid there on my back dazed and confused, all of a sudden I felt this excruciating pain in my head. It felt like my hair was being ripped right from my scalp. I was terrified when I quickly realized it was true. My husband was standing on my hair with his rubber bottom boots, brutally snatching his foot back (Like a bull getting ready to charge.) He did so much damage, that day I had to cut my hair very short, which is still the way I wear it today."

"Evelyn when your husband was hitting you did you think he loved you?" Ebony asked sincerely.

"Well, I didn't really know. I guess I did," Evelyn responded.

Evelyn was like a lot of women who was raised without love, they never really knew what true love was. It's our human nature to want to be loved, but if abuse is all we've ever known, we can confuse abuse for love. It was very important that women not be confused on this matter again, so I want you to get the picture, I advised.

A Man Hitting You Is Not ACCEPTABLE.

And It Is Not LOVE.

True Love… SHOULD NOT HURT!

"Evelyn what made you leave?" Lyric asked.

"I knew if I didn't leave one day he would eventually kill me. With nowhere else to go, I went back to my parent's home. Mother was furious that I was back, so I knew I couldn't stay long. The next morning I asked Eve, who was still living at home with mother and dad, if she would watch my two-month-old twin boys and she agreed. I knew I was wrong but I just needed to get away and clear my mind for a while.

I returned three weeks later to find out that my angry mother, in her last attempt to destroy me, contacted my husband. He agreed with her that my babies had been abandoned by me. He wanting no responsibilities or anything to do with them and quickly gave up his rights. Since the boys were in the care of my mother, she was able to sign them over to Child Protective Services, where they were eventually adopted.

Angry With God

"OH GOD WHERE ARE YOU? DON'T YOU SEE WHAT'S HAPPENING? WHAT KIND OF GOD ARE YOU? WHY DID YOU LET BAD THING HAPPEN TO ME?" Evelyn reminiscing angrily shouted out. It was clear that back then she was angry with God.

"After my babies were taken I allowed my hurt, and anger, to take me on a path of destruction. I recklessly got married two more times both lasting less than a year. I knew my life needed to change. So, after my third divorce and being tired of running from *myself*, I invited Jesus in my life to be my Lord and Savior; that's really when my journey began. I learned that *I am* lovable and that Jesus has always loved me even when no one else did, even when I didn't love myself. I learned that I do belong to someone, Jesus, and He bought me with a high price, His life. I learned from the Bible that Jesus knows me so well that He knows the number of hairs I have on my head, that I am fearfully and wonderfully made, I am valuable, worthy, and worthy to be loved, and that I am somebody. I also learned that if I truly loved the Lord, I had to FORGIVE those who hurt me; *I have*, and I pray for them. To this day my parents still don't want anything to do with me, but I no longer let *their* issues hold me back.

I've been married to my fourth husband and a true man of God now for ten years. I didn't really realize how messed up I was from all those years of abuse starting with my mother and dad. My husband didn't know what he was getting into when he married me either. We've had some very rough and difficult times in our marriage. It has not been easy for him. He is experiencing with me the effects from my horrible past. But God has

189

taught my husband and me through my husband, that love is patient and kind.

Even after we both accepted Jesus in our lives, holding our marriage together was still a challenge. However, we put our trust in Jesus to get us through the difficult times; and He does. God has also blessed me with two more sons, and I pray daily to God thanking Him for wisdom and compassion so that I wouldn't be like my mother. It brings me so much comfort when my husband puts his arms around me and says, 'You're nothing like your mother; you are a *good* mother.'

Now my life, to be honest, almost seems too good to be true, knowing that there are people who really love me for me. I used to wonder if my husband would have stayed with me through my healing if he had not been a man of God; I just thank God he is. Now I consciously try to wear a smile on my face every day, because I remember the years I had nothing to smile about. So if you see me and I look like I have an attitude, I don't. I have too much to be grateful for. It might just be one of those days that I forgot to remind myself that I survived my mother's hate, and that each day I'm overcoming."

Evelyn's story had certainly opened some painful feelings; it also helped set some people *free*.

•

Discussion Question:

Men: It takes a strong, patient, praying man to love a woman through her healing. Are you that man?

Women: Evelyn has gone through a lot. However, it is her love for Jesus that made it easier for her to forgive. Has someone wronged or betrayed you and you just can't find it in your heart to forgive them? Then ask yourself the question, is the love you feel for Jesus stronger than the hate you feel for the person?

Abandoned And All Alone

I was prepared to share the story of an abandoned child. Having been a foster mother, I've seen many children in this predicament, but before I could speak, LaRita called out in her normal rough and forceful tone, "Ms. Jerri, you know when you said Mona's mother just up and left them, and y'all know how I told y'all that my mama and daddy are in prison and stuff? Well, the truth is," LaRita said as her eyes appeared to become teary, "I never really knew my daddy; and my mama, well, one day when I was eleven, I waved bye to her as I left for school; I never saw her again. Ohh, I miss my mama. I still don't know what happened to her."

The women were surprised, but relieved to see LaRita's softer side. In all the years they had known her she had always come across as hardcore. However, obviously not wanting to appear vulnerable, she immediately retrieved back to her hardcore attitude and said, "I mean I know she ain't dead. The people at the foster care said she gave up her parental rights. It seemed her new boyfriend, who was moving to another state, didn't want a woman with kids, so she just up and left us," LaRita angrily confessed.

No longer able to keep up her facade she hung her head and said, "But, why did she do it? What did we do? Why did she not love us anymore? I still wrestle on the inside with those questions," she said.

The women were beginning to understand that LaRita's angry attitude was coming from pain and an emotional wall she had built around her heart.

"When my mama abandoned us, my whole world fell apart. When I came home from school she wasn't there. I waited all night for her to return, but she didn't. Yes, my mama had stayed out all night with her different boyfriends many times before, but this time something was different; all her clothes were gone. I was worried sick out of my mind. The next day I got my younger sisters and brothers dressed and we went to school. I asked my teacher if she could help me find my mama. By the end of the day, I was in a foster home.

Strangers, that's what they were to me, and I didn't want to be there. Although the foster family was nice and kind to me, I didn't want to be with them, I wanted to be with my mama. I needed to get out of there. I needed to go back home and wait for her because, 'She's coming back for me,' I thought. 'If I stay here in this foster home, she won't know where to find me.'

I didn't want to go to a different school. I wanted to go back to my school. All my friends and teachers were there. I didn't even get a chance to say bye. The first few days at the foster home, I refused to talk, smile, or eat; well I ate a little something, but as little as possible. My foster family tried to make me feel welcomed, but I wasn't having it. 'Stay out of my face and leave me alone, this has nothing to do with you,' is what I wanted to say to them. I just wanted to scream out, 'Mama please come back and get me, I'm sorry for whatever I've done.'

After several weeks had passed it was obvious that my mama was not coming back to get me. By that time, I think I had cried out every tear I had in my body. All my hopes for her coming to get me were gone. All I had left was anger. So I became angry; I was angry with my mama, I was angry with myself, and I was angry at the world. And over the years my anger turned into hate; that's right, I hated my mama for abandoning me, and I hated myself because I was her child.

I was told that when my mama's rights were terminated, my younger sisters and brothers were adopted into different families. But me, because I was eleven going on twelve, I was considered too old. Not too old to be adopted, it's just that the request to adopt older children is not on the top of the list. So the foster care services contacted my relatives, and that's how I came to be with my Aunt Bessie, which was another nightmare.

I would have rather stayed in foster care. My mama stole my innocence, the day she chose to walk out of my life, and not allow me to have closure. I tell people that my mama and daddy are in prison, because that's what I've heard; and if it is true, then good. As far as I'm concerned that's where they belong. I've been told that one day I'll have to forgive my mama in order for me to move on with my life. But uh, I ain't there yet! I'll admit it, 'I'm an Angry Black Woman with an Attitude.'

Ms. Jerri I am so glad the topic is on these scandalous women, because I think that any woman who would put a man, especially one that she ain't even married to, before her kids, is **'Scandalous.'**

Before I could address LaRita, she looked over at Ms. Veronica and attackingly said, "Ms. Veronica, at the shop I've heard you brag about how you married your husband for the money. I mean, no disrespect, but obviously you got married with the wrong motives. It sounds to me like you were a gold digger. I bet when your husband found out what you did he was hurt."

"LaRita!" I said surprised.

"No, she's right Ms. Jerri," Ms. Veronica said. "My motives for getting married were wrong. But, the person who got hurt, was me."

Although LaRita wasn't ready to forgive, she had made a huge step by taking off the mask and admitting her pain and the root of it. Unbeknownst to her, her walls were beginning to slowly come down.

"I have found that abandonment issues can affect women on into their adult life. Many women become clingy, angry or needy; they depend on the company or emotional support of other people; or may need constant reassurance or acceptance. A clingy person can be very draining because no matter how much love, care, and support that's given to them it is never enough. Clinginess can take its toll on the people around them. It is my opinion that many times a clingy person can be obsessive and/or paranoid. If things don't go the way they feel it should, their feelings can easily be hurt. Being clingy can also set you up to be hurt. It can cause you to refuse to give up something such as a belief, tradition, or a person you have grown fond of even if that person or the situation is not for your good," I concluded.

"But Ms. Jerri, I know a lot of women who was raised with both of their parents and they are just as clingy," Lyric said.

I turned to Lyric and said, "I have found that abandonment issues aren't just developed from physical detachment, it can develop from emotional detachment as well. So if a father and/or mother are in the home but have nothing or very little to do with a child, emotionally, that child could feel abandoned or they may hide behind the facade of being hard like LaRita; but as you can see, even LaRita has a soft side. And I'm so proud of her for letting it show. I personally understand how hard that is."

If you are reading this and deep within feel you could be a clingy person, know that everyone at some time or another need help, support, and encouragement. However when it's all said and done, it's YOU who have to stand on your OWN two feet, and walk through YOUR own situations. Man CAN'T carry you but GOD CAN.

•

Discussion Question:

Men: Did you realize abandonment could cause such serious issues, whether physical, mental, or emotional? After reading this chapter do you know someone who's been abandon? Are there similarities?

Women: Is your tough or hard attitude a protection, but deep within there's a soft side you would like to show? Have you noticed people you know love you, distancing themselves from you, but didn't connect the reason until now? Have you ever lied or made up a story to cover your pain? Are you ready now to tell the truth? John 8:32 says, *the truth will set you free.*

Marrying With Wrong Motives

"LaRita had exposed my motives, and yes she was right, I was a gold digger. After everything I had gone through in my life, I had plenty of baggage. By age forty I had developed the attitude, 'I will do whatever I need to do to have the best.' Therefore, when Henry, a distinguished older gentlemen thirty years my senior, began showering me with the finer things in life I moved to Atlanta and married him. I thought I would have all the luxuries of life, but what I did not know, was it came with a price.

Immediately, I noticed Henry's strange behavior. He flirted with every woman he saw. Now I know you're probably thinking, 'Child, he's just being a man,' which is what I thought at first, but, it was almost as if he went out of his way to make sure I saw it.

Because Henry was older, I dismissed his constant flirting as an insecure way of trying to let me know he still got it. However, it was a few years later that I found out, my husband, the man that seemed too good to be true, had a secret life. He was heavily involved in Internet pornography. *Who was this man I thought I knew? How was he able to keep it from me for so long? Is that why he is so obsessed with women? Could that be why he no longer seems to be interested in having sex with me?* All these questions and doubts that began to consume my thoughts, I wondered what those women on the Internet were doing that made Henry spend every moment from the time he arrived home from work, into the wee hours of the night, on the Internet watching pornographic videos.

Whatever it was, he didn't want me to see it because he put a password on the computer that only he knew.

A few more years had passed and we were no longer sleeping in the same room. And as far as sex, well, that stopped about a year after we were married. No longer able to stand the rejection, one day while working out at the gym, a young man approached me in a complimentary, yet flirty way. When I say young man, I mean that literally, he was in his mid-twenties with a body and smile to die for.

I wasn't the type of woman to sleep around so I don't know if it was his compliments, if I just wanted sex, or if I just wanted to feel desired but that night I had an affair. I don't really know why I did it. Maybe it was the years of rejection I felt, or the loneliness I felt even

> Being married and lonely, is a miserable feeling.

though I was married. By no means am I making excuses for my actions; it was my choice. It was wrong, I had committed a sin.

Although that was a one-night stand, being in the arms of another man made me realize how lonely and miserable I was with Henry and I was no longer able to stand the rejection; a few weeks later I packed some of my things and moved back to my hometown.

Still married, a year later I returned home, to care for Henry who had undergone prostate cancer surgery. It was explained to me by the doctor that Henry would probably have retrograde ejaculation. Retrograde ejaculation means that when he has an orgasm, his sperm goes backwards into his bladder, rather than out through his penis. This is because the valve that normally shuts off the route to the bladder, when a man climax, no longer works properly.

I understood Henry's situation and over the next few months cared for him. However, the whole ordeal was overwhelming, so after he was better, once again, I moved away.

Confused but trying to fulfill the commitment to my marriage, six months later, for the second time, I returned home, determined this time to make my marriage work. The day I arrived, Henry wasn't at home and unaware that I had returned. The first thing on my agenda was to give the house a really good cleaning. Just looking around at the dust, it was obvious that while I was away the house hadn't received any T.L.C.

Hoping to maybe spark a little romance, the first place I started was the master bathroom, but was instantly startled when I entered the shower and saw semen drip stains all over the walls. Thinking my mind was playing tricks on me, and knowing that Henry could not produce sperm, I just ignored it; putting the thought in the back of my mind. I cleaned the bathroom and went about cleaning the rest of the house. When I began cleaning the office, on the desk, I noticed something that could not be ignored; a birthday card that someone had given Henry. I noticed it because of the sweet smell coming from it. Curious to know who this woman was, I opened the envelope, pulled out the card and it read, 'The last three months were great. I miss you so much.' It was signed, 'Love Larry.'"

All the women in the room gasped.

"Hold up! Wait a minute, did she just say *Larry?*" asked LaRita.

"Uh huh, that's what she said," Shaquanda egged her on.

"So Ms. Veronica, you mean to say, all those years you thought your man was watching women on the internet, he was on the down low and you didn't know it?" LaRita asked in shock.

"I was devastated to find out that not only had my husband been having an affair, it was with a man. I too was in shock LaRita; worried, scared, and frustrated. I franticly searched through his desk drawers looking for any clues; I wanted to know how long it had been going on. What I discovered was another life Henry had been living. I also found that he'd had multiple affairs with different men."

It Messed Me Up

"I sunk even more into depression; my self-esteem went even lower. Any and all affairs are bad, selfish, careless, and devastating, but to choose a man over me was a slap in the face! A woman I could compete with, but how was I supposed to compete with a man for my position?"

It wasn't easy, but like in the past, Ms. Veronica has always had the ability to turn her situation around by putting on a mask and pretending it didn't bother her.

She Has Always Worn A Mask

Ms. Veronica was born into a family of ten girls: she is the second to the oldest.

She was raised on food stamps and very little money by a single hard working mother, who was a factory worker. Her mother was a tall large plus size woman, and all her girls took her build. Well, all except for Ms. Veronica that is, she was slim and petite.

Growing up Ms. Veronica, being the smallest, felt her sisters disliked her because of her size. She had good reason to think so because although her sisters would take up for her against anyone outside of their home, inside their home they made her life a living hell. Their envy and jealousy was apparent because they would talk out loud to each other about her, saying things like, "She thinks she's all that; she thinks she's better; she thinks she's prettier just because she's small; but she ain't nothing."

Growing up hearing those constant remarks, Ms. Veronica developed low self-esteem and low self-worth. At first she would put herself down to try and show her sisters that she was not trying to be better than them; but, with her mother working long hours, many times pulling double shifts, there wasn't much adult supervision there for the children. Ms. Veronica's overbearing, and controlling sisters, treated her like a stranger in her own home.

Ms. Veronica soon learned how to survive her sister's harsh abuse by pretending their words didn't hurt or bother her. Therefore, when they would make comments like, "She thinks she's prettier," Ms. Veronica would respond with, "That's because I am prettier." She would also make comments to hurt them, like, "I'm glad I don't have a problem fitting into my clothes like some people do." The sisters grew up with a love/hate relationship.

Deep down Ms. Veronica was very insecure. To escape the brutality of her sisters, while still in high school (eleventh grade to be exact) she became pregnant and immediately married Isaac, the baby's father, before the baby was born. Although she had become a mother, Ms. Veronica also graduated from high school with her class; her mother demanded it; Isaac graduated the year before.

Being so young, marriage wasn't what either of them thought it would be. They spent more time cussing each other out than they did making love. Once, Isaac hit Ms. Veronica, (believe me that only happened once) immediately called her sisters who came right over with knives, bats, and broken bottles. Afraid, and in shock, he ran into the bedroom and locked

200

the door refusing to come out. Eventually, the sisters left; but, not without putting all four of his tires on flat. Needless to say, he never tried that again.

However, that didn't stop his infidelity. In fact, he became so bold, or crazy, (whichever one you'd prefer to call it) that one night on the way to a motel with a woman he just met at the club, the woman mentioned that she really needed to use the restroom. Since they were near his house, Isaac actually stopped there and took the woman inside and told Ms. Veronica, "This Tonya. I just met her at the club and she needs to use the bathroom." He had become so bold with bringing women home that another time, instead of taking a woman to a hotel, he brought the women to their home to "stay the night" telling the woman that Ms. Veronica was his sister. That time, well I guess that was the straw that broke the camel's back, because that time she cussed both him and the woman out, and then put her out, and dared Isaac to take her home. Oooh that woman was mad at Isaac for putting her in a situation she knew nothing about, as she walked down that dark street with those stilettos on, (I know sister girls feet was on blaze when she got were she was going). But even that didn't stop him, although he never brought women home to stay all night, he still brought them by the house to use the restroom.

After a while, I don't know if Ms. Veronica had became sick of him or just mentally sick in general, because the next time he brought a woman into their home, all she did was point the woman to the bathroom. My guess was she was becoming mentally sick. After fourteen years of his continual adulteries, Ms. Veronica finally divorced Isaac and moved out, taking their sons.

> Because sistas, y'all know there is not a black woman in her RIGHT MIND that's going to allow that.

Ms. Veronica's self-esteem had taken a plunge, but with four sons she had to raise to become men she didn't have time to stop, look back, or dwell on the past. She did what she'd done many times with her sisters, she put on a mask and pretended it didn't bother her. She had learned to put up a front. Ms. Veronica needed to feel good about herself, so when her sons became young men, for Mother's Day she would tell them to buy her very expensive gifts, even if it wasn't really in their budget.

Trying to keep a certain lifestyle, Ms. Veronica became a hard worker, working much overtime or whatever it took to buy expensive things. She also did whatever it took to make herself and her sons look their best, including keeping her a sugar daddy or two.

I Only Date Younger Men

After everything she had gone through with Henry and Isaac, Ms. Veronica made a decision to no longer date older men or even men in her age group that she felt could hurt her again. Her attitude was, "I'll only date younger men. I'll love'em and leave'em. From now on, I'm in control!"

Ms. Veronica was only fooling herself. She worked out six days a week and watched what she ate to keep her figure tight. She'd say, "I'm going to do whatever I have to do to stay young, because baby, I have to keep up with my young Tender-Roni's."

Desperate and willing to do anything to get a man, she works two jobs to support her man.

Ms. Veronica wouldn't have to look for love in all the wrong places or try and pretend that she is "all that" if she would only allow Jesus to love her and teach her to love herself. Ms. Veronica is still single and yes, still dating younger men.

Unless the Lord builds the house,
its builders labor in vain.
Psalm 127: 1

•

Discussion Question:

Men: If you are a young man dating an older woman, what do you expect from the relationship? Do you think she should feel privileged? Do you feel it's love, all about sex, or is it just a game?

Women: Do you think marrying with wrong motives sets you up to be put in bad situations? After Henry, Ms. Veronica boxed herself in, when she made the choice to only date younger men; have you made a choice for your life based on a bad situation? Could you be missing out on a blessing? Do you think a wife should every have to compete for her husband? Even though people can change, disappoint, and hurt you, do you believe the Bible when it says in Hebrews 13:8 that Jesus never changes?

Food For Thought

Scandalous Acts

Most women who commit scandalous acts, have little regard of the consequences. It may seem that their lives are happy or they have won, but in truth, deep down within they are unhappy. As we can see from these stories, their acts usually stem from pain, hurts or insecurities that they have not dealt with. However, we *are* accountable for our actions (For the wages of sin is death. Romans 6:23). Even the Apostle Paul in the Bible knew the important of accountability…

Therefore, I urge you, brothers and sisters, in view of God's mercy, to offer your bodies as a living sacrifice, holy and pleasing to God—this is your true and proper worship.[2] Do not conform to the pattern of this world, but be transformed by the renewing of your mind. Then you will be able to test and approve what God's will is his good, pleasing and perfect will.
Romans 12:1-2 (NIV)

Truly examine yourself if you are a woman who has committed scandalous acts and want to change; you can. You can ask God…

Create in me a clean heart, O God, And renew a steadfast spirit within me. Do not cast me away from Your presence, And do not take Your Holy Spirit from me.
Psalm 51:10-11(NIV)

When we sincerely "Repent" Jesus says in His word…

"For I will forgive their wickedness and will remember their sins no more." Hebrews 8:12 (NIV)

I shared these stories of women who commit scandalous acts, not for us to pass judgment, but to forgive, pray for and uplift our sistas. Let's not forget what most of us DID or WAS before we accepted Jesus in our lives and He began a healing in us.

"When we know better we do better." Maya Angelou

Sixth Session

THERE ARE STILL GOOD MEN OUT THERE

The President
& Men in Power

Men raising their
sons to be men

Men of God

Men supporting their
Children through college

Good Husbands

Corporate Men

Just Food For Thought

Before we talk about the good men, I have some "WHY IS IT THAT," questions for the women.

*Why is it that when we meet a good fine brother, who seems interested in us, we act like we're not interested? Or we play hard to get? Okay now, there's an old saying, woman that play **too** hard to get, DON'T GET GOT!*

OR

Why is it that we can act so ungrateful, or don't appreciate the little things that our man does; especially when it's from the heart?

AND

Why is it that when we have a good hard working man, we will call his job stressing him out with drama that has nothing to do with him, just because we're having a bad day?

OR

Why is it that when we have a good man who we know love us, we treat him like he's no big deal?

AND THIS IS A BIG ONE

Why is it that before we get married, we are wanting, and/or having sex practically every day?

BUT!
*When we get married, and **IS** supposed to have sex with our husband, we act like we don't want to be bothered.*

Did you know having sex with your spouse when you are married, is pleasing to God?

I will talk more about sex in the marriage in another upcoming book series, "THE MISTAKES I MADE IN MY MARRIAGES COULD SAVE YOURS"

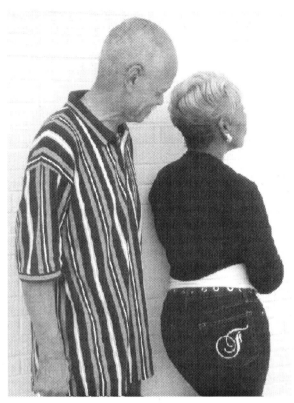

AND PLEASE TELL ME

Why is it that a woman in her sixties can still turn her husband's head?

AND YET

Some of these younger women make their husband's just want to turn their head.

Can't Judge A Book By Its Cover

After Ms. Veronica finished telling her story, I could tell some of the women were having some trust issues with men by their comments.

"See that's what I'm talking about, MEN ARE DOGS! All they want to do is run games on you," Shaquanda said.

"Uh-huh" LaRita angrily agreed.

Shaquanda, "You can't judge a book by its cover, and you can't put all men in the same category. THERE ARE STILL GOOD MEN OUT THERE. Like these men for instance, they are college graduates, and business men who are doing good things in their community, *and* taking care of their families." I replied.

"Well, maybe there are a few, but I still say, most men are dogs." Shaquanda said, becoming more heated.

"Yeah, especially the ones in prison!" LaRita threw out there.

"Un-un LaRita, it ain't just the ones in prison." Shaquanda said as she and LaRita went back and forth.

"I know Shaquanda, just look at Shawn he's a NFL player; let me tell y'all about him," said LaRita.

Not wanting the women to see all men as dogs, and since I knew Shawn, another one of Mike's clients, and some deeper details of his life, I decided to let LaRita talk; I had a motive for doing so, which I'll share later.

The Ladies' Man

"Shawn's the big man in town. Shawn has made it to the top. He's a twenty-five year old NFL wide receiver. Although Shawn is married with two children, he is still quite the ladies man. When Shawn was dating his wife he was also seeing three other women. After she found out about those other women, in fear that he may lose her, Shawn married her.

Getting married didn't stop his temptation for 'the honeys,' especially after he signed that big contract. Women were coming at him like flying torpedoes. Yeah, that big contract brought Shawn plenty of women. It also brought the opportunities for plenty of parties and drugs. Yep! Shawn was the big man all right; living large. Not to mention, he is six feet three inches tall, chocolate, has a six-pack, and good looking. Oooh-wee! He kinda remind you of Tyrese. Oh yes! He had it all.

That was until his wife got tired of his infidelities and finally took the kids and left. Shawn was hurt when his wife left. But, instead of getting himself together and trying to get back with her, he tried to get back at her, by partying even harder with women, spending money all around town, and refusing to give her child support for the care of his kids. He actually thought his actions would force her to want to come back. Child Please!"

My motive was right, it was just as I thought, LaRita, only told half of the story, but there was so much more and this was my opportunity to show a balance. So I started by saying, "Can't judge a book by its cover, there is so much more to Shawn that you all don't know." The Bible says:

> *Train up a child in the way he should go:*
> *and when he is old, he will not depart from it.*
> *Proverbs 22:6,*

A Changed Man

Although Shawn's mother raised her only child in church, like many professional players do, he got caught up in the fame game. But after all the years of sleeping with different women, scandals, partying, and the pain Shawn took his family through, he eventually cried out to God for help.

What Shawn's mother had instilled in him as a child was finally paying off. After crying out to God and asking Him to save and restore his marriage, Shawn was shocked when God didn't do it immediately. Shawn felt since God was the originator of marriage He would instantly fix and correct any wrongdoing; however, God needed Shawn's faith to grow. He needed to teach Shawn to depend on Jesus as his source instead of man and money.

As a little boy Shawn remembered his mother saying, 'Faith without works is dead,' therefore, while Shawn believed God would restore his marriage, he began to line his will up with the Will of God for his life.

212

Shawn made a conscious choice to honor his marriage and turn away from the different women and ways of his past. By doing so, Jesus worked through him to restore his family. Shawn shares the lesson he learned through song."

Caught Up In The Fame Game

It was the fame game that I thought I could play.
Contracts, money, and fame came with my name.

Women, parties, even drugs I had at my feet,
No time for wife or kids, it was all about me.

Spending money all around, I was the big man in town.

Getting women pregnant didn't matter to me,
I felt using protection was their responsibility.

Caught up in the fame game,
I was the big man with the great name.

But when I was alone, my face wore a frown,
It was something inside me; my spirit was down.

One day I fell to my knees, cried out Jesus!
Help Me Please! Forgive me for what I've done wrong.

I'll confess it was me, and I take full responsibility.
And that's what a real man should do.

I just didn't understand what it took for me to be a man.
Or how much I love my family, you see I was...

Caught up in the fame game,
I was the big man with the great name.

Spending money on others was easy for me.
But child support, no one could see.

But when I kneeled and prayed, I learned a valuable lesson that day,
one, I'd want to pass on.

There was a robber going around, robbing children in need.
__But I had no idea, that the robber was ME!__

"So you see LaRita, Shawn learned a valuable lesson." I said as I got real with them, "AND if you are looking for that **'perfect man'** let me tell you, THERE ARE NONE. However, a man who has made mistakes but has learned from them and has repented can become a **good man**.

LaRita, you also mentioned you felt men were dogs, especially those in prison, well, again I say we have to be careful about putting all men in the same box because every situation is different. For instance, I'm sure Mike wouldn't mind me sharing his story with you," I said while thinking to myself, *instead of me trying to speak for another man, why not let him speak for himself,* so I asked the women if it would be okay if I invited Mike to our next session.

•

Discussion Question:

Men: Can people change themselves? Have you, or Do you know someone who has made bad choices, and now is clearly a changed man?

Woman: What role or effect does God have on one's situation or character? Do you know a man who has made mistakes, and now his life has turned around for the better? Do you think he is a good man now?

A Painful Lesson

"I won't stand here and tell you that I'm perfect, or that I have the Christian walk. After being caught in the act of infidelity and losing my wife and half of everything I owned in a divorce. I realized a little too late that the 20 percent I thought I wanted wasn't worth losing the 80 percent that I already had. I learned a painful lesson from my first marriage that I'm willing to share," Mike addressed the women.

"I'm thirty-seven years old; born and raised in the streets of L.A. I saw it all, including the inside of prison where I spent four years for an armed robbery that I committed while in a gang. Upon my release, I vowed not to return.

Immediately afterward, at age twenty-two, I met and married my first wife Rachel. We were married for fourteen years and she was very instrumental in helping me stay on the right path and becoming successful. She and I have two sons, ages twelve and ten. We lost our first child to a miscarriage, that child would have been fourteen.

I really loved and adored Rachel we had many happy years. However, I'm not going to make excuses like so many other men do, I began listening to some of the fellas talk about how much fun they had being single and being with a different women. And of course they would brag about all the freaky things that women were willing to do just to have a man. Ladies trust me, there are men who will take advantage of your desperate desires to have a man, to fulfill their freakiest pleasures; and depending on how soon he can get you to do those acts, tells him what type of woman you are. Okay let me keep it real, even though we as men want sex right off the bat, when you give it to us right off the bat, we wonder about your morals and value, usually you won't be the woman that we'll marry.

Now don't get me wrong, as men, we want our wives to keep it spicy in the bedroom; if I can be honest, after we're married we would like our wives to do some of those bad girl freaky things, but we are afraid to ask them to. Now, I will speak for myself, instead of appreciating my wife for her loyalty and devotion, I began to imagine myself with other women and them doing all those freaky things to me. I allowed lust to enter my mind, and when it did the grass started to seem greener on the other side.

I didn't consider the consequence of my actions or the hurt and pain I was responsible for causing to my family. I know this is not something that a lot of men will admit, but I will. As I mature, I realize I was being selfish and at that time, it was all about me."

Mike's honesty came as a surprise to the women who were listening closely to his every word. Then Mike surprised them even more as he opened a letter and shared the heart and emotions of his ex-wife. It read:

"I came home early from work that Monday afternoon. I was excited to surprise you with an unexpected afternoon of what I called a human hot chocolate sundae treat. So I stopped by the store and picked up some whipped cream and cherries, imagining myself being the chocolate, covered with whipped cream and a cherry on top. Since Mondays were your off days from the shop, I figured you would still be in bed where I left you just a few hours earlier. I quietly entered the house and began walking up the stairs to our bedroom with whipped cream in one hand and cherries in the other hand and a big smile on my face that quickly began to fade as I heard strange sounds of moaning coming from our bedroom. Instantly a sinking sick feeling hit the pit of my stomach as my knees began to buckle. All kinds of thoughts began to run through my mind, 'surely my husband, the man I love, and thought loved me, would not betray me by

> Listen to that inner feeling it will warn you when something's not right.

216

having another woman in our bed.' But it was no denying what I was hearing. I knew then that my life would be changed forever, and in a split second I made the choice to go down to the kitchen to get a knife. In a fit of rage, I burst in our room determined to kill you and the tramp that would have sex with a married man in his house.

You can't begin to imagine how devastated I was walking in catching you naked in the act, and even more devastated to see who the tramp that was also naked, and straddled across the top of you was. It was out of hurt, anger, and rage that I stabbed her and if you had not wrestled me down, taking the knife out my hand, I'm sure I would have stabbed you too. Oh how I wish I would have just walked away. I wish I would have known that I deserved better than a man who would cheat on me. It just didn't seem fair. You cheated on me and I'm the one who has lost everything and is locked up while both of you are free to live your lives. And after all that, you two are not together.

I've allowed the anger to consume enough of my time. I'm learning to take responsibility for my actions. I hate that I didn't control my emotions that day. I guess I just couldn't get past the fact that your mistress was my BEST FRIEND; a person I trusted, confided in and thought had my back.

There was a time when I thought I couldn't live without you. I loved you more than myself, and worst, more than God. What I've learned over the years sitting in prison was that loving anything more than God should never be. I realize now that Jesus has to come first.

Well Mike, now that I've said everything I had to say, I want you to know that I'm sorry for what I've done. I have made peace with myself, and I have forgiven the two of you. I realized I had to forgive in order for me to be set free in my mind. And I pray that my forgiveness will set you both free as well. Please give my boys a kiss for me and tell them I will be reunited with them soon."

When Mike finished reading the letter he just stood there for a moment, then he said, "It has been years since that happened, but to me it seems like it was yesterday. Although Rachel is locked up, there's not a day that goes by that I don't regret the choice I made to cross the line and have an affair with her best friend. I could stand here and say that her best friend came on to me, that she seduced me, or that she lured me in by the seductive clothes she wore, or that she persuaded me to have sex with her.

Bottom line, I made the choice, I destroyed my family, and I hurt a lot of people. All because I was selfish, I can admit now, and believe it or not, I learned how to from Rachel. It's because of her forgiving me that I'm now learning to forgive myself."

I was proud of Mike! He is now remarried to a born again believer who does not have any children of her own but is helping him raise his two sons. Mike is truly sorry for the hurt and pain he caused to his first wife and sons, and has vowed to try and help other brothers by encouraging them to do the right thing before it's too late. Mike has even begun attending church services with his new wife. Even though Mike's first marriage didn't work out, he has learned a valuable lesson that has made him a changed man, a good man. This is Mike's spoken word:

I Made a Lot of Mistakes

I made a lot of mistakes; caused a lot of hurt and pain,
I'm just being a man, but that don't make it okay.

You see being a man is not what's in my pants.
It's not the hurt from my hands that makes me a man.

It's the love that I show
It's the respect that she's owed.

It's the joy in her heart
When we're on one accord.

It's the care that I give
When I give all I can.

**It's the love I have for the Lord and taking care of my family.
That makes me a man.**

I was so thankful to Mike for openly sharing his story I think it really made an impact on the women to see a real man admit and take ownership for his mistakes. Not only did Mike step up and admit to his wrong doings, he allowed the women to ask him some pretty harsh questions. I wanted to help the women see that some men do change. On that note, I **dismissed** the group.

•

Discussion Question:

Men: Have you done something that you truly regret, and now would like someone to forgive you? Is it possible you could have contributed to a black woman having an attitude?

Women: Do you think forgiveness should be given based on what a person has done, or, his sincerity and change?

Seventh Session

WHAT BLACK WOMEN DEFINITELY NEED TO KNOW

Now It Was Time To Go To
The Next Level and Work On SELF.

TELLING IT LIKE IT IS
Sistas, I'm just going to tell it like it is.

Name Calling and the Effects

Name-calling is a form of disrespect. Disrespecting a black woman or any woman, through name-calling is not and should not be accepted from anyone. For many women name-calling started at home with their parents. What value do you have for yourself when your own mama and daddy called you a "B" or "hoe?" I want people to know, THERE'S POWER IN WORDS; so think about the words you say. Do those words make you feel proud? Are they words you would call your mother? Or say while praying to your heavenly Father? I've heard some men say, "It's just a joke; no harm is intended; that's just the way we talk; are they just words?" There's an old saying, "Sticks and stones may break my bones, but words can't hurt me." That's not true, words DO HURT!

Now, LADIES: When are we going to stop disrespecting one another? How can we expect for men to not disrespect us and we are disrespecting ourselves and each other, through name-calling. When I hear women refer to THEMSELVES as a "B" I think, *if she knew her value, and the price that was paid for her, she would know that she is worth so much more than that, and does not deserve to be referred to as such.*

You may be wondering why I'm using "B" instead of spelling out the whole word; well, I refuse to give those words glory or power for what they represent in my book.

[29]Do not let any unwholesome talk come out of your mouths, but only what is helpful for building others up according to their needs, that it may benefit those who listen. Ephesians 4:29 (NIV)

How To Know Who You Are

The only way we will really know who we are is by spending time with Jesus. I used to hear older wise women of God say this, and to be honest, I didn't want to hear it. However, now that I have become an older wise woman of God, I can now speak from experience.

We spend time with Jesus by reading His Word, talking, praising, praying, being grateful, and fellowshipping with other believers. Developing a relationship with Jesus is just like developing one with anyone else; we must invest the time. The more time we spend with Jesus, the more clearly we will see our value. That's because Jesus' Word is filled with love for us, and we can't help but become wrapped in that love if we regularly consume His Word. When we develop that deep relationship with Jesus, we won't stand for the foolishness of others.

Spending time with Jesus is vital to developing a strong sense of self.

Good Enough To Shack-Up With, But Not Good Enough To Marry?

Sistas, now that you have begun spending time with Jesus and you are learning to love yourself, you are beginning to see yourself through His eyes. And now that you understand that you are valuable and worthy, your self-esteem is rising.

It's time you let your man know who you are. It's time he realized your value and self-worth. It's time for you to ask him, "If I'm good enough to shack-up with, why am I not good enough to marry?"

222

Some people might call this an ultimatum; no, what this is called is you getting yourself together. Once you know where he's going with the relationship, you will know your value in his eyes, and what you need to do. Remember, people will treat you the way you ALLOW them to treat you. In other words, if you want to be married, then he needs to step up to the plate or get out of the game...

> You don't need a bench warmer.

How can we teach our children if we don't know?

Once while sitting at park with my three little granddaughters, I happened to notice two teenagers, a male and female. They looked to be around fifteen or sixteen years old. As I watched them, I noticed that the female was punching the male. It was obvious there was some kind of attraction there and she wanted a certain kind of attention from him as she continued to punch him. Even though he tried to play it off by slightly smiling and putting his hands up to protect his arms, shoulders, stomach, or where ever she decided to punch him I could tell he was becoming aggravated as he constantly asked her to stop. Playfully he even tried to put his arms around her to give her a hug; however, nothing worked. As a last attempt to get a certain reaction from him, she punched him in his face. All of a sudden, he punched her on her arm. Well it seemed as if that was the attention she wanted, because after he hit her back, she stopped punching him. He apologized and put his arm around her; she put her arm around him; they kissed, smiled, and happily walked off arm and arm. If only she had been taught her value and self-worth she would know that's not the way to get a guy's attention.

Now that young lady happens to be a teen and didn't seem to know any better, but sad to say, there are grown women who act that same way trying to get a certain reaction from their men. Maybe not punching him, but nagging or aggravating him until he either says something to hurt her feelings or hauls off and hits her. Some women are not satisfied until that happens.

We must start teaching our daughters about self-respect and their value at an early age, so they won't have to go down this road. Likewise, we have to teach our sons how to respect women by helping them understand and appreciate a woman's worth. More importantly, we must instill in our children Biblical principles by sitting down with them, talking, reading, and encouraging them to read the bible on their own, followed by a brief discussion or Q&A. This will keep them as they get older, even when *we can't*.

> *Direct your children onto the right path,*
> *and when they are older, they will not leave it.*
> *Proverbs22:6(NLT)*

Stop Stalking that Man, He Don't Want You!

Sistas please, please, please, don't be like Pam. She runs all over town after (stalking) men who don't want to be with her; even worse, she drags **her children along with her. Don't act like you don't know Pam; we all** know a Pam. A good looking man passes her in the grocery store, she happens to notice that he's not wearing a wedding ring, then like a bee to honey, she zones in on him.

She casually strikes up a conversation with him. Somewhere in the conversation she asks him where he attends church; probably not thinking anything of it, he tells her. Guess who shows up Sunday at his church along with her children? Pam, coincidence I think not.

She goes up to him after the service. He's somewhat surprised as he tries to recall where he met her; nevertheless, he's happy to see her come to church. In the midst of him trying to leave church, again she engages him in a conversation as her children follows behind them. This time he happens to mention where he work, and that he will be required to go in a few hours next Sunday morning, so as not to miss church altogether he would be attending an associate church that evening.

Well, guess what? Yes, Pam showed up there along with her five children. Okay, now it's obvious to him that this is more than a coincidence. Now he feels that she could be stalking him, but, with her children though? Surely not.

Hmmm, stalking? Well when we want a man we don't exactly call it that; now do we ladies?

But that's not all, on Monday guess who he received a call from while at work? (You know these days with the Internet you can find out any and everything about a person). That's still not all, the next morning as he's attempting to leave for work, he finds a nice little love note on the windshield of his BMW 745, which had been parked outside of his door in his gated apartment complex.

Pretty scary, huh? And this is not the only man Pam has done this to; just one of several. With one man, she actually went out and bought a wedding dress the next day after meeting him.

Well to the Pam's, I say this out of love, GET YOURSELF TOGETHER; learn your

> STOP STALKING THOSE MEN. THEY DON'T WANT YOU!

self-worth and value. Remember, what we do affects our children; so instead of acting insecure and desperate, be confident and about your business and men will be attracted to you. What you're doing could make men think, that all black women are crazy.

•

Discussion Question:

Men: Do you think it's okay to call a woman a "B"? Have you ever asked a woman how she feels when you call her that? Are there some women you won't call a "B"? Would you call your mother one? If you are shacking up with a woman, is there a reason you won't marry her? Some parents have said, "Don't do what I do, do what I say do." Do you feel parents have an obligation to lead by example? Hitting a woman in front of your children, how do you think it makes them feel?

Women: Do you call yourself a "B" or allow anyone else to call you a "B"? Have you ever looked up the meaning of a "B"? Do you still think it's okay to be called, or to call someone a "B"? And, how does it make you feel with the reality of being good enough to shack up with but not to marry? Thinking back, are there things you have said, done, or allowed, that you are not proud of, and now you see your child doing the same?

Niecey Finally Gets It!

Just as I was finishing that example, again Niecey spoke up. It was obvious she no longer cared about keeping up an image; Niecey wanted to be free because she admitted, "Selfish, religious, judgmental, and shopaholic is what I've been called. Oh sure, I've heard the comments that even some of you have made about me at the shop, '*Niecey's only concerned about herself. Everything must center around her. She's greedy, out to get all she can any way she can. She's never satisfied. It doesn't matter how much she get, it's never enough.*'"

The women waited for her to continue as they were preparing to defend their comments. But Niecey shocked everyone when she said, "The truth is, you all were right, I was all those things. It wasn't that I wanted to be, it came from my pain. I will admit I was being selfish and greedy by spending money I knew we really didn't have. I used shopping for comfort, but ended up feeling even worse after I checked our overdrawn bank account. I knew we really couldn't afford it.

I've been told I can't hold a conversation without every other word being, 'Praise the Lord!' Well to be truthful, it wasn't always that I was really praising the Lord; it was out of habit that I would say it. I grew up being in church all the time. I learned all the moves, language, and mannerisms that 'Church Folk' are supposed to know. For instance, when I get up to speak before the church I start out by saying, 'Praise the Lord everybody!' and of course the church would respond back with, 'Praise the Lord.' I guess it must be customary to repeat that three times because everyone I know does. Oh yes, and, whenever someone asks me how I'm doing, my answer is going to be, 'blessed.' It's what I've always heard my parents say. They acted as if they never had a bad day.

Following in their footsteps, I can now see how being in my presence was uncomfortable because by the time I finished putting up a holy front, talking about how perfect my life was, and pointing out what all that person is doing wrong in their life, people would walk away feeling bad. And I know I could be judgmental; would walk past certain sisters and not speaking because I decided I don't like their lifestyle. Well the truth is, like Ms. Jerri said earlier, 'hurting people hurt people,' and the *religious* attitude that I portrayed, is what I hid behind. It's all I knew. It's what I was taught; a secret my family hides behind. But no more, I'm tired of the facade. Now when I say, 'Praise the Lord,' I want it to be a real praise that comes from my heart."

The women's attitudes toward Niecey was sympathetic; however, most of them knew Howard from the shop and felt she had a good man. They told her she needed to realize it and not take her husband for granted. It seemed she'd began to, because Niecey admitted to the group, "Keeping my rapes a secret could have destroyed my marriage. I'm married to a good man. Howard caters to my every need trying to make me happy; even working extra hours and taking on additional shifts to pay for my out of control spending. But no matter how much debt we accumulated providing me the best, it's never enough. I feel worthless on the inside. I constantly shop to feel better, but it doesn't work. Although I have no job, I'm in control of our finances. Several times I caused our bank account to be overdrawn; but I couldn't help it, I had allowed the hurt, and un-forgiveness I carried from my past into my marriage, to cause my attitude to be, 'whatever Niecey wants she gets,' even if we can't afford it."

Niecey finally gets it. She realized the pain she's caused her husband all those years. She also realized her selfish behavior was a way to cope with what happened to her and that she needed to be healed.

"I know I've been blessed with a good man," she tearfully confessed, "and my 'Selfish, Holier-Than-Thou Attitude,' almost pushed him away. Now I'm truly ready to respect my husband, develop a real relationship with God, be the woman He has called me to be, and STOP PLAYING CHURCH!'" Niecey humbly concluded.

•

Discussion Question:

Men: Have you ever been stalked? What did you think about that woman?

Women: Have you ever run after a man you know didn't want you? How did you feel? How do you think that made him feel about you? What is she teaching her children about her sincerity of Jesus when she's going from church to church following after men? Do you feel that excessive shopping, eating, drinking, working, or any type of addiction can be a sign of inner turmoil? Do you or do you know any of these habits? Do you feel these habits could be a cry for help? Can you tell when a person finally gets it? What's different about them now?

Let's Stop Playing Church

I'm so glad Niecey was courageous enough to expose some truths about *playing church* because that is serious; it affects our relationship with God.

You CAN'T always tell what's in a book by its cover. Talk about a faithful woman. You cannot find one more faithful. Every time the church doors open, she's there. She sings in the choir. She's on the usher board. She's on the event planning committee.

She helps out in the kitchen and with the bake sales. She's even a front line pray warrior. Wherever you look, she's there. She sure seems to be sold out for Jesus. But what if she had to choose between Jesus and her man?

JESUS, Or My Man? I Choose My Man!

As you are reading this, I know you are probably in shock that there are women who would choose their man, a fleshly human, over The Almighty God. Well sad to say, it is more common than you think and usually the reason is just that, the man is flesh. You see, until we develop an intimate relationship with the Father in the spirit, we will run after the intimacy of a man of the flesh. Jesus is waiting for you to choose Him.

Is Your Relationship With God Real?

Don't fool yourself, your man is watching you. After interviewing several men, one of the main points I walked away with was, men really want to see a real woman of God; that's not just talking the talk, but walking the walk. Therefore, make no mistake; our men are watching us to see if we are real about our relationship with God.

One man mentioned Fake Church Women. He went on to say, "You know, the one's who go to church on Sunday, and is quick to tell a man that she's a Christian. But, the other six days of the week, make her mad, and she will cuss you smooth out. Oh yeah, you can find her in the club, she'll be the one dropping it like it's hot or backing that thang up; or, she's somewhere getting high or drunk. Sometimes she even behaves this way on a Sunday! Then, she will be ready to make this big announcement about, 'I'm waiting on the Lord to send me a husband,' but before she can finish her sentence, she is ready to jump in the bed and have sex."

Another man said, "One evening after a woman had finished her, 'I'm a Christian and I'm waiting on the Lord,' speech, I was impressed. So, I told her, 'I respect your standards and values, therefore, I won't make any attempts to have sex with you.' By the end of the evening, *she* was seducing *me*!"

Sistas, come on, we have got to stop playing church and get it together. We are stumbling people; not only the men who want to love us, but other sistas who are *really waiting on God* and trying to do the right thing, and looking up to us as true women of God, only to find that there are many women secretly having premarital sex regularly.

There's a song that says, "Everybody talking about heaven ain't going there." Yes that's right. Nowadays, everybody's talking about God, but are we doing His Will? Or, are we just playing church? You know what I'm talking about. We can lift our hands and look like we're praying or praising God, but when our eyes are closed, are we really thinking on things of the Lord?

Or, are we remembering what we did last night with Eric?

233

We are going around talking about how we "Want a sincere man of God." Well, are we sincere "Women of God?"

The Bible tells at Matthews 7:22, 23 (NIV)

Many will say to me on that day, 'Lord, Lord, did we not prophesy in your name and in your name drive out demons and in your name perform many miracles?' [23] *Then I will tell them plainly, 'I never knew you. Away from me, you evildoers!'*

Sex

Shun immorality (fornication) and all sexual looseness [flee from impurity in thought, word, or deed]. Any other sin which a man commits is one outside the body, but he who commits sexual immorality sins against his own body. 1 Corinthians 6:18 (AB)

[19]*Do you not know that your body is the temple (the very sanctuary) of the Holy Spirit Who lives within you, Whom you have received [as a Gift] from God? You are not your own,*
1 Corinthians 6:18 (AB)

I was in my twenties when I found this out, which is no excuse because it is our responsibility to seek God's Word. (Remember Jesus words, 'My people will perish for lack of knowledge'). One day at work, a co-worker and I were having lunch. After she had finished eating, with the time she had left, she pulled out her Bible and began reading it. (Now if you noticed I did not say while she still was working and on company time, I said during her lunch break. Remember, we want to be women of integrity.)

At that time, not being a Bible reader myself, I began to ask her questions about what she was reading. She shared with me that she was reading from 1 Corinthians 6:18 where the Bible talks about fornication. Then she turned to me and asked if I knew what *fornication* meant? I told her I did not. To be honest, as long as I had been in church, all my life, and has been a choir director, I had not even heard of that word nor recall my pastor ever preaching on that word. My co-worker, Mrs. Johnson, whom I had noticed and come to respect as a true woman of God from the months we'd been working together, went on to explain to me that fornication was having sex without being married, which she explained, is a sin against God.

WOW, What a wake-up call! Talk about taking the blinders off? I didn't know that having sex without being married was fornication, and that fornication was a sin. I didn't know that every time I had sex *without* being married, I was *sinning* not only against my own body, but, against God. That day changed my life.

That same evening I went to my boyfriend and shared what I had learned. I explained to him that after learning the truth, that having sex without being married was a sin, I could no longer continue down that same path. Although he was not ready to change he respected my decision and we agreed to sever our relationship.

For a while I refused to have sex, but sad to say, after a few months I became involved with another man and was back involved in sexual sin. This went on for years, however the blinders had been taken off, so each time I had sex, the guilt of knowing I was sinning against God was so heavy that I could no longer enjoy it. (I know there are many of you who understand what I mean.) I have even gone so far as to blame God for my choice to have sex. I know this might sound crazy, but it's true.

After years of guilt, in my late thirties, I decided to be celibate. And just like those women that the men mentioned earlier in this chapter, I was one of those Christians who gave the big announcement about how I was, "waiting on the Lord to send me a husband before I have sex." But, the truth is, I was playing church. I would go as far as I could; kissing, touching, hugging, rubbing, and all the foreplays of sex without penetration. But eventually, my flesh wanted more, and once again, I finally made the choice to go all the way and have sex; and when I did, afterwards, I was so upset.

I don't know if it was because I had deceived myself into feeling I had broken my two years of celibacy or what, but I was upset. So I went to God in prayer and said, "You said I wasn't going to have sex until I get married." God replied, "I said you are *not to* have sex until you get married." Then God said, "If I would have said, you were *not going* to have sex, then it would have been *MY* responsibility to make sure it didn't happen. But, when I said you are *not to* have sex, then it was your responsibility to make sure it didn't happen." Still not fully understanding, I went back to my journal to recall, years earlier, what I had written the day God spoke those words to me. Sure enough, there it was plain and clear; God's words, "You are not to have sex until you get married."

I learned two very important things that day. The power of words, and that we must take responsibility for our choices. So now understanding, and being sick and tired of the guilt, I made a commitment to **truly** *wait on the Lord.*

Dressing for Church, or the Club?

Church on Sundays has become the social event for fashion. Nowadays you see women dressed in some of everything. It's amazing how we will go out and buy clothes specifically to wear to the club, and then wear those same clothes to the church. Are we taking that statement "come as you are," too far?

When we are able to commit to living according to what we find to be right in the eyes of God, we are showing a level of self-love that will enable us to not only continue healing, but it will enable us to help others heal. Sistas, healing starts with our own relationship with God.

•

Discussion Question:

Men: What is your relationship with God? Do you think the commitment to truly wait on the Lord and not have sex until you get married is only for women?

Women: Let's Get Real. Could the sistas playing church be you? Have you started to view your relationship with God in a different light after reading this book? Do you see how important God is to your healing? Is God now real to you?

Teach Him How To Treat You

Do you realize you teach your man how to treat you? Oh, you didn't realize that? Okay, well, let's break it down. Have you ever noticed a man who will walk over one woman, can get with another woman and walk on eggshells? That's because you teach him how to treat you. Think about it, when you see a man walking on eggshells with a woman it usually has very little to do with her looks. If you really pay close attention you will notice it's her confidence. She knows who she is. She also know her self-worth and her value. She's a wise woman, and this wisdom has nothing to do with age. It's the wisdom of knowing how to allow a man to be a man, without acting like she's the man. It's the wisdom of knowing not to compete with him (that's way too tiring anyway); it's much easier to complete him. A wise woman also knows she can teach a man, not by her demands, but through her loving, kind, meek, and caring presence.

WAIT!!! Now <u>*PLEASE*</u> *Hear This!*

Before your mind starts scheming, don't go out and get any little piece of a man, or a man you know don't want you, or a man who has shown you who he really is: he don't have a job and not making a real effort to get one; he don't have a car; and he's in his thirties and still live at home with his mama. Yes, he proudly goes with you to all the events, *you* pick him up, *you* buy him a new outfit, and *you* pay for the both of you to attend. Oh yes, and to make it look good, while you two are out having dinner, you slip him the money so that when the bill comes it can look like he paid it. And you actually feel privileged to even boast about how much time he spends with you? Think about it, he doesn't have a JOB! If your man is not helping you financially, he is probably hurting you financially. I'm not judging because I've been there, done that, and got a T-shirt.

After I had enough, I got real with myself, and prayed for myself. I prayed for wisdom, knowledge, and strength because I realized the fact that I didn't need a man to do bad; I could do bad all by myself. So again I'm saying, don't just get any man and expect to change him or teach him. You can't change people, only God can. I'm talking about a man who shows he loves you and wants to be with you. (If you noticed, I said a man who shows he loves you, NOT just say it.)

A man who is willing to be taught, who feels the relationship is worth it. A man, who although may not understand it all, realizes that the bad attitude you *used* to have, came from past hurts and has very little to do with him. (I say used to have, because at

> There's a different between a man who say he loves you and a man who shows he love you.

this point in the book, your attitude should be changing.)

Excuses

We make so many excuses for how we allow our men to treat us. One woman admitted she dreaded being on the phone with her husband because he never listened to what she had to say, and always ended their phone conversations by hanging up in her face. When I asked her how it made her feel she said, "Bad. It's as if he doesn't notice me, or he thinks I'm nothing. He doesn't seem to have any respect for me. In fact, he treats me like I'm one of the guys."

As we were talking I noticed she had on what looked like her husband's jeans and his ball cap with her hair sticking out underneath. She had on an oversized T-shirt that was so wrinkled it looked like she just picked it up off the floor. Her tennis shoes were dirty, and she had no makeup on; not even lipgloss. There was nothing about her that looked feminine, appealing, or inviting. And she wondered why her husband didn't notice her. Well, could it be he sees her as one of the guys?

Wanting to help her, I knew that in order for her situation to turn around she had to first begin to feel good about herself. So I started by telling her who God says she is. At first it was hard to get her to see herself through the eyes of God. She even made excuses for why her husband treated her that way, taking all the blame. But I continued to speak the truth about who God says she is, until eventually she began to agree with God. Now with her feeling good about herself I next had to address her outfit. "Men are visual," I explained to her, "and you *can* make him notice you." Next thing was her hair, which she had already made her first appointment with Tracy for that afternoon. Lastly, we addressed the way she spoke to her husband. Jumping on the defense she said, "I know I talk rude and crazy to him but that's the way he talks to me."

Sensing her defense I had to go there with her, so I said, "do you realize that if you keep doing the same thing you're going to keep getting the same results? You are the one who has to *want* your situation to change and *you* have to do something about it, not me." Then with love I said, "If you want respect from your husband you have to give him respect." She seemed too had gotten the point.

Now equipped with the tools she needed, aware of who she was, and having a full understanding of how she wanted to be treated, I told her to let me know the outcome.

Sure enough, I received a phone call late that night, about 11:45 p.m., waking me out of my sleep. She apologized for calling so late, then she excitedly yelled, "It worked!" She went on to say that after she left the beauty shop, she felt so good about herself from the talk we'd had and because her hair looked better than she ever thought it could. "I felt so good that when I got home I took a shower, put on some perfume and a nice outfit, and made sure my husband saw me before he left for work. His eyes got all big, with an even bigger grin on his face. He grabbed me and gave me a big kiss, and said, 'I can't wait to see you tonight.'

Later that evening he called and we had a small argument. As usual he did all the talking and not listening to me. But, before he could hang up in my face, remembering who I was, my self-worth, and my value I said, 'Wait, I have something I want to say, and I need you to listen.' He said, 'What!' Then I *briefly* told him how disrespected I felt every time he hung up in my face and how he never listened to what I had to say. After twenty years of my husband treating me that way, he said he was sorry and that from now on he will work on being more respectful."

I shared this woman's story to help the women appreciate the POWER in knowing who you are, your value, and self-worth.

"Ms. Jerri do those principles only work when you're married?" Lyric asked.

"No. There was a woman who was in a serious relationship that confided in me that although she really loved her man, he was a good man and provider, the one thing she disliked was that he wasn't thoughtful or considerate when it came to special occasions, holidays, or birthdays. In fact, he only brought her a gift when she would mention it, although she always went out of her way to make those occasions special for him. She said once after she made a big deal (crying) about him not doing anything for her birthday; he finally went to Wal-Mart, bought her a card, and gave it to her still in the bag. He didn't even sign the card or put it in the envelope that came with it, nor did he even take the time to write her name on card."

"WOW! Talk about careless. Ms. Jerri what did she do?" Niecey asked.

"I know what I would've done," Shaquanda voiced her opinion with an attitude. "I would've kicked him to the curb."

"Well it's not always that easy Shaquanda. Remember she said he was a good man and a good provider? So what she, and any woman, has to ask themselves is, *does the good outweigh the bad?* In other words, no relationship is going to be perfect; there's going to be some type of issue that he or she is going to have. However, I believe you should be true to yourself and think about if that issue, or issues, is something that you can live with or not. You owe it to yourself, and him, to seriously think about this; it can save you much heartache later down the road.

Now after you have done the above and have come to the conclusion that your relationship with him is worth it, don't allow your emotions to control your feelings on special occasions. Have a *brief* conversation (do not use that time to vent); be honest with your man; let him know how much those occasions mean to you; and even if he can't buy you a gift, then maybe he can surprise you with a creative atmosphere (it doesn't always have to be about money). However, you want to also reiterate to him that if he does not acknowledge you at all on those days, and although you will be disappointed, you will still love and acknowledge him (you never want to play the game, tit-for-tat). I believe if he really love you and is a stand up guy, you won't have to worry about it."

"But Ms. Jerri," LaRita interjected, "I think teaching a man how to treat you only works when he's a REAL MAN. Not a Mama's Boy."

In most cases you're right LaRita and I believe that's usually because most mama's boys are not mature enough to realize his benefits down the road. Let's talk a little about mama's boys.

•

Discussion Question:

Men: Does your woman dress like one of the guys? Would you like her to dress more appealing or sexy? Do you think men have the tendency to treat women the way we act, or allow you to? Personally, can you do a better job making your woman feel special?

Women: Do you think there is a difference in trying to change a man and teaching a man how to treat you? To teach him, what did she have to do first? If you think the thing you dislike about your man is something you don't feel you can live with, should you continue to stay with him and even marry him hoping he will change?

Food For Thought

Mama's Boys

Is there a difference between men who love their mamas, and a mama's boy? Every woman in the group collectedly agreed, the answer is a loud resounding, "YES!!!"

The man that loves his mother, now, he's the one you want, because if he loves and has respect for his mother, he will love and respect you. Now on the other hand, if he does not love or show respect for mother, or if his love for his mama is unbalanced, meaning he's a grown man still "sitting in his mama's lap", because she won't let him stand on his own two feet.

Watch out!!! Stay as far away from him as you can.

WARNING!!!   WARNING!!!   WARNING!!!

Mama's Boys And Their Mamas

I was just about to talk on this subject when LaRita interrupted and said, "Oooh Ms. Jerri, I know you usually give the talks! But can I pleasssse speak on this one?"

I could tell that LaRita had firsthand knowledge on this matter, so I took a seat and gave her the floor.

"Now y'all gonna have to excuse me if I don't sound all professional and stuff, but when Ms. Jerri said stay as far away from a Mama's Boy as you can, child, she was telling the truth. I just have to warn y'all because if y'all get a *mama's boy,* he will probably be like, well, I'll call him TJ because y'all might know him; Mike cuts his hair and I'm not trying to put his business out there like that. And if y'all don't know him I'm sure y'all know somebody like him, so anyway...

TJ is a thirty-six year old mama's boy who was raised by a very controlling mama who never taught him responsibility; or to take responsibility for his actions. He has a rival older brother who is very jealous of him being the lighter-skinned one with 'good hair.' (Thought only women acted like that. Hmmm). Now if Ms. Jerri was telling this story she would probably say it like this, 'It is obvious being in their presence that TJ's brother feels TJ is better looking than he is;' but I'm gone just keep it real and say, he know TJ looks better than him. Now get this, he also know that he is smarter and got more common sense than TJ. On the real though, it don't take much to have more common sense than TJ."

"LaRita," I said, trying to keep her mindful of her words.

"Well it's true! But anyway," LaRita said as she continued, "you could tell his brother gets joy in making him look bad because every opportunity he gets, he puts him down and belittles him; in front of *anybody*.

You can tell growing up that TJ was a mama's boy, because he can gossip harder than ANY woman and he can update you on *any* television show."

"LaRita!" I said again, "Can you please just get to the point?"

"Well anyway, like I said, TJ is a mama's boy and a woman's worse nightmare."

Niecey raised her hand and says, "LaRita, how do you know so much about TJ's personal life?"

"Because he tried to get with me, that's why! And baby I would've caught a case if his mama would've been all up in my business, trust me. Anyway, like I was saying and stuff, even though TJ is in his thirties it's like he's stuck at a juvenile age. I ain't lying y'all, just start paying attention to different men; you will see this trait in a lot of mama's boys. Now, in TJ's case he seems to be stuck at about age fifteen, from his actions. In just one year TJ either quit or was fired from about forty jobs. Before that, he hardly worked at all.

Once he applied for a job and the woman called several of his references, and he answered the phone. Against everyone else's better judgment she took a chance and hired him anyway as a valet driver. I mean, I don't know what it was, she must've felt sorry for him or knew his people or something cause I know she couldn't hired him based on his resume; cause it sure was jacked up with all them two and three day jobs he had listed on it. I guess he thought he was making himself look important or something cause on all his jobs he put down that he was the supervisor. Even on his applications where it asked for his supervisor's information, he put his own name and phone number down. See, just ignorant. I knew that woman was gonna regret hiring him and it didn't take but one week for her to realize her mistake.

Now listen to the reason TJ told Mike why he got fired, 'It wasn't my fault. See what had happen was, after I parked a car in the parking space, somebody must've put a concrete pole behind it cause when I got ready to bring the doctor his car back, I didn't see that pole when I was backing out, so I hit it. I tried to tell my boss that pole wasn't there when I parked that car, but he gon' fire me anyway. My mama said it wasn't my fault that they put that pole back there.'

Mike asked him why he got fired from so many other jobs, he still didn't take responsibility. He said, 'Man it don't be my fault. See on that last job, I was just borrowing some gas so I could get to work. So as a driver, when they gave me the gas card to fill up the company car, I borrowed it and filled my car up too. They come talking about they got proof of me stealing gas several times, adding up to more than $295. I wasn't stealing they gas, I was just borrowing some so I could get back and forth to work to do *they* job, and anyway; I was gonna pay them back. My mama said they oughta be glad that at least I was tryna get to work.'

TJ's just ignorant, and his mama too. But wait it gets worse. One day while I was over speaking to Mike and the fellas, I overheard TJ telling Mike'nem his philosophy on life. He went on and on and on with some of the most ridiculous stuff I've ever heard! Y'all got to hear this.

TJ's Philosophy on Life

'Ah, man shoot, there's so many ways to beat the system and get out of paying child support. Like when my son was born, I went to the hospital right away. It might've looked like I was there cause I was happy, but the real reason I showed up was cause my mama told me to go and take pictures of the baby so she can see if it was mine, and to ask the Dr's and nurses about how I can get a paternity test; and don't sign the birth certificates until I can get one.

I delayed having the paternity test done for a few months so I wouldn't have to pay child support but then, when we had to go before the child support review board, I took a chance again and told the review officer to wait before he set the child support cause I didn't even know if that baby was mine, and I wanted to have a paternity test first. In fact, I told them don't set the child support for my daughter, that was born a year before him, because I really didn't know if she was mine either, and that I wanted them both tested. And sure enough, IT WORKED! Even though the test came back 99.9% that both of them were mine, it still delayed me from having to pay child support for about four or five months, and by that time, I had quit my job, so they had to set it low anyway.'

Mike and the fellas in the shop were really giving TJ a hard time about how they couldn't believe that he took his kids through that, or treated his girlfriend that way. But TJ shocked everybody when he said,

'MY GIRLFRIEND, THAT WASN'T MY GIRLFRIEND! SHOOT... THAT WAS MY WIFE!' TJ proudly boasted.

'TJ, man, are you serious? Did you really degrade your wife like that? Come on man you got to grow up, no wonder you are no longer married," Mike exclaimed.

"I never even knew you were married TJ," Howard said in shock.

"See the reason why no one really knew I was married was cause I stayed at my mama's house most of the time cause me and my wife kept getting into it and breaking up all the time and stuff; and since she already had the house before she met me, I went back to my mama's house.

Anyway, my wife and her family was trying to control me, by asking that lady to give me that valet job talking about my wife needed insurance because she was pregnant. Shoot, I told her to go get on Medicaid like everybody else do.

Even though I didn't work there long, when I got my paycheck she actually wanted me to take my whole check to help her pay the mortgage. Shoot, that was her house! I wanted to have fun, not use my money to help pay bills. I wanted to use my money to go to the movies, and to go out to eat and stuff. So I figured if I wasn't gonna be able to spend my money my way, I might as well not work at all.

Plus the main reason I left her was cause I got tired of her putting her hands on me. Man, she was crazy. One time she went to jail for putting her hands on me. See what had happen was, we had been separated for a while and I had moved in with my friend Ke Ke and her kids.'

'TJ, man, I know you didn't move in with another woman while you were still married," John remarked. "Did Ke Ke know you were married when she let you move in with her and her children?' John asked.

TJ said, 'Yeah! She didn't care! But then, after about two weeks Ke Ke started tripping though; talking about I eat too much, and I need to help her pay bills if I'm gonna be living there. But shoot, she knew I didn't have no money or job, so man I left her and I got back with my wife.

But then my wife said she wanted me to use a condom when we had sex, cause she read a text this other girl had sent me. I told her, 'I ain't finna use no condoms on my wife,' and anyway she was already two months pregnant so I didn't know what she wanted me to wear a condom for. But then she started tripping and took my cell phone. So I went after her and we started tussling cause she wouldn't give it back to me. Yeah, I pinned her up against the garage door by her throat. Then she scratched my face to get me off her, but that made me madder, so I kept her in that chokehold until she stopped trying to fight me, then I dropped her. She gave me my phone back and I went in the kitchen and made me a sandwich; shoot, I was hungry. But, then she went and got her phone and called the police.

When they got there she told the police she scratched my face to stop me from choking her. And they could even see it a little bit cause I'm real light skinned. When the police asked me did I choke her, I lied and said no! Yeah! I lied, cause to be honest, shoot I was scared. I done been to jail so many times and she hadn't been to jail at all so I knew it was gonna be easy for me to ask my mama for some money and just go bail her back out the next morning. Plus, I didn't want no domestic violence on my record. Anyway, since she told the truth about scratching me, the police said they were gonna have to take her to jail. What!? So, I didn't care that it made me look bad to let my pregnant wife go to jail; shoot she ain't never been to jail before; at least now she know what it feel like. Maybe next time she won't be so quick to call'm. And I didn't feel bad or sorry for her. She shouldn't took my phone.

She was always tripping, and it be for nothing though, like just cause she had to go back to work just two weeks after she gave birth to my son, shoot! I said, what's wrong with that? Black women back in the old days did it. Man I got tired of hearing her mouth.

Black women always want a brother to have a j-o-b if he gone live with her. But shoot, what I'm gonna work for, by the time the employer take child support from my check for the two kids I got with my wife and the other four kids I got out there, I won't have no money left to have fun. How am I suppose to have a life with all the child support being taken out of my check? Man, so I called my mama and asked if I could come back home. She said yeah, but only if I leave my wife and the kids for good. Shoot, me and mama decided what would be best for me was to move back in with her," TJ concluded.

Mike shook his head and said, 'Man you need Jesus.'

LaRita wrapped up her story by saying, "But TJ just don't get it. His response to Mike was, 'Shoot, I don't know what you talking about, my mama get me up every Sunday for church.'

LaRita said with a look of disgust on her face, "And black men wonder why black women got attitude??? Well maybe it comes from dealing with ig'nant men like TJ. OOOH, HE'S SO TRIFLING! And he had the nerves to have a philosophy on life."

Some People Never Change

"Man, you need Jesus," is what people say to me. But I don't know what they talking about, my life seems pretty good to me.

I stay with my mama, ain't got no bills to pay.
Eat, sleep, and watch TV, is what I do all day.

Yeah I done hear about JESUS, and what HE can do for me. But as long as I can stay with my mama, I ain't gotta take responsibility.

They say some people never change, I guess they talking about me.
Cause change would make me have to man up, get a job, and

act responsibly.

But take it from me; you can live like this too.
It don't take much effort… Just being LAZY will do.

(TJ yells out, as he scratches his belly while slouched across the couch,
'MAMA, is the food ready yet?')

As I took the floor, I thanked LaRita, for sharing her experience and story
of a mama's boy, and for "keeping it real." That's what WOMAN TALK
is all about. LaRita also hit on another important issue, "The Mamas." So I
addressed that issue as well.

Moving away from TJ, I asked the women if any of them ever felt
they had a good man, but his mama kept interfering in their relationship.
Several of the women raised their hands. Well from one mama to another I
would like to *say*,

To The Mamas

If you really love your
son, then do this for him,
ZIP YOUR LIPS! BACK
OFF! And allow him to
GROW UP! Don't make
him have to choose
between his wife and his
mama. THAT SHOULD
NEVER BE!

For this reason a man shall leave his father and his mother, and be joined to his wife; and they shall become one flesh. Genesis2:24

For this cause shall a man leave his father and mother, and shall cleave to his wife; Mark 10:7

Because of this a man shall leave his father and mother, and shall be united to his wife, and the two shall be one flesh.Ephesians5:31

Those scriptures have already been quoted for the mama's boys. This time they are being quoted for the MAMAS.

> We should never put our sons in a situation to have to choose.

I will admit that in the past on several occasions I, being a mama have crossed the line. However, my sons respectfully out of love let me know that their situations were just that, *their* situation. What I had to learn was, regardless of what I may have felt about their choices, it was out of respect for my sons that I had to back off.

A wise mother and Woman of God shared with me her wisdom on how she handles her son when he comes to her for words of encouragement. First, being unbiased, she lovingly tells him what is right, not just what he wants to hear. And when he comes to her for wise counsel, she respects him as a man. Her tone is respectful and warm, she said she **do not** use phrases such as; *get you better, what you need to do, stop being silly,* or *do what I say.* Get the point?

Mothers, what we may not realize and need to understand is, the way we raise our sons has an impact on the type of men they will become, therefore, it is our responsibility as parents, to:

LOVE THEM, RAISE THEM, TEACH THEM, and
LET THEM GO!

For this cause shall a man leave his father and mother, and shall cleave (be joined) to his wife: and the two shall be one flesh.
Matthew 19:5 (KJV)

•

Discussion Question:

Men: Do you have a mama who you love dearly and you know love you, however, you wish she would back off? Why is fear keeping you from letting her know it? Remember, love never fails.

Women: Do you feel you married a mama's boy? Do you see some of TJ's traits in him? Do you feel his mother is bias? Do you feel that the other woman is your mother-in-law, and that you have to compete with her for your husband's love? Would you like for him to lovingly step up, and ask his mama to let you two handle your own business?

Surviving The Battlefield In My House

Although the past sessions were intense, I was proud of each of the women for willing to be open; it helped them identify the root cause behind their attitudes.

"Ms. Jerri, can I ask the ladies something?" Shaquanda asked, "Now I know we have spent a lot of time identifying the root cause behind our attitudes, and I'm just gone keep it real and say this, it do seem like most of our attitudes come from something that a man or our parents did to us. But, is it just me, or do some of y'all's attitudes come from dealing with y'all's kids? I don't know about y'all but sometimes my kids act like they can't stand me. And to be honest, sometimes I can't stand them either. In fact, sometimes I feel like I'm in a war, and the battlefield is in my own house.

Now I know none of y'all's kids do this, so I'm gonna tell ya'll about my kids, well, my boys at least, because Quanny *don't do no wrong* I mean, yeah she might cuss somebody out, but that's only if you mess with her. And yeah she done been suspended for drinking liquor at school. And yeah she done sneaked boys in her room through the window.

Well anyway, have y'all ever woke up in the morning and got out of bed to find that the ground you were standing on was a battlefield, and that the battlefield was in your OWN house, and by the time everybody wakes up, the battlefield has become, an all out war? I have, and let me tell y'all how it started.

First of all let me go back to the evening before. I came home from work, y'all know most mamas today are working mamas; I made dinner, well at least made sure the kids ate *something*. I looked over their homework and acted like I knew what I was looking at; I guess kids think mama's are supposed to know everything, but I'm gonna keep it real, I didn't. So anyway after I did the routine things, I gave my kids a short list of the chores I expected them to do that night before they went to bed. I watched a little TV with the kids for about thirty minutes and counted that as family time. Then I took a hot shower and got in bed with a good book hoping to read a few pages, I didn't get to finish reading because I fell asleep with my eyeglasses still on my face and the book laying across my stomach.

When I woke up the next morning, already disappointed that I fell asleep without getting to finish what I was reading, I got out of bed not realizing that the ground I was standing on was about to become a battlefield. I wiped the crust from my eyes, and you know my breath was tart because I hadn't brushed my teeth yet or wiped the drool from the side of my face. I wanted to make sure that the kids were up and getting ready for school before I took my shower and started my routine of getting ready for work.

When I went in Jawan's room, I couldn't believe what I saw. The room was a mess! Clothes were all over the floor. I was tripping all over shoes, and games, and all kind of stuff that was just left in the middle of the floor. I said to myself *this little colored boy must be out of his mind.* Then I went into Jacobi's room and it looked the same way! And don't even let me get started on what I saw in the kitchen; dirty dishes still in the sink; food that had soured and spoiled because it had been left out all night on the stove; the trash was stinking and running over; and instead of somebody taking it outside and putting it in the barrel for the morning trash pickup, which by the time I saw it, we had already missed. My lazy kids sat the overflowing trash on the floor and counter top next to the trash can. Now do that make any sense? That was just stupid. Oooh they make me sick!

So now I realized that the chore list meant nothing to them. Now they were getting ready to see a mad black mama with an attitude. I yelled for everybody in the house, including the dog, to get up and I meant *get up now!* But y'all ain't gonna believe this, when my kids got up, they had the nerve to look like they had an attitude towards *me*.

They eyes looked like they wanted to roll, and they mouths looked like they wanted to say, 'We can't believe she woke us up this morning confronting us about some chores we didn't do the night before. She must be tripping!' Now this is what I assumed they *wanted* to say because trust me, if they had said it to my face..." Shaquanda paused and rolled her eyes as if her kids were sitting in the room. "Well, anyway now I'm upset and my whole day is ruined because shoot, now I got to spend about thirty minutes fussing at them about they chores. Then I got to follow them around the house and stand over them making sure they do'em; and not only did they have to do the chores I gave them that night, but shoot, now I was finding stuff for them to do as I go along.

So, by the time all that's done and we get dressed; now they done missed the school bus. I should've made them walk, but it was raining cats and dogs outside, so now, I got to take them to school; which meant that I was gonna be late for work. So now I gots to use my cell phone daytime minutes to call my boss and make up a lie, because I'm too embarrassed to tell the truth; that the reason why I'm going to be late was because my lazy kids didn't do they chores the night before.

Now you know I was mad when he said he had to write me up because that was the third time that week I called in late. So now you're talking about, **a black woman with an attitude,** Oooh wee! Them DOGGONE kids gets my pressure up! Shoot that's why they can't never go nowhere; cause they always on punishment. I can't wait til I get me a man and get married so that my new husband can deal with my kids, because I'm sick of them. I'm tired," Shaquanda admitted.

"Now Shaquanda, you know if you can't control them 'Bebe kids' of yours, what makes you think your new husband is going to be able to?" Ebony asked.

"And is it even fair to a man to have to come in and do what you should've been doing all along?" LaRita asked.

"Ebony, I know you not talking; and what's that, LaRita?" Shaquanda defensively snapped at her friends.

"Teach and train your kids how to be respectful for one, and two, listen and do what you say. Because ain't no man gonna want to have to deal with all your mess. Until you get some kind of order in your house, trying to put all that responsibility on a man is just a disaster waiting to happen. And you know I love you, but I'm just saying," LaRita said, helping her friend understand the point.

"Well maybe you're right, I hadn't thought about it like that. But I just got one more question; now I'm not saying this is my case, I'm just asking on behalf of single mother's period." Then Shaquanda asked, "Why are mothers always the blame?"

•

Discussion Question:

Men: What are your expectations of marrying a woman with children?

Women: Is your house a battlefield? Do your children sometimes act as if they can't stand you? Do you sometimes feel you can't stand your children? Do you think calling your children names like, 'lazy' or using phases like 'stupid,' affects their self-esteem? If you are a woman with children desiring to be married, do you feel it is important to get your house in order?

Jerri Lynn

Food For Thought

___

Why Are Mothers Always To Blame?

When a man makes a choice to leave his family, his wife and children, people usually blame the mother. No matter what his reason is, or how good of a wife and mother she was, people, including the children, typically blame the mother; which makes her a victim. Excuse me, a SURVIVOR.

Being a mother is not only a blessing, it is one of the most important jobs a woman will have. And if we're being real, it is one of the hardest jobs we'll ever have. Think about it, mothers get blamed for everything; It's always going to be our fault. A Father can cheat on the mother and go on to be with other women, leaving the mother with no money or support. While on the other hand, the mother works hard, sacrifices her needs for the needs of her children, she juggle her days taking off work early so that she can make the school activities, as well as make time for their evening and weekend activities, and stays up late helping with homework assignments and school projects.

She puts her love life on hold so that her children can have all of her attention. When she's able to fit in a little time for a date, (Excited to interact with an adult) she feels guilty for leaving them, or has to sneak out of the house by pretending she was at Wal-Mart for three hours, even though she didn't come home with anything, so she wouldn't have to answer a thousand questions her kids would ask about the man.

A mother will put a smile on her face so her children won't worry. While her heart is weary, she tries to figure out how she's going to pay all the bills and buy those *much-needed* shoes for her children with what little money she has. Mothers will by the grace of God, manage to stretch the money, pay all the bills, and still get the shoes. However, by the end of the month, she truly has no money left. When her children come to her and ask for money for school activities or other needs, she has to fight to hold back the tears and the lump in her throat when she says to her children, 'I don't have it.' It pains her to see the disappointed look on their face because they don't understand why she never has any extra money for their school activities or do things that other kids are doing.

Mother's Story, Daddy's Glory

Fathers can show up once a month, if that, hand the child a crisp twenty dollar bill; without giving anything to the mother who could honesty use it to provide for his child. Then again if he gave the money to the mother, he might not get the praise and honor from his child for doing what he is supposed to do anyway. So he gives it to the child who now sees him as The Hero.

The mother who is there with her child every day and night is usually made to feel like that she's no big deal. And yet the father comes around every now and then, and child gets all excited and lights up like a Christmas tree. Children as young as four and five years old hold dear in their minds the one time daddy gave them five dollars when he came to visit.

What's sad is watching the children who hold on to the false promises from their fathers. I can remember as a young child holding on to the false promises my father made to me every time I talked to him on the phone. Of course he never called me, it was me trying to keep what I imagined in my mind to be a father-daughter relationship. Although I had yet to meet him face-to-face, I often asked my mother if I could call him. Somehow over the years she always managed to track him down on the phone. Then just like every other time I talked to him, he gave me false promises of how he was going to come see me on my next birthday, or Christmas, or whatever occasion was coming up. I can remember once telling all my friends that my daddy was going to come on a particular day. I sat out on the porch all day with my prettiest dress on, anticipating his arrival. Hours had past when my friends who had been waiting with me were called to come in the house, it was dark when my mother called me in. I don't know what it is that would make an adult give a child false hope. Maybe it's just the innocent trust of a child, but even though my mother was there daily caring for me, I didn't appreciate her or her daily sacrifices. And like most kids, when my father didn't show up, and he never did, I blamed her; the one that was there fixing the broken pieces.

> I truly believe that most single mothers are doing a great job with their circumstances, but usually get the bad rap.

This is so true and really sad, especially for the mothers who are really sacrificing to be good mothers to their children.

Jerri Lynn

Food For Thought

Where Has The Courtesy Gone?

And now for the sistas who *know* they have a bad attitude…

And you wonder why you can't keep a man! Or a Job!
Could it be your attitude?

My boss come talking about customers be complaining, they say I got a bad *attitude.* I ain't got no bad *attitude*! But anyway, what you want? Oh, I forgot I'm supposed to say,

"Can I help you?"

Don't be mad at the customers, you applied for the job.

Sometimes we get annoyed with the customers, even ticked off, because we're not in the mood to work; yet we want to get paid. Now this is <u>NOT</u> the case for all black women; however, I've seen enough to realize it is something that needs to be addressed.

Be approachable, teachable, and coachable!

When given instructions, are you approachable, teachable, and coachable?
Or do you get an attitude when receiving constructive criticism?
Now again, this is <u>NOT</u> the case for all black women. *I'm just saying.*

What to Know
Before A Job Interview

As a black woman who worked in corporate America for more than twenty years before starting my own business, I have seen it all! I have worked as both an employee and employer. For eleven years, I worked as a staffing coordinator and recruiter. The main part of my job, and the most important, was finding qualified candidates for certain positions. However, being qualified was not enough; a lot of the decision had to do with their attitudes. Yes, that's right! The number one thing that a recruiter notices first is your attitude.

Okay let's get real and back up; first, before you even get to the interview, be prepared. Take time to learn something about the company you want to work for. Start preparing for your interview the night before by deciding what you are going to wear. Dressing appropriately for the interview is a big factor on the outcome of the interview. For instance you shouldn't wear jeans when applying for a corporate job. It wouldn't be wise to wear stiletto heels or a mini skirt when applying at a hospital, especially when you know you will be doing a lot of walking.

Please don't wear a mini skirt, short dress, or a shirt showing your bare stomach when applying to work with children or seniors. Make sure your accessories, such as earrings and handbags, are not large or flashy. At no time should you ever wear low rider pants that show the top of your thong underwear when you bend over, or the split in your behind when you sit down. Be mindful of cleavage showing during an interview as well. Wearing loud colors could be considered inappropriate and offensive to the hiring manager. It's best to stick to neutral colors such as black, navy, brown, tan, and white, especially if you are interviewing for a corporate job.

Remember, first impression is everything. The interviewer may think if you have put on your best for the interview then your dress may become worse once hired.

Your hair should be clean and styled appropriately; dirty hair smells. Make sure your clothes are clean and free from spots and wrinkles. Clothing that you have worn several times, although they may look clean, could still have a not-so-fresh smell no matter how much perfume you spray on them. Also make sure the hem in your pants, dresses, skirts, and jackets are intact.

Take a Look in the Mirror

PLEASE look in a full-length mirror front and back, to see how you look. Remember what you see coming and going is what the interviewer sees. It is best to do all these things the night before; it will make things go a lot smoother the morning of your interview.

Get Sleep

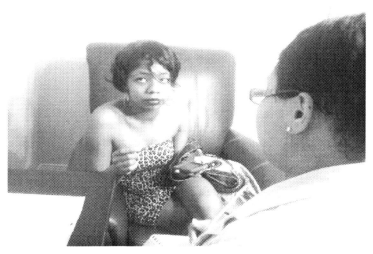

Get adequate amounts of sleep so that you are refreshed for your interview. You don't want to appear dazed or drugged. It would also help you stay alert, so you don't appear to be out of it, or look as if you're staring off into space.

Make sure your résumé is updated. Run a spell check to make sure the cities, states, months, and other words are spelled correctly. You would be surprised how many résumés have misspelled words. Your birth date shouldn't be on your resume. Believe it or not, age discrimination is real, that is still a way for employers to discriminate against you. List accolades from the last school attended.

If you have had twenty or thirty jobs in the past year and have only worked a few days, or a week or two on some of them, I understand you want to list them all to show your experiences, but don't. What that really shows is a lack of stability, consistency, and commitment. List the jobs you worked the longest; sometimes less is more. Remember as a rule of thumb, keep the résumé as close to one page as possible and free from a background design; résumés are meant to look generic. It is appropriate for your résumé to be more than one page if you have been working for more than ten years at multiple facilities.

Do not put references on your résumé. You don't want to give employers the opportunity to check your references before formally considering you. Another point about references, ONLY list those who will give you a GOOD reference. You would be surprised how many times employers call the references and receive a negative review. And if it's a personal reference, PLEASE inform the person that you are going to put them down as a reference so that they will answer the phone and/or be willing to answer questions about you. Again, you would also be surprised at the number of people who will say, "I can't discuss their business." Have all the contact information the interviewer will need. Remember it is your responsibility to provide names, phone numbers, addresses, dates and times. I can recall several applicants telling me, 'I don't have some of the numbers and addresses. But you can look up the numbers in the phonebook, if you want to.' Well you can imagine where their application went.

Do not use a complicated email address. Email addresses are usually the first point of contact an employer will use. It is wise to use firstnamelastname@domain.com for professional use. If your personal email account has random letters and numbers please create another one. Yahoo (Ymail) and Google (Gmail) are a few of the host who offers free email addresses.

Finally, PLEASE! Don't have signatures in your email such as: "Hot Chocolate, All About Me, Big-N-Beautiful, Sexy Mama, Black Pearl, I Love My Kids, and Day Day 'nem." Excuse me, you want to work where? Keep your correspondence professional. Sincerely and Thank You, are good professional closers to use. Okay, now you are all prepared.

In the morning after you have showered and brushed your teeth, PLEASE DO NOT pour perfume all over your body and clothing. Whoever told you that that was a turn on was lying to you. It does not matter how good you smell, no one wants to or should be able to smell you a mile away; it is offensive and a turn off. Only people in your immediate space should be able to smell you. The smell of your perfume should not be lingering in the office an hour after you leave.

Relieving Possible Stress

Now that you have double-checked your entire do and don't do list, it is time to leave for your interview. PLEASE allow enough time for travel and unforeseen traffic. You should arrive at least fifteen minutes before the interview, giving you time to wind down, and of course stop by the restroom for one last look over. Fresh breath is a good thing to be aware of, because if you are interviewed in a small office it's very offensive for your breath to stink up the place; however, still remove any gum or candy from your mouth. Chewing gum in an interview is considered rude. Nothing is more distracting then watching gum roll around in a person's mouth and hear them smack while they speak.

Smile, be warm and pleasant, and show confidence that you are the best person for the job, be confident, but not a know-it-all. Listen, don't talk too much or try to tell the interviewer more about the job than he or she is telling you. Don't be loud; use an appropriate inside voice. Remain professional, and don't act like you all are home girls. And PLEASE don't tell all of your person business, especially if it doesn't pertain to the job.

Don't tell the interviewer your car was repossessed because you didn't have the money to pay your car note. Or, if they can't get in touch with you on your cell number, then call your mama's house and leave a message because your phone might be cut off next week if you or your boyfriend don't come up with the money to pay the bill; or you got a cut off notice on your electricity and you're hoping to get that job so you can pay it before they cut it off.

Don't act desperate. If the interviewer asks you which positions you are interested in don't say, "I'll take anything." Companies may feel you are only taking the job because of your situation and if and when something better comes along, you'll quit.

And PLEASE, PLEASE, PLEASE only use (vocabulary) words you are familiar with and understand the meaning of. It is not impressive using words that you really don't know, or used in the wrong context, to try to impress.

Put Away Your Cell Phone

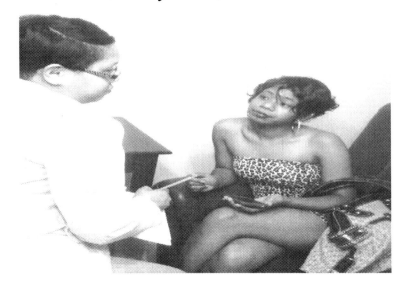

Don't sit through the interview with your cell phone in your hand, telling the interviewer you're waiting on an important call from your man, Joe Joe, who will be calling you from jail.

Never Tell the Interviewer to Wait

By all means never tell the interviewer to wait while you answer your cell phone. In fact, your cell phone should be on silent and out of sight during your interview. If the interviewer hands you a script and asks you to role-play, PLEASE don't ask them to role-play with you. Once a woman was handed a script and asked to role-play, she asked the interviewer to role-play with her, and then suggested that the interviewer go first so that she would know what to do. The interviewer's response was, "I don't do role-play, I have a job." Let the interviewer see that you are, teachable, trainable, and coachable.

Now that you have been giving some pointers, the chances of you getting a job should be much greater.

Breaking Through the Barriers to Get to the Top

CONGRATULATIONS to all the black women who have, and are making it to the top of their career goal. Climbing *the Corporate Ladder is not easy, but* **WE'RE DOING IT!** Although we have to work three times as hard to get to the top as black women, I'm proud to say we're getting there. Not only do we have to be just as good, or better than our peers in our field, we have to excel above the white man, the white woman, and our black men as well.

This could put a strain on our relationships, and all-too-often cause division. Especially if our man is insecure and feels he has been beaten down by the system and society. Along with everything else we have to carry as black women climbing up the ladder, we have to also stroke our black man's ego by encouraging and reassuring him that he's still the man of the house. However, he needs to understand that at work, **she's the boss** and it's not personal; it's corporate!

Many of us have had to start from the bottom and work our way up to the top, having to endure the isolation of many times being the only minority in most companies. In many situations we've been overlooked while watching our peers, who many times are less qualified get raises and promotions, even training many of those who became our bosses. Women at the top realized that we have work three times as hard in our field.

So again I say, Congratulations! You represent us, and I'm sure you deserve to be there!" We are proud of you. Seeing you reach your goals shows us that we can reach our goals as well. You Go Girl!

●

Discussion Question:

Men: When you see a successful black woman in an executive or leadership position, are you proud and supportive of her, or resentful and insecure?

Women: Do you believe a person's attitude affects their job? How has your attitude affected your job or career? Has it helped or hurt? Do you know any sistas who you feel has made it to the top? How do you feel about sistas in leadership positions: are you happy and encouraged, or mad and jealous? What does that tell you about yourself?

Eighth Session

SISTAS, WE GOT TO GET OURSELVES TOGETHER

Why Is It Hard To Love A Good Man

For many women, our rejection started with our fathers not being in the home, or even worse, being in the home but not having a presence. I believe the presence, or lack of, have a lot to do with the attitudes of some black women.

As little black girls most of us watched on TV how the little white girl's father came home from work with a big smile on his face, picked her up, threw her in the air, gave her a big hug, and told her how much he loved her. For most little black girls, this was a scene played out only on TV because the reality for most of us growing up was we hardly knew our fathers, if we knew them at all. Then we wonder why we can't love a good man. Well, what is a good man? And what examples have we had to recognize one when we see him? In the early years even on TV, little white girls had examples like, "Father Knows Best," "Leave It to Beaver," "The Brady Bunch," and so on.

As little black girls we had programs such as, "Super Fly," "The Mack," and "Shaft." These "bad boys" were our examples and our reality. We watched the disrespectful ways they treated our mama, big mamas, and aunts. With no real example of what a good man is, we grow up under the same generational curses as the rest of the women in our families.

Oh yes, and if you think generational curses don't exist, start paying attention to your family's history. See if you see a pattern.

For instance, if a mother worked two or three jobs while her children were growing up, more than likely her daughter will work several jobs while her children are small or growing up. If your mama's man doesn't work or keep a job, you will usually attract men who don't work or keep a job. But, this doesn't have to be your future. Good news! Generational curses can be broken!

> [26] *See, I am setting before you today a blessing and a curse* [27] *the blessing if you obey the commands of the LORD your God that I am giving you today;* [28] *the curse if you disobey the commands of the LORD your God and turn from the way that I command you today by following other gods, which you have not known. Deuteronomy 11:26-28(NIV)*

You see, we can break generational curses by choosing to obey the commands of the Lord. As we become more educated and empowered, we realize we no longer have to live under the curses of the past. We have now moved up in the world, got a little something, and now realize we don't have to "put out" to get what we want. Now, not only are we becoming more independent and more confident, we are now becoming angry and vengeful for all the things we allowed those "bad boys" to do to us.

So when we finally meet a good man who wants to love us, has a job, not on the down-low, not trying to live on, take our money, molest our children, and even willing to love us and our 'Bebe Kids," *WHAT DO WE DO?* We complain that he's too nice saying, "I'll run all over him." Or, we search until we find his flaws then pick him apart looking for something, *anything,* because we say he's 'too good to be true' All because we don't think we deserve a man like that. Therefore, we become a black woman with an attitude, and our attitudes keeps us *running back* and *attracting* the same type of *"bad boys"* that we feel we *deserve.*

●

Discussion Question:

Men: Did you realize how important your presence and involvement as a father is to a child in helping them to develop a healthy balance?

Women: Do you feel having or not having your father in the home had an impact on how you view men? Why do you think you are attracted to "bad boys?"

Jesus, The Healer

"**A**s it has been mentioned several times, Jesus is the One and Only who can heal your brokenness. Until we allow Him to heal our broken pieces, we will keep going around that same mountain. In other words, we will continue to remain in our same situation," I began.

"You are so right Ms. Jerri. I truly believe that by allowing Jesus to come into my life, He was able to heal my hurts and pains of all those other men from my past. And, had Derrick and I not made the choice to wait until we were married before having sex, we would probably not be married today," Tracy said. "I would probably be like many women today who jump into sex right off the bat, then later realize that the relationship was centered around sex. They never really got a change in the beginning to really get to know one another."

After this statement most of the women nodded in agreement as Tracy continued on, "When couples who base their whole relationship on sex begin to spend time together, most often they find out they can't stand one another. Then two things can happen; the woman may stay in the relationship for the sex but eventually develop an attitude toward her man, or she may decide that the sex is not worth being unhappy and ends that relationship and begins the search for her next man. Either way, her wall goes back up. Yes, a woman wants a man, but the wall she has built is keeping her from being willing to take a chance and really getting to know the next man for who he is.

In fact, before we can really get to know a man, we need to first get to know ourselves; to learn what we want, or don't want. Sadly how we learn
278

this is often through our past experiences and mistakes. Once we have gotten to know ourselves and what we want in a man, we won't have to waste our time—or his, by going on an emotional roller coaster ride every time we meet a man; which affects the man and our children. It's just not fair."

"Thank you Tracy for sharing that. It is so true and I'd like to add that the way we treat our men has an effect on how they will treat the next woman. You don't care? Well think about it this way, what if the next woman was *you*?" I said, seriously wanting the women to think about it.

She Prayed For a Husband with Problems

"Ms. Jerri, what do you think about this?" LaRita asked. "I know a woman name Jordan who said she prayed for a husband with problems, and got what she prayed for! He won't work and he's abusive towards her. He treats and talks to her like a dog. He will cuss her out, calling her names in front of anybody. Now I know that no one is perfect, and everybody has something they deal with but, to ask God to give her a husband with obvious problems; what's up with that?" LaRita asked puzzled.

"Well LaRita, first let me say, for any woman to pray for a husband with problems, especially financial problems, is out of order. The Bible makes it clear that a husband should be able to provide for his wife and family, and that his wife is supposed to be a helpmeet, remember, in order for a wife to help, the husband has to already be doing something.

As women, it's in our nature to nurture. But, many times when we have low self-esteem, from years of being put down, abused, told we would never be anything, and feeling like we're nothing, we begin to feel inadequate. Because we have grown up not feeling loved and feeling

279

lonely, we have the tendency to want someone that we think is our own. So in a low self-esteem state, we subconsciously deceive ourselves into thinking if we lower our standards and find a man who is low on the man pole, he will be so thankful to us for bringing him up, he will never leave us. So we will attract or draw men who we feel are lower than we are so we can nurture and take him on as our little project. However, those plans don't usually work out the way we expect, just like Jordan's case.

People marry according to where they are mentally located or according to their situation at that time. Let's say a woman or man is dealing with low self-esteem caused by abuse; again I say they are more likely to subconsciously marry someone who will abuse them."

"Wait! I got a question for Tracy," said Ebony. "Tracy was that the reason why you and Derrick made the choice not to have sex before y'all got married for spiritual reasons?"

Before Tracy could answer LaRita said, "So Tracy you're telling us that you really didn't give your man sex for eight months before y'all got married and he stayed with you? Dang, I don't know nobody that didn't have sex before they got married. In fact, I don't know no man that would stay with a woman, no matter how fine she is or how much he say he love her, if she ain't giving him sex." There was clearly a look of doubt on LaRita's face regarding Tracy's story.

"That's because you probably don't know any true Men of God LaRita. If you notice, I said a true Man of God, not these men who claim to be but having sex with every woman who opens her legs. They use excuses like, 'God knows a man got needs,' or this one 'God made sex for man to enjoy.' Both are true but it's to be enjoyed in marriage, Praise the Lord!" Niecey explained.

280

"And LaRita," Tracy chimed in. "We both knew that having sex without being married was fornication, and that fornication is a sin against God. Now it wasn't easy, because when you love someone you want to please them. However, we both had been there and done that, and are still healing from the wounds of doing things our way and not God's way. Now, in our maturity, we were able to see a bigger picture of God's plan for our lives. Ebony I'm not trying to preach to you, or act all holier-than-thou, or sit here and act like I'm so perfect and got it all together because I'm still learning. And I'm sure Ms. Jerri is too!"

"Yes Lord!" I said agreeing with Tracy.

Tracy continued, "But I have learned that we can't keep on making the same old choices and expecting different outcomes. And really at some point we all should begin to mature; our thinking should not still be on an immature level; especially for those of us professing to be Christians."

"Woo, I never thought about it like that!" Ebony confessed.

"Maturity is a process; it is learning to think before we react. Mature people know that there are consequences for their actions, and understand that the choices they make affects not only them, but everyone around them. Maturity comes from wisdom and experiences. When it is developed, especially mentally and emotionally, our lives will change.

•

Discussion Question:

Men: Are you one or do you know any true men of God?

Women: Do you now believe that Jesus is a healer? Do you feel you are maturing? What is one example of how you feel you have matured in life?

Let's Stop Degrading And Talking Ignorant To Our Black Men

Now that the women were understanding what they needed to do in order to heal, there was another area I thought we should address. So I said, "Sistas it is time for us to stop degrading and talking ignorant to our black men."

As a black woman who wrote, '*The Black Woman's Attitude and The Men Who Want To Love Us*' I will be the first to admit that I never really thought about the concept of this philosophy. Everything I've seen, heard, been around and even watched on television led me to believe that the black woman talking ignorant to and about the black man was right, acceptable, and normal. It has also been depicted on some television shows as somewhat humorous for the black woman to talk crazy and rude to her man. It seems that the more she belittles him the more popular these shows become.

This is such a sensitive subject to me because for years I was notorious for tearing a brotha down. I would "hit below the belt," as the old saying goes, by saying anything I felt like saying with no regard or care to how it made him feel. I would rip him to shreds, beat his spirits down, bring him to his knees, and then despise him for being weak; and this was all done with my tongue (and NO curse words). The tongue well, this is what the Bible says about the tongue:

> [8]*But the tongue can no man tame; it is an unruly evil, full of deadly poison. James 3:8 (KJV)*

[17] But the wisdom that comes from heaven is first of all pure; then peace-loving, considerate, submissive, full of mercy and good fruit, impartial and sincere. James 3:17 (NIV)

[29] Do not let any unwholesome talk come out of your mouths, but only what is helpful for building others up according to their needs, that it may benefit those who listen. Ephesians 4:29 (NIV)

[18] Reckless words pierce like a sword, but the tongue of the wise brings healing. Proverbs 12:18 (NIV)

I know there are many women that will say, "Well that's not me. I don't act like that. I'm not loud or rude to my man." Well are you confrontational? Do you make every situation an issue? Better yet, does everything he say turn into a debate? Now I will admit, there's nothing wrong with a good debate every now and then, but not over every little thing he says. You will tire the man out! Or worse, he may even shut down, and just stop talking altogether.

I know a woman, who always had to prove her point of being right with her man. I mean she would go there, (hit below the belt) and wouldn't let up or stop until she had proven her

> Hitting below the belt (Words) can not only be very hurtful, you can't take them back.

point; which most of the time meant proving him wrong. And it would be over something as minute as the shortest route to the grocery store. *Is it really that serious?* Sometimes sistas we are so determined to win the battle, that we create a war. Learn to pick your battles and realize everything doesn't have to be one. When we learn this, we will find love is better than war.

I like to be clear on matters, so for the many women who are like me, I broke it down so that we won't have any excuse: First, we have to go back to the originator, our Father God, who said to Adam in the Garden of Eden, *"I will make you a helpmeet."*

And the LORD God said, (It is) not good that the man should be alone; I will make him an help meet for him. Genesis 2:18 (KJV)

Notice God said a "helpmeet." This means he needs to be productively functioning at a task, in order for us to help him meet it. Are you starting to get the picture? As women, we are to uplift, encourage, and support our black men, not beat down their spirits, belittle them, and, the one that boils me the most, talking ignorant to them. I know someone's going to say, "What if the man pushes you to that point?" I didn't say it was going to be easy and I didn't say that there won't be times when he probably deserves it. "What I am saying is this, if we as a black race are ever going to be healed, bonded, united, and become strong foundations for our families, it has to begin with both the black *man* and the black *woman*.

WOMEN, we are very powerful, and we can truly set the stage for our surroundings. For instance, when we think of power many times we think it means being strong and hard. But did you know that being feminine and soft is just as powerful? In fact, it is *more* powerful. It takes power to hold your tongue when you want to say something crazy to him, or not go ahead of him when you both have agreed to wait on something that you know you really could have taken care of right away. We first have to get ourselves together by renewing our minds, as we develop positive thinking, physically, emotionally, economically, and spiritually. When women are equipped for success the *entire* family benefits.

I spoke on this subject at one of my WOMAN TALKS, and when I finished, during the question and answer time, a woman came up to me and asked me if I was suggesting that women should allow men to run all over us. NOT AT ALL! Remember, once you know your value and self-worth, your wisdom will remind you that you no longer have to prove who you are or compete with him. Your power is in knowing that.

Okay let me break it down for you. In other words, stroke his ego and 'allow' him to be the man. In the long run he will get what he needs and be happier in the relationship; you will get what you want and be happier as well. Because everyone knows, that when women are happy, the *entire* family will benefit.

> When MAMA is happy, EVERYBODY is happy.

It would be sad to stay in an unhappy relationship or marriage because we were not willing to practice these principles. For those with sons, how are our sons supposed to think we feel about them, when they hear us belittling and degrading men?

•

Discussion Question:

Men: Do you feel disrespected by the way your woman talks to you? How does it make you feel?

Women: Do you talk ignorant to your man? How does it make you feel? When you see other women degrading and talking ignorant to their men, how do you view those women? Is it important to you to always have to be right or prove your point? What do you gain? Have you ever tried being kind and loving to your man? Did he respond in the same way?

Jerri Lynn

Food For Thought

Seek Wisdom

If you are really serious and ready to get yourself together, one of the first things you should do is have someone to be accountable to. When I say someone, I'm not talking about a homegirl who's in the same boat as you, or a neighbor, or co-worker, wanting to hear gossip. No! I'm talking about seeking wisdom from a Woman of God who you trust, who will listen without judgment. Someone who will not just say what you want to hear, but will give you Godly council. Be honest with yourself. If your mother is that woman, great! However, if she is not, seek a Woman of God you trust and respect.

> [26] *When she speaks, her words are wise,*
> *and she gives instructions with kindness.*
> *Proverbs 31:26 (NLT)*

286

Fulfilling His Needs
When You're Not Married

It is true everyone has needs. And yes if possible, everyone would like his or her needs met. But, how can you fulfill his needs when you're not married? What do you think of when you think of fulfilling a man's needs?

Ebony raised her hand, "I think the only way you can fulfill a man's needs is by giving him sex. And I personally don't see nothing wrong with it; after all like you said yourself Ms. Jerri, everyone got needs. So when I need some money, I will call one of my babies daddy's over and I will fulfill his needs by giving him sex, and he will fulfill my needs by giving me money. Shoot, I don't see the problem."

"See Ms. Jerri, it is that kind of ignorant thinking…," before Elaine could finish her statement, Ms. Veronica cut in.

"Ebony, I've already told you, your babies' daddies are not doing you a favor when you have to fulfill their needs before they will give you any money to take care of the needs of their child."

"And it's not just any money," said Tracy. "It's called 'child support,' it's what they are supposed to give you to help take care of their child."

Well, I hope Ebony got the point. But she also has a point, most of the time women think to fulfill a man's needs it has to be through sex. However, there are many ways to fulfill a man's needs. You could ask yourself what are some of his needs? Or you can pay close attention to his routine. Now his needs can be anything from cooking him a hot meal, to knowing when to give him an encouraging word, or simply be quiet and giving him a moment to himself. I said wanting the women to think creative.

You will find many of the answers to this question by getting to know his character and morals. By communicating with him, which in most cases means listening; paying close attention to what he is saying; observing him; watching for his likes and dislikes; his reactions to different topics; pay attention to what he says are goals for his life, then look at the direction he is going in to see if it matches.

Or you could simply ask him what his needs are. This could even be a way to start open communication with him, laying everything on the line up front. For many men their first answer maybe "sex." If so, don't be alarmed; use this opportunity to openly explain your stance on sex before marriage, and then ask what some of his other needs are. If he is an upright man, who respects you, he will respect your stance. Although it may not be easy for the two of you to abstain from sex, you should feel no pressure to have sex before marriage from anyone. Also use this time to really take a look at him, be honest with yourself, and truthfully ask yourself some questions. *How do I feel around him? Do I feel good or bad about myself when I'm in his presence? Are the things that irritate me about him something I can live with? Where he wants to take me am I willing to go? What price am I willing to pay? Does he respect my choices?* Remember filling his needs should not mean compromising yours.

[18]*Flee from sexual immorality. All other sins a man commits are outside his body, but he who sins sexually sins against his own body.* [19]*Do you not know that your body is a temple of the Holy Spirit, who is in you, whom you have received from God? You are not your own;* [20]*you were bought at a price. Therefore honor God with your body.*
1 Corinthian 6:18-20(NIV)

Discussion Question:

Man: Do you feel in order for a woman to fulfill your needs it has to be through sex? Do you think a woman should compromise her beliefs to prove she loves you?

Women: Do you think it's possible to fulfill your man's needs without committing sexual immorality? Do you feel abstinence can be practical in today's dating relationships or is it old-fashioned? Is there ever a reason you should compromise on sex? Which do you feel is more important, satisfying the flesh, or obeying God?

Are You Preparing Yourself To Be A Wife?

That walk down the aisle is what many women dream of

I have heard so many women say they want to get married, they're ready to be a wife, and when asked the question, "Are you preparing yourself to be a wife?" Most women say yes, because most single women think just wanting to be married is being prepared. Just as I have thought in the past.

However, after three marriages and divorces God spoke to me and said, "You will get married again, but I'm going to have to teach you how to be a wife first."

I replied, "But God what do you mean *teach me have to be a wife?* Then, as if God didn't already know me, I said, "I been married three times."

God said, "Yes you've been married three times, but, you've never been a wife."

Message! God let me know marriage is a ministry, and He joins husband and wife together for that purpose.

"Oh God, I did not know that marriage is such a serious commitment not only to my mate but also to you. I also didn't realize it is a ministry." So I had to humble myself and be willing to allow God to teach me how to a wife.

"Well praise the Lord! I never thought about it like that. How do you prepare to be a wife Ms. Jerri?" Niecey asked.

"Yeah! That's what I'm wondering!" Shaquanda curious to know too.

You can begin by going to the Bible and looking up scriptures on the role of a wife.

The Bible tells us:

> *"He who finds a wife finds a good thing,*
> *and obtains favor from the Lord."*
> *Proverbs 18: 22 (KJV)*

Now if you noticed, it didn't say he who finds any woman, a mother, child, boss, provider, trophy, doormat, gold digger, harlot, or a slave. No! It said a "wife" which means before we get married, we have to start preparing ourselves to be wives. And how do we do that? Well let's go back to the Bible and look at some of the qualities of a wife:

And the Lord God said, it is not good that the man should be a long; I will make him a helpmeet for him.
Genesis 2:18,

A wife of noble character who can find? She is worth far more then rubies. 11, Her husband has full confidence in her and lacks nothing of value. 12, She brings him good, not harm, all the days of her life.
Proverbs 31:10-12,

However, each one of you also must love his wife as he loves himself, and the wife must respect her husband.
Ephesians 5: 33,

A foolish son is his father's ruin, and a quarrelsome (Nagging) wife is like a constant dripping.
Proverbs 19: 13,

Wives, submit to your husband's as to the Lord. 23, For the husband is the head of the wife as Christ is the head of the church, his body, of which he is the Savior. 24, Now as the church submits to Christ, so also wives should submit to their husbands in everything.
Ephesians 5: 22-24,

I heard Bishop T.D. Jakes say, "A half person will attract a half person, and together they will become two halves. However, when a half person becomes a whole person, they will attract another whole person and together they will become one." And that's what we want our marriage to be, whole. However, if you notice, we too must be whole.

Remember earlier when we talked about how a person can't give what they don't have? Well it's the same principle. We can't go into a marriage with a half attitude and single-minded thinking and expect the marriage to be whole.

Was it really that important to be on Facebook and texting, on your wedding day?

•

Discussion Question:

Men: Do you feel Biblical advice about marriage is still relevant today? Do you think divorce should be an option in marriage?

Women: Did you know before you were married that marriage was a Holy commitment to your mate and God? If you want to get married, how are you preparing to be a wife?

Black Women Can Be Each Others Worst Enemies

"Why sistas can't help sistas out? Although we don't talk much about it, this is a big issue in the black community, and it needs to be addressed. When will we learn that we don't have to be each other's enemy? There's a quote by Eleanor Roosevelt:

> Great minds discuss *ideas*.
> Average minds discuss *events*.
> Small minds discuss *people*.

Think about it. What are you discussing? Now be honest, have you noticed yourself, or do you know people who are always discussing (talking about/gossiping) people? You hate to see them coming, or to even answer the phone when the caller ID shows their name, because you already know, they're not going to discuss ideas, or events; all they're going to do is talk negative about other people or themselves.

Sadly, and I know this fact all too well, many times people who talk about other people do so to take the focus off of them, their flaws, imperfections, ignorance, and/or pain. I know for myself, I've talked about people just to make other people laugh; or simply just to have something to talk about. However like the quote, I have noticed the more ideas I came up with for great potentials, the less idle time I had to discuss people," I paused and looked at the women.

"What I want to know is this, when a sista is happy and has a good man, why can't other sistas just be happy for her?" Ms. Veronica asked.

Immediately, LaRita and Shaquanda took turns calling out names as if they were on a tag team.

"Because some women are really wolves in sheep clothing, resentful, two-faced, jealous, envious, or haters," LaRita said.

"Uh-huh! They are messy, will gossip about you and stab you in the back!" Shaquanda tagged in as she continued, "And don't forget there are some sistas you can't help anyway because they are freeloaders, lazy, trifling, and ungrateful."

"Offensive, difficult, suspicious, and rude, just to name a few!" LaRita wrapped up. "These are some of the reasons why sistas can't help other sistas, ain't that right Ms. Jerri?"

"Dang! Shaquanda, LaRita, y'all called those names out like y'all got firsthand experience," Ebony said.

"Well ladies, the main points that I would like us to focus on, are positive ways to strengthen the unity and bond between sistas," I explained, "However, I will agree that what LaRita and Shaquanda brought up could be valid reasons."

"Actually, I have heard many situations where black women have been burned by other black women, all because a sistas with a sincere heart wanted to help another sista out. Praise the L....Well, I guess I don't have to say that after *every* statement I make anymore," Niecey, said, catching herself and not wanting to go back to appearing religious.

"Another area where black women have been burned, is in the work place; where they compete against one another, is favored over another, or will negatively discuss one another, (this I know because I have lived it)," I said.

"But don't get it twisted, although we as black women might do or say these things about one other, and I'm not saying it's right, but let another race talk about black women as a whole and we will jump on the same side and on the defense," LaRita said.

All the women nodded their head in agreement.

I intervened, "Well, bottom line, in any case, it's wrong! Getting back to the sistas; when are we going to stop hurting (ourselves) those who are trying to help us? One sista's success does not mean another sista's failure. So when a sista succeeds in her endeavors don't get with other sistas and hate; CONGRATULATE! Learn from her success and succeed in your endeavors."

Remember, If They Will Talk With You...

Then, they will talk about you.

•

Discussion Question:

Men: Have you ever encountered sistas bickering back and forth, gossiping, and verbally hurting each other? What are your views on these types of women? Does it affect your attraction to them?

Women: Do you or do you know another sistas that gossip, backstab, or create drama with other sistas? Have you ever helped a sistas out and got burned? Now, be honest, have you ever burned a sistas who helped you out? In either case did it destroy the friendship? Did the sistas ask for forgiveness? Have you repent to God, and then ask her for forgiveness?

Ninth Session

LET THE HEALING BEGIN!

When Women Are Equipped For Success, The Entire Family Benefits

Sistas, It's Time To Be Healed

Well it was our last group session and everyone was feeling good about their breakthroughs. Everyone was there; accept Tammy, who I especially wanted to hear the topic that I was going to speak on, "Healing, and Learning to Love Yourself." I asked if any of the ladies knew why she was not in attendance, but no one had heard from her that day. Although concerned, I started my talk.

"Now, we have already indentified many of the reasons we have attitudes, and have established that for the most part, the reasons are legit. However, it is time for us to be healed. It is time for us to stop letting our past hinder our future. Honestly, we as black women are a very important part of this universe, and it is time we get it together because we have places to go and people to see.

We have husbands who need our love and support, sons we need to help raise to be respectable and responsible men, husbands, and fathers; and daughters that we, by example, need teach how to be loving wives, mothers, and successful black women with positive attitudes. We also have parents we want to make proud; brothers and sisters who look up to us, and friends and associates who may need our encouragement. Most importantly, we must develop an intimate relationship with GOD, so that we will know our value and who we are as we walk in our purpose. And speaking of purpose, as an author, speaker and life guide, *my* purpose is to empower you by exposing the hidden taboo issues of life, so that you too can be healed and live life abundantly; free from bondage and chains, as you walk into your purpose. Oh! You didn't know you have a purpose, and that God wants you to live life abundantly? Well, check this out:

Purpose:

> *Now it is God who has made us for this very purpose and has given us the Spirit as a deposit, guaranteeing what is to come.*
> *2 Corinthians 5:5 (LAB)*

> *I raised you up for this very purpose, that I might display my power in you and that my name might be proclaimed in all the earth.*
> *Romans 9:17 (LAB)*

Life Abundantly:

> *The thief comes only to steal and kill and destroy; I came that they may have life, and have it abundantly*
> *John 10:10 (RS)*

Now that you *know* that you have a purpose, it is your responsibility to seek God to find out what it is and how He wants you to walk in it.

> No matter what we've done, have or gone through, EVERYONE HAS A PURPOSE.

We, as black people, are a very smart and creative people. We've been down through the years. It is now time for us to take that same creativity that has helped us to survive, to take our lives to a higher level. It is time for more of us to be owners of businesses, own properties, be lenders (not borrowers), and employers. We must change our attitudes of "just getting by" and develop an attitude of being the head and not the tail, above and not beneath, because we are more than conquers.

Many of us and/or our children will become millionaires or even billionaires, so we have to get our attitudes ready, equipped, and prepared for success. The first thing we must do is allow Jesus to heal us through

His love and forgiveness. As we learn this, we will begin to love and forgive ourselves, and others.

Accepting material wealth begins with spiritual wealth. If our broken selves acquire wealth or increase before our spiritual selves are ready, we risk losing whatever we've acquired because we may not see the greater purpose for the blessing. We may think the blessing (wealth or increase) is just about us and never realize the purpose behind it.

We can't afford to lose anything God blesses us with because our families depend on us; as well as our communities. When we receive wealth or increase, we must understand it is not just a gift for ourselves, it is to make meaningful contributions to the world around us.

•

Discussion Question:

Men: Have you begun to realize how important the women in your life are to you and their purpose? Now that you realize it, do they have your full support?

Women: Have you begun to explore your purpose? What do you feel God is calling you to do? Will the hurt you've experienced lead to a ministry where you can help others in a similar situation? Do you have a talent or gift you feel called to use? Do you have a unique way of looking at life that can be used to help others in some way?

Lord Teach Me How To Love

The best thing you can do for your family is to love yourself first. Yes, you heard right. I know this is hard for some of us to hear because for some of us, when we think of ourselves, we think, *self-last, self-doesn't- matter, or self-not-important.*

News Flash: if we are thinking this way, then our thinking is wrong. Self **does** matter. In order to give our family our best, we have to be up to our best. Love is such an important factor that it plays a part in every aspect of our lives. For instance, let's recall when I talked about growing up not loving myself. Remember I shared with you, when a woman doesn't love herself, she can't give love, or receive love? We also talked about the fact that without love, there's low self-esteem? When there's low self-esteem, there's no self-worth or value; and where there is no self-worth or value, there's no self-respect. You see how it all works together. Now let me continue…

LOVE Is The Key

Love, that four-letter word is the key that unlocks power. Love isn't about that warm tingly sensational feeling we get when we think we're in love, that kind of love is called infatuation; which we can confuse for love because when we meet that potential person that we're interested in, typically we feel those little flutters inside. But can we really call that love? In fact, love is not the way that a person feel, are what they say, or about their emotions. LOVE IS ACTION. It's doing, caring, commitment, and sacrifice.

Love is one of the very characteristics of God, "Agape." This love is the highest form of love.

For God so <u>loved</u> (agape) the world, that He gave His only begotten Son,
that whoever believes in Him should not perish, but have eternal life.
John 3:16,

Our love is usually conditional and based on how other people act or treat us. But God's love is unconditional regardless of who we are, or what we do.

Since you have in obedience to the truth purified your souls for a sincere
<u>love</u> of the brethren, fervently <u>love</u> (agape) one another from the heart.

1 Peter 1:22

This capacity for love is not something we can do on our own. Agape love requires a relationship with God through Jesus Christ. As Christians, our goal is to become emulators of Christ, in love.

Now for this very reason also, applying all diligence, in your faith supply
moral excellence, and in your moral excellence, knowledge, and in your
knowledge, self-control, and in your self-control, perseverance, and in
your perseverance, godliness, and in your godliness, brotherly kindness,
and in your brotherly kindness, <u>love</u> (agape).
2 Peter 1:5-7

He sent his one and only Son into the world that we might live through
Him. This is <u>love</u>: not that we <u>loved</u> God, but that he <u>loved</u> us and sent his
Son as an atoning sacrifice for our sins. Dear friends, since God so <u>loved</u>
us, we also ought to <u>love</u> one another.
1 John 4:9-11

We <u>love</u> because he first <u>loved</u> us. If anyone says, "I <u>love</u> God," yet hates
his brother, he is a liar. For anyone who does not <u>love</u> his brother, whom
he has seen, cannot <u>love</u> God, whom he has not seen.
1 John 4:19-20

No one can serve two masters. Either he will hate the one and <u>love</u> the
other, or he will be devoted to the one and despise the other. You cannot
serve both God and Money.
Matthew 6:24

Jesus replied: 'Love the Lord your God with all your heart and with all your soul and with all your mind.' This is the first and greatest commandment. And the second is like it: 'Love your neighbor as yourself.'
Matthew 22:37-39

My command is this: Love each other as I have loved you. Greater love has no one than this, that he lay down his life for his friends.
John 15:12-13

'Do not seek revenge or bear a grudge against one of your people, but love your neighbor as yourself. I am the LORD.
Leviticus 19:18

Hatred stirs up dissension, but love covers over all wrongs.
Proverbs 10:12

The most famous Biblical chapter on love is from

1 Corinthians 13:1-13

If I speak in the tongues of men and of angels, but have not love, I am only a resounding gong or a clanging cymbal. If I have the gift of prophecy and can fathom all mysteries and all knowledge, and if I have a faith that can move mountains, but have not love, I am nothing. If I give all I possess to the poor and surrender my body to the flames, but have not love, I gain nothing.

Love is patient, love is kind. It does not envy, it does not boast, it is not proud. It is not rude, it is not self-seeking, it is not easily angered, it keeps no record of wrongs. Love does not delight in evil but rejoices with the truth. It always protects, always trusts, always hopes, always perseveres. Love never fails.

It wasn't until I cried out to God,

"*Lord Teach Me How To Love You, So I Can Love Myself And Others,*" that I began to learn to LOVE. I also realized that Love goes hand and hand with forgiveness. Speaking of forgiveness, I have also learned, *you must forgive to live. The Bible says...*

"Make allowance for each other's faults, and forgive anyone who offends you. Remember, the Lord forgave you, so you must forgive others."(Colossians 3:13 NLT)

Oftentimes, Jesus will ask us to do something that makes no sense *to us as humans,* however, we have to trust that He knows what's best.

"And we know that God causes everything to work together for the good of those who love God and are called according to his purpose for them."(Romans 8:28 NLT)

Therefore, when Jesus asks us to forgive, it means do what He asks out of obedience to Him. It's through our obedience that we are set free from bondage. *Forgiving ourselves, and others, is what sets us free.*

•

Discussion Question:

Men: Do you now understand women better? Has this book helped you learn some things about women that you didn't know? Have you realized some things about yourself you didn't know?

Women: Has this book helped you to know yourself better? Do you now understand how important it is to love Jesus, yourself, and others? Since reading this book, have you allowed Jesus to heal you in your broken areas? Are you ready to make significant changes in your life? What will some of those changes be?

A New ATTITUDE

Well, the eight-week group sessions had come to an end. And as I expected, God is faithful: He showed up, and showed out. Each of the women were in some stage of healing. Although this was something I usually don't do, at the last session I asked the women if they would write a summary, in Spoken Word, of what they had learned over the eight weeks and bring it to be read for our close-out.

Ebony took heed to the advice she was given and filed child support on all her children's fathers. With sufficient child support, Ebony has broken a generational curse; she has come off the welfare system and is taking parenting classes. After the birth of her fifth child she plans to attend cosmetology school. She has cut all sexual ties with her children's fathers, and now has routine scheduled visits for them to spend time with their children. Her Spoken Word:

Satan Almost Had Me

Sleeping around was no big deal to me,
Do whatever you have to do for your kids, was the lie Satan told me.

I was being deceived, Satan was laughing in my face. He knew at the rate I was going my future would be in his place.

Having sex without being married the Bible say is fornication,
a sin, and now that I've accepted JESUS, my soul, Satan won't win.

And anyway ignoring wise advice is a heavy price to pay.
If I hadn't listened, and gotten myself together,
I would be stuck, in that same old life style today.

Forgiving my mother has broken the chains off me;
"All things are possible," Jesus said. It's now up to me.

Hearing Ms. Jerri's story encouraged me. Now I'm instilling
in my children that they can be whatever they want to be.

Niecey has made great changes. She exposed her secret past to her husband, Howard, who now understands where Niecey's attitude stems from. He has lovingly and patiently supported her through her healing. As for Howard's job, he was not one of the ones to get laid off. In fact, due to the extra workload, he received a promotion. I'm also happy to announce Niecey and Howard are excitedly expecting their first child in eight months. Her Spoken Word:

Marriage is a Ministry

Marriage is a Ministry, now I understand. When I disrespect my husband's
headship, I make him feel less than a man.

I took him for granted, thinking he would never leave me,
But it was his commitment to the Lord that kept him true, indeed.

So if you have a good husband, don't be like the old me;
Don't take him for granted, instead treat him like a King.
Love is a two-way street; now I see. Marriage is about him too;
It's Not Just All About Me!

LaRita and John ended up getting together. Yes, surprisingly the woman John was describing was LaRita and now they're engaged to be married in the spring. Since neither of them have children they are considering adopting. Being with John, LaRita has calmed down a lot, however in her words, "But don't get it twisted, if you mess with me or my man, I will *still* set it off!" Some things don't change. Her Spoken Word:

Drama Free

It seemed like everywhere I went there was drama around me.
But if Drama was always where I was, then maybe it was me.

People say your attitude makes a difference in life.
But the attitude I had was, "I'm ready to fight."

Being a Drama Queen is no longer cute you see;
Being loud and rude is not how a Queen should be.

In the Bible it says as long as it's up to me
Have love for one another and live peacefully.

And now that I've accepted Jesus and is in His royal family
I'm now a Queen who's Drama Free!

Facing her past has truly set Elaine free. She now realizes that the anger and unforgiveness she held for others was keeping her from being happy. Although she is still a workaholic, after spending time with the women at WOMAN TALK, she better understands that even though everyone's walk in life is different, the hurt and pain of our experiences are the same. Elaine no longer judges or looks down on people. Her Spoken Word:

Independent Woman

I'm an independent woman; I have all that I need. I climbed the corporate ladder
to the top and found success waiting for me.

I own my own home, drive the finest SUV.
So what did I need a man for? What could he possibly do for me?

"When do you have time for Jesus?" One day Ms. Speaks asked me.
Why should I take up Jesus time, when there are poor people in need?

But I'll talk to Him anyway; I guess I'll give it a try.
And when I did, I fell to my knees and began to cry.

What is this feeling that's come over me? I don't understand.
Jesus knew my deepest thought; He knew I wanted a man.

I thought it was too late. "Nothings impossible," Jesus said to me. "I fed over five
thousand with five loaves of bread and two fish from the sea."

"Your husband is waiting on you, but before it could be, I needed you to
understand that you have to be ready to receive."

So like Tracy, I'm now preparing myself to be a wife.
For true joy and happiness, and the "Boaz" God is bringing in my life.

Although Shaquanda thought she had forgiven her father, she didn't realize that the anger she displayed towards men including her sons were the result of the anger she felt for what her father had done to her. After hearing Tammy's letter and accepting Jesus in her live, she has now stopped running games on men and is spending quality time learning to love and respect her sons. Her Spoken Word:

They Called Me Ghetto Fabulous

They called me ghetto fabulous; people were always staring at me,
I thought it was because of my beauty, but hmm--could it be?

From the colors in my hair, to the way I dressed, provocatively;
I wanted to get attention, but not negatively.

"A product of the *ghetto* environment," is what people expect of me.
But really I'm very intelligent, and now I see.

If I want to be taken seriously then it's up to me,
I'm not saying that it's right, but people do judge you by what they see.

But more importantly I've learned,
That the way I act and dress, should reflect the Christ in me.

It is Ms. Veronica's preference to date younger men, although it is nothing wrong with her choice, she now realizes it was her motives that were wrong. She is now in a serious relationship with a younger man, and they both seem happy. Her Spoken Word:

Age Ain't Nothing But A Number

"Age ain't nothing but a number," is what I always say.
But giving men money to spend time with me, is not OK.

Hair done, body fit, staying young was important to me,
But when I take a look back, I had the wrong mentality.

I dated younger men because I knew I could,
But deep down inside I still didn't feel good.

I thought I had it going on, but everyone could see
How low my self-esteem had gotten and how I needed to be set free.

I was looking for love in all the wrong places,
Sleeping around with many young faces.

Little did I know in order to be set free,

<u>I had to allow Jesus to show me how much He loved me!</u>

Tracy has fully committed to helping Lyric find her daughter. She also wanted to express her feelings in Spoken Word:

Leading But Bleeding

Leading But Bleeding is what my name should be--
People seem to always tell their problems to me.

But what they don't know is I have problems too,
And if it wasn't for Jesus I wouldn't know what to do.

After the birth of my twins I went through postpartum depression blues,
I didn't bond with them at first and didn't know what to do.

The stress of dealing with their father was overwhelming me,
I thought I would go crazy with all the pressure on me.

The night before their birth, my ex-husband went to jail;
But then he bailed out and made my life a living hell.

My girls were six days old when I went back to doing hair;
Because the bills were all due and someone had to care.

Sixteen days later he abandoned us.
I said a prayer to God, and then I had to trust.

"You seem so strong," is what people say to me.
But what they didn't know, it was Jesus carrying me.

Well, that was my past, now I've moved on.
Doing things Jesus' way, you can't go wrong.
<u>Now I'm remarried, happy, have a "Boaz", and a new home.</u>

After we wrapped up that final session, as the women left the building they seemed more positive. I was excited about the strides they had all made. **To God be the Glory!**

As it had been in the past, Tracy and I were the last two people to leave the shop; however, this time would be different.

An Unexpected Call

Tracy received a call on her cell phone. It was from a relative of Tammy. She asked if Tracy would put her on speaker so that we could both listen in. The call was to inform us that Tammy was found dead earlier that day. Then she went on to read a letter Tammy had written, in the form of Spoken Word, that was also found.

It read: If you are reading this letter then it's too late for me. But I want people to know while they still have time…

The Choice Is Yours

I was a good person trying to be the best I could be,
But in three months my life changed drastically.

Hiding my bruises, I thought no one could see,
But the only person I was fooling, was me.

Because I didn't protect my children they were taken from me.
The state ruled they would be better off in a foster home then home with me.

I sunk into depression, my life seemed hopeless to me,
A brighter day, I didn't believe I would see.

So I went deeper in sin allowing Satan to come in.
Drugs and alcohol became my best friend.

"Come to Jesus Tammy, HE will protect you, you'll see,"
Was what Tracy was trying to tell me.

But I didn't take that stand; I chose to stay with my man,
Trying to convince myself that he loved me.

I thought I had plenty of time later to accept JESUS; you see,
Even though you were right Tracy, my man was beating on me.

But between the beatings and the daily torment from the demons inside,
I couldn't take it no more, so I COMMITTED SUICIDE.

When the call had ended, we both just stood there for a moment in silence. We were shocked and saddened to hear the news.

Poor Tammy; her story didn't have to end that way. Like many who are in abusive relationships, she didn't realize that her choice to stay with her abuser could cause her death. But ultimately, it was Tammy's lack of self-love that Satan used to cause her to reject the love of Jesus, and to feel that she didn't deserve love. Feeling unworthy she just refused to be loved. It doesn't matter how much Jesus wants to dwell within us, He cannot, until we invite Him in. Choosing to accept Jesus in your life, as your personal Savior is a choice that only *you* can make; no one else can make it for you.

Before Tammy's death, she expressed to some of her closest friends that she wasn't ready to accept Jesus into her life; she felt it would change her life and she might lose what she thought she had (Her man). If only Tammy understood, when you accept Jesus, you don't lose; you gain. And as for your life changing...

Well Tammy was right about that, your life does change. You become a new creation in Christ and the old things will begin to fade away. That happens as you spend time with God. The more you spend time developing an intimate relationship with Jesus, the more you learn who you really are.

Right before Tracy turned off the light, she gave me a big hug and said, "These past eight weeks have truly been a blessing. I have learned so much from being in your presence these past few years. One of the things I learned was not to judge a book by its cover. Although you are considered a statistic, Ms. Jerri, you didn't allow society to stereotype nor define who you are. You have defied all the odds.

Ms. Jerri, not only are you a powerful, strong, and dedicated Woman of God, you are a dynamic speaker, guide, writer and author, I believe you are and will be an inspiration and source of hope and encouragement to the many women whose path you will cross in life. Although I'm really going to miss you as my assistant Ms. Speaks, you made the right choice to terminate your employment here at the shop with Mike and me, as you walk full-time in your purpose, and pursue your calling to help women heal and be set free through WOMAN TALK. May God continue to bless you," Tracy concluded.

As I walked out of the shop for the last time as an employee, I felt blessed to have been a part of the healing and new beginnings of those women's lives. I felt even more blessed that God had taken my mess and turned it into a message of hope. By allowing Jesus to heal my hurts and pains I was able to receive my gifts and walk in my purpose.

Now that you have been enlightened and you are equipped for
SUCCESS with a **NEW...**

ATTITUDE

GO AND WRITE A NEW SCRIPT FOR YOUR LIFE!
Remember, Victory is in knowing who you really are.

Food For Thought

What Women Want Men To Know
"We are all Beautiful Black Women."

Black women are unique. We are different shades of color, different sizes, different body shapes, different heights, and different ages. We have different hair textures, our voices are different and, yes, we have different Attitudes.

We need to know that you care.

We need to feel that we are #1 in your life.

We need to feel protected; physically, emotionally, verbally, and spiritually.

We need you to be our head (Our covering).

We want to follow but we need to see you leading.

We want to be appreciated and valued.

We need to be heard when we speak softly, so we won't have to get loud.

It's hard to be submissive when we're the breadwinners.

We don't want to compete with your mother for your love.

We want you to step up and be the man of the house so we won't have too.

We can be hard, but we can be soft.

What Men Want Women To Know

We need to be respected.

We need you to be patient with us.

We need you to understand that we are human and we have feelings.

We can be sensitive and we can get hurt.

We want you to allow us to be the man.

A smile and a kind word goes a long way.

We need you to know that we don't always know the answer however, if you would allow us to, we will try and find out.

We sometimes need our egos stroked.

Sex is very important to us.

We would love it if you would sometimes initiate sex.

Tell us what you need.

We want to love you and we're trying to learn how.

We want you to know that when we married you, we married all of you, and we want you to give all of yourself to us.

The New Release Sequel
Set to debut the Summer of 2013

When Loving Him Is Hurting Your CHILDREN

Jerri Lynn

WOMAN TALK is an adult forum where Jerri Lynn speaks open, bold, and direct on real life issues. She holds nothing back. She tells it like it is. So if you are ready to hear the truth, book Jerri Lynn/WOMAN TALK for your event.

Send an email to jerrilynnspeaks@yahoo.com and include information about your event, the event's purpose, proposed event date, and estimated number of participants. We will contact you. Go to www.jerrilynnspeaks.com for more information.